Fixing You

JORDAN SIEWERT, DO

This book is dedicated to my Natalie Paige. You came into my life and taught me what it means to be someone's Dad and how to be a more compassionate doctor along the way. While our journey has been a difficult one, it has been my privilege to be your father and stand by your side through it all. You mean the world to me.

CONTENTS

PREFACE

Many times, over the years, I thought about making a memoir about my experiences with my daughter, Natalie. In 2018, during one of the "good patches", I was watching the movie "Cider House Rules" with my wife and recognized a childhood friend as an extra in the movie. Seeing him brought back many memories, both good and bad. I remembered that he had brain cancer during middle school and had undergone treatment. By the time I met him he had undergone treatment and was a "normal kid". I remembered him talking one time about how he had starred in a movie but it was something we never had discussed in detail. Seeing the movie now in the present and recognizing him, I immediately became curious. How did he get in the show business? Was he still acting? I was bored and so I looked him up on google, trying to get the details of his acting career. After placing his name and the name of the movie in the search box, an obituary was the first hit on Google. A sinking feeling came over me as I learned that my old friend had died last year in New York from cancer, one week after his wedding. In reflection, I feel this is something that I may have heard before as a rumor, but it had passed from my memory, much like many things that come through our daily lives. The obituary, speaking on his triumphs through his battle with cancer, reminded me that he had written a book as a teen about his experiences. Interested and feeling a little bit guilty about my sketchy memory, I bought the book and received it a few days later. Upon starting it, I was instantly inspired. While his journey was different from ours, it was something that spoke to my inner demons that I frequently hide from the world. I decided to start writing down some memories. I was surprised how many specific details I was able to remember. I kept writing and soon found myself several Chapters into a story. It was fun to walk through the halls of memory lane and it was almost therapeutic to a point. This is what motivated me to keep going.

Some things were much more difficult than others to get down on paper. There were some parts that were very difficult to work through and lead to crying spells. What follows, is from what I remember. I am sure it is not perfect, and is very one sided, but hopefully it stays as close to the truth as possible. I can only pray that this book is able to bring you some of the same insight and wisdom that I was able to obtain from the work of my friend John Cathcart.

PART I

A New Beginning

CHAPTER 1
MY NATALIE

What can I tell you about my Natalie? Well, the first thing most people notice about her is that she is pretty small for her age. We get asked frequently if she and her younger brother, Lucas, are "twins" even though she is two years older than he is. It has been debated that her short stature could be due to her heart condition or her absolute refusal to eat like a normal child. It is likely a mixture of both. Personally, I think it is just Karma. You can't tell it now, but I was a terribly picky child and remember how hard it was to get me to eat much of anything. Who knew that kind of thing could be inherited.

Natalie has short, dirty blond hair, and a wide smile. The next thing people seem to notice about her is her large brown eyes. Most people comment on this as well. "Oh she has such beautiful eyes" we heard frequently, especially when she was younger. Her voice is pretty high pitch, coming out almost like a squeak at times as she giggles or squeals with laughter. She loves to sing and is not soft spoken.

Natalie is a fun loving, goofy and definitely the Queen of excuses. From the moment she could speak there was always a reason she couldn't do what we asked of her. Almost nightly at the dinner table she would go through her lists of what had worked for her in the past in an effort to try to get away from eating. From being "too scared", "tummy hurts" or "too tired to eat", I don't think she has ever finished a meal in her entire life.

Don't even get me started on bed time. For almost a year, she would scream out to us about how she had a "bad dream" five minutes after we turned off the light. After we cured her of this, she moved onto her next excuse. She would call out, "I need someone to sleep with me!". For quite some time, she was terrified of the Shadow Monsters (Thanks Caillou). Currently, she insists on sleeping on a camping cot, mostly because her bed "hurts". I believe she gets the ability to make excuses from her mother. Who knew excuses could be inherited too?

Her smile can light up a room. Nothing makes me happier than when I walk in the door after a long day at work and hear her scream out "DADDY'S HOME" and listen for those little footsteps as they come pounding across the floor. I wait in anticipation for the smiles and hugs that are sure to follow. It is an amazing feeling, one of appreciation and love, and it is really hard to describe. It is likely very typical for most children to react this way when a parent comes home from work, but that does not change how special it makes me feel.

Natalie loves to be the "big sister" to both Lucas and little Joey. Lucas follows her wherever she goes. While he adores her, Natalie tells my wife, Kelly, in private that she "Loves Joey and not Lucas". Her favorite pastime, at least at the age of 4, are playing at the park, making up songs, Paw Patrol and Sprout. She also loves Dinosaurs. Her favorite park is Wildwood in Toledo, known to Natalie as the "big" park, with the swings, bridges, slides and climbing tree.

Let me take a moment here to be honest. Natalie is spoiled rotten and has her Dad wrapped around her finger, so some of these statements are likely a little bias. When she calls out, "Hold You Me!" I have no choice but to do as she asks. When your kid wants you to pick her up and cuddle her, what parent can say no? While she can be demanding, most would agree that Natalie is super sweet. She also can be pretty shy. Almost at random, she will ask us, "Mommy, can you help me find a friend today?"
 She has an amazing mind that is sharp and overflowing with creativity and imagination. When she first started in on Paw Patrol at age 3, she renamed all of her little dinosaurs after the puppies on the show and to this day that those are their names. The little yellow duck named "Skye". Chase is a 1 inch "Longneck" who lost his head after months of constant playtime. It is not just her toys. She loves renaming many things in her life. Her Plavix is the "Big Nasty". She nicknamed her Aspirin pill "Big Spicy". We even made up a song about it that we sing together whenever she has to take her medications at night.

4

The last thing I will share about our amazing girl is both sad and a blessing. Somehow, throughout all this, Natalie doesn't recognize that she is sick. When your entire life has consisted of hospital visits, procedures and scars, how would you know it could be any different? I remember before one of her procedures her calling out "It's Lucas's Turn!" I have held her down as she begged, "Don't let them hurt me!" Things like that hurt you deeply, a deep gnawing pain that digs at the back of your mind at night, and I do not know if there is a cure for that. How do you tell a three year old she is not normal and it will never get better?

With that said, we are blessed with times of normalcy. Sometimes things are going so well that we seem to forget that Natalie is sick. Many families with sick children get to say that. We have always tried to allow her to live a normal life. We did not want to be those "helicopter parents." Our Heart doctor told us that she will "titrate herself", meaning she would learn her own limits with her heart. This has worked for the most part as she will "take breaks' during play to catch her breath. She doesn't wear oxygen, goes to preschool and runs outside like a regular little kid. She gets to sing and dance and play all day, rocking out to 'troll songs". For now, we just hope and pray that this honeymoon lasts forever. All that said, this journey did not start that way.

CHAPTER 2

WHO NEEDS KIDS ANYWAY?

As far back as I can remember, the idea of my wife, Kelly, being able to have children was always in question. Back in our teens years, the concern from her doctors stemmed from her heart condition. My wife was born with a "Cyanotic" heart defect known as Truncus Arteriosus. To describe it simply, the large arteries that come off of her heart never separated when she was developing, creating a system where her blood never was able to fully oxygenate. Most children born with Cyanotic Congenital Heart Defects before the 1980's did not survive very long. There was simply no way to fix the heart condition. Due to this, most heart babies would follow with their Pediatric Cardiologist for their entire life and never make it to adult hood. As medical advancements developed treatments, this helped increase survival, and more patients survived. Pediatric Cardiologists are not fully trained in dealing with some of the heart issues of adults, so many patients found themselves in need of an adult heart doctor as they reached their 20's.

Luckily, my wife was able to be treated as a child and had done well. She was set to establish with a new cardiologist in 2007 when she was 20. Up until then, she had followed with the same heart doctor since birth. At her last visit with her pediatric cardiologist, he told us that there may be a chance Kelly would be cleared for a pregnancy. It was difficult for her to leave the care of someone who had taken care of her for so long, but we looked forward to our future together with optimism. Her new Adult Cardiologist however, felt otherwise. She felt that it likely would not be a good idea for Kelly to try to have children of her own. While her heart was surgically "repaired" as a child, she still had occasional symptoms as an adult. It was possible that pregnancy could lead to heart failure or worse. We accepted this actually pretty easily at first and had planned to adopt a baby at some point.

One year later, at her next scheduled follow up, Kelly had to establish with yet another cardiologist as hers had moved on. Her new doctor seemed to think a healthy pregnancy could be possible, but he wanted the opinion of a Obstetrician. His adopted daughter was diagnosed with Tetralogy of Fallot and he had been looking into the research and felt it may work out. We were very excited as we left that appointment. I had a year off from school and we decided it would be the perfect time for a child. That said, the cardiologist doesn't manage pregnancies, Obstetricians do. We wanted the blessing from the Obstetrician before proceeding with that recommendation. Kelly saw an Obstetrician in St. Joseph, Missouri that summer who seemed overwhelmed by the idea. She told Kelly, "I would not want to be managing your case." and basically shut down the entire idea. After that visit, we were pretty devastated and relatively confused due to all of the conflicting opinions. We reluctantly decided to just "not worry about it and went back to the "Adoption" mindset. The anxiety and stress of that day slowly faded away and we moved on. I had been accepted to Medical School in Kirksville, Missouri and things were going otherwise very well in our lives.

In 2010 during the spring before we moved away from Saint Joseph, Missouri, I had a rather bizarre experience. I was with my mother driving down I-29 to meet the family at a local restaurant when we encountered a stopped delivery truck on the side of the highway. My mom pulled over to see if the driver needed assistance. The driver was an Indian gentleman and, in mildly broken English, told us he needed a ride to Kansas City to pick up a part for his truck. His phone had died and he was having a hard time getting a cab. Kansas City was an hour away and he was preparing to walk. My mom and I looked at each other and spontaneously told him to jump in. It was a very enlightening and edifying experience. My mother is of short stature and rather "small" but she has never been shy to speak her mind or ask questions. On the way down to Kansas City, we discussed about this gentleman's life and what brought him to Missouri. He explained that he had come to the United States to supporting his family, and he was sending money back to India every month.

We continued to speak about life in India as we made our way to Kansas City. It was fascinating how different life was there. The man wanted to know how he could repay us. My mother refused payment, explaining that it was not necessary. He persisted, offering support in other ways. He asked if there was anything else we needed in our lives, as he wanted to pray for it. This somehow brought up the topic of myself and my situation with kids. It was a very uncomfortable topic for me, but that didn't seem to matter to my mother. Any topic is a good topic if it drives conversation. Something odd happened that night though. Right after we picked up his part and turned back towards St. Joseph, the man leaned forward from the back seat told me that he had a vision and wanted to pray for me. He placed his hand on my shoulder and said I would be blessed and would have multiple kids. It seemed so farfetched to me, and I dismissed it. My mother did not. When we arrived in St. Joseph, he attempted to pay my mother a few hundred dollars and she refused again. He insisted, stating that we had blessed him and it was part of his culture. My mother took a $10 bill and we left him where we found him. We sat in silence on the car ride home. I reflected on this peculiar encounter. It made me feel uncomfortable. It had been awkward, curious, peculiar, and particularly mystifying. I was upset emotionally as well. Deep down, having children was a hard topic to me, but I did not want to tell my mother. The wounds were still fresh from Kelly's doctor appointment and it almost felt like a mockery of the whole situation. I was not upset with the man. I knew he was genuine and only meant to help.

When we moved to Kirksville, Missouri for medical school, Kelly had to establish with a new local cardiologist. It was getting to be a trend. She made an appointment with a local Cardiologist named Dr. Valtos. He was young, friendly, very smart and just a little bit arrogant. At our appointment, he brought up children, asking when Kelly planned to start the process. "Clock's ticking… You know.." he had said with a smile. Both Kelly and I were taken aback by this, having cemented in our minds that having a child naturally was just not in the cards for us. We voiced our concerns about pregnancy and past recommendations against such. Dr. Valtos listened intently, then held up a single finger. He left the room for a second and then brought in a large textbook. Slamming it down on the bed next to Kelly, he pointed to a paragraph that indicated something that was beyond my understanding at that point. It was something along the lines of "Pressure over the pulmonary valve as a major determinant of outcome". He was quick to point out that Kelly's pressures on the last echocardiogram were basically normal so we should be safe to proceed. We left this appointment walking on sunshine.

We tried for 3 months without any luck. This is not abnormal for many couples. Oddly enough, my education was in stride with our experience. We were discussing basal body temperature and infertility in

8

class at school. While most couples are supposed to try for a year before you really worry about infertility, I decided that I knew where to start and had my wife keep basal temperatures. This is where you take your temperature every morning when you wake up. If you trend it, a normal pattern can develop that can hint to when you are ovulating. It was clear after three months of tracking that Kelly was not ovulating. Her temperatures were all over the place. We saw a specialist who agreed with this assessment and gave us medications to help with that. A round of Clomid (a drug designed for assisting female fertility), and further testing later revealed what the problem was. We were told that we could not have children, but this time it was due to me. This was difficult to hear, especially as this was the first time I was the problem. It can be hard to be told you cannot have children as a male. It can mess with your mind, making you question your "manhood". Now I have never been a man's man, but still it was upsetting. The doctor did present other options, including in vitro fertilization. Kelly was not a fan of in vitro fertilization as there is increased risk of multiple pregnancies and her cardiologist strongly recommended against twins. Kelly shrugged the idea off entirely. By now, we were informed on the "adoption" option and decided to simply proceed with that.

Now, I know what you are thinking. This is a book about my daughter, why are we talking about infertility and such. Hold on, we will get there! Obviously, we became pregnant. It is funny how many stories with infertility start this way. Years of trying and failure, only to have success when you stop trying. For us, it was all out of the blue. The pressure to get pregnant was off and instead we became focused on just living our lives again. I was completely consumed by school, and Kelly was working at a local clinic. We focused our spare time on each other and having fun. It was one of the best times of my life.

One afternoon during my last year in medical school in 2013, Kelly was getting ready for a girls trip to Kansas City and asked me if she should take a pregnancy test. Her cycle was late and she was considering it as a precaution. I remember laughing at her as I sat in the bathtub, telling her that it was "stupid" and she always has an irregular cycle. Later, during my night shift in the ER, I felt I was probably a little too harsh on her. I sent a text and apologized. I remember texting her the old saying, "Better Safe than Sorry". She sent me an image late that night of a positive test. I was sure it was a joke. Turned out to be very real. Somehow, we were going to be blessed with a child! I remember running round the hospital, trying to tell my friends the good news.

We were originally seeing a rural Obstetrician in mid-Missouri and a maternal fetal specialist in Columbia, Missouri. Due to Kelly's heart condition, we required a specialist for delivery. We had some special tests ordered due to Kelly's history, and everything was coming back great. I remember at her first anatomy screen, waiting very anxiously to hear about the babies heart. They had to call in the doctor to find some special "views", but everything came back great. As things progressed though, Kelly struggled with palpitations and feeling tired. We saw the heart doctor and the Obstetrician, who reassured us that Kelly was doing well.

Applying to Residency is not straightforward. It is not like a normal job, where you apply and get an offer if they like you. There is a complex computer algorithm that takes your preference as an applicant and compares it to the preference of the Residency program. It can be very stressful and there are many graduating medical students who do not find a place to go. It had been difficult to decide where to apply for Residency. I had looked in Missouri, Illinois, Michigan and Ohio. Being from Toledo, there had been a draw to "go back home", but there were many obstacles. I wanted to attend a Residency where I would be challenged. While the Family Residency in Kirksville or Quincy, Illinois would be fine, the program at Toledo Hospital was large and had an excellent reputation. I would have to take care of very ill patients. I had heard a saying once that 90% of how you practice medicine is based upon what you learn in Residency. I had never really felt confident in myself or my skills, so I wanted to go where I would be force fed knowledge. I did not think I could count on myself to learn on my own. The idea of leaving most of my family behind in Missouri was a hard one, but I felt that, for the future of my growing family, it was one I had to make. I looked at programs that were larger and more complex, hoping to hear back about a possible position.

Lucky for us, Kelly's pregnancy was pretty uneventful. This allowed me to travel around the country for interviews and audition rotations. I was given positive vibes from several large programs in Ohio and Missouri. In the end, after prayer and reflection, I made the choice to select the program at Toledo Hospital in Ohio as my top choice. Kelly and I were thrilled to hear back that I had matched with them in February 2014.

The pregnancy was progressing as well. There seemed to be nothing about the baby that the doctors were concerned with, just more concerned with my wife and her risks. Our Obstetrician still wanted a Cardiologist who specialized in heart defects involved with the Birth, and Columbia was becoming less and less an option. We were told Kansas City or St. Louis had excellent centers who would be able to assist us. It was our choice, but a necessary one for the safety of my wife and future child.

It was a difficult choice. My Mom lived about 60 minutes away from the specialty hospital in Kansas City, Missouri. We decided it would be best for Kelly to stay with my mother for the last month or so of pregnancy while I finished medical school and prepped the upcoming move to Toledo for my Residency in Family Medicine.

As the year progressed, Kelly continued to do well. The fatigue and palpitations that she had experienced in the second trimester seemed to have faded away. After getting established with a new Obstetrician in Kansas City, she had frequent visits with her doctors, at first every 4 weeks, and then every two. They felt that she was tolerating pregnancy very well. They repeated some testing, all of which came back "normal". I recall feeling almost overconfident. To us, it had seemed that the rural doctors had overestimated the risk to Kelly and her heart. It felt really amazing to be normal and the optimism about the upcoming changes in our lives was absolutely palpable.

I was scheduled to start Residency in Toledo, Ohio on 7/1/2014. While Kelly stayed with my mother in St. Joseph, I worked with the moving company to clear out our house in Kirksville and take most of our material things to our new house in Toledo. Kelly had picked out a nice 3 bedroom house when he had visited the area in December of 2013 and we were blessed to be able to purchase the house when we matched in Toledo. The Residency Program paid for the moving cost and hired a moving company to assist. It was the first time I had experienced having someone else come and pack up my stuff and I can tell you that it is beyond good. My advice, if you can afford it, always hire someone to do this work for you. It may be pricey, but it does save your back and gives you piece of mind. I drove to Toledo with my two cats and dog to assist in the unpacking. I was there for several weeks, enjoying time with family, unpacking boxes and setting up the nursey. Kelly and I had decided early on that we wanted to be surprised come delivery day on the sex of the baby. That uncertainty brings even more excitement at the time of the child's birth, but it also makes picking out the color and décor of the nursery much harder. With that in mind, we picked out nice neutral colors for the room. With the help of my Grandfather Marvin, we painted the room light green and a pale yellow. It looked pretty good and went well with the "Classic Pooh" as the theme we picked out. We placed some things amongst the newly constructed furniture that would go with that. It was simple, but I was really proud of myself. I was excited for Kelly and the new baby to see it. By the time I left the new house in May 2014 to stay with my wife in St. Joseph, everything was ready for our new larger family.

Kelly never went into labor. She hardly even had a contraction. A week or so after her due date, it was decided by her doctors that she needed to go into the hospital for induction. This is where the doctors use several different methods to stimulate labor. Kelly's heart had tolerated the pregnancy very well, but there are risks in allowing pregnancies to go too far past the due date. We were not very concerned. She had been doing so well and all of the prenatal testing had come back great. So there was nothing to be worried about, right?! The induction was scheduled to start on a Wednesday night. It was uncertain how long it would take, so we packed quite a bit of activities. We were checked into a large birthing suite at St. Luke's in Kansas City and the process was started. Much like any normal labor and delivery room, our room was large, with faux wooden floors, a small dresser, a small pull out couch and no windows. It was clean, but dark and rather boring. Kelly really hated it. After settling in, we were told that we would only be allowed to have 1 additional visitor at any one point and time. This was frustrating as many family members had made the drive.

First, Kelly was started on something to help thin her cervix. It is a type of pill. The baby did not seem to like it, having changes on the monitor. Next, A mechanical device was used to help move things along, but that is probably more details than most people care to hear about. To keep her from pushing too hard, an epidural was placed pretty early on. I will spare you the details, but what I will tell you is that it was a long induction and it was not until Friday night that Kelly was even close to pushing. I spent the time reading up on neonatal resuscitation, a required class that I was set to take next week for the Residency Program I would be starting soon. I also played Drawing with Friends, Farmtown and Clash of Clans on the iPad. Nothing like mindless Facebook games to pass the time. Kelly, for the most part, tried to sleep and only complained of intermittent back pain occasionally due to being stuck in the bed. She also was not allowed to eat.

On Friday, the labor was still in progress and Kelly was getting uncomfortable. The nursing staff pointed to some changes on the fetal monitoring, explaining to us that these changes told them that Kelly was likely going to have a baby that day. The changes that they saw are called "Decelerations" and can be due to multiple possible causes. Sometimes, they are normal and due to the baby's head being compressed during contractions. These are called "Variable Decelerations". The further the baby goes into the birthing canal, the more of these variables you may see. Sometimes though, decelerations can be due to blood flow issues. These "Late" decelerations can be a sign of trouble.
Kelly was having decelerations off and on throughout most of the day, mostly variable. I had no idea how to interpret these, but the random spikes and dips had my mom worried. My Mom and I had mentioned

concerns to the nursing staff whenever they would discuss it with us and they had responded appropriately. They had repositioned Kelly, forcing her to move side to side and placed her on oxygen which seemed to help things for a while. The doctors who came and checked on us from time to time told us that they had been watching and felt encouraged that things were going ok. As the shift change approached, Kelly had been stuck "at a nine" for several hours. She was growing frustrated, was in pain and the tension began to rise in the room.

Around 9:30 Pm that Friday, the babies heart rate started to show signs of trouble on the monitor. We were seeing more and more of the second kind of decelerations as were coming up on the fetal monitor. I voiced my concern to the nurse. While I was a novice at these thing for sure, I had looked at some of the text that I was reading up on while we waited and something didn't "look right". It was not until the Anesthesiologist came in and asked us about the decelerations that things changed. He asked us how long they looked like this, pointing to the monitor and my mother and I both simultaneously said "All Day". He left quickly and came back with a crew of support, obviously concerned.

Suddenly, the doctors were in a hurry. The Obstetrician came in, joining the Anesthesiologist and explained that they did not like the way the babies heart beat looked on the monitor. They considered forceps, but decided that a Cesarean Section was required. Kelly was upset by this, she wanted to have a natural birth, but reluctantly agreed. Once this decision to have the surgery was completed, things moved very quickly. Little did I know that this moment was the last "slow" moment we would have for the next few week. I can tell you honestly that what would come next is easily the best and worst day of my life.

CHAPTER 3

10:43 PM

It was a girl! As mentioned before, we had waited to find out the sex of the baby, looking away during ultrasounds, and even had two names picked out. We had decided months ago that we would name the baby Lucas if it was a boy and Natalie if it was a girl. My mind was racing with excitement as the doctor held her up so I could see her over the large blue drape. She was to be my Natalie and she was perfect. After the long induction and the decelerations, it was a relief to know she was out and she was safe. I had been all worried with the way the heart monitor had looked for nothing. I walked over to take a look at her as the nurses cleaned her off. Natalie was screaming, which was always a good thing to hear for a newborn. Her skin was a pinkish purple in color, her blue hands flailing back and forth. Discolored hands is not abnormal for babies when they first come out. Natalie opened her eyes for the first time at me and I was shocked by how dark they were. It was like nothing I had ever seen. After snapping two photos with my phone, my attention turned back to my wife, who was feeling effects of the medications. She laid there, arms out to her side with an Anesthesiologist by her head as the surgeons worked to finish the procedure. I told her how beautiful Natalie was, struggling to find the right words. Kelly seemed almost like she didn't care. She closed her eyes, telling me that she was done. Her life work was completed and she was ready to die. Looking at the Anesthesiologist as well as her vitals,

14

everything seemed stable. I leaned in to tell her not be silly, but suddenly stopped. Something was off. I noticed that the nursing staff was really working on Natalie. They had gotten out some equipment and were hooking her up to monitors. I immediately noticed that they were quite advanced on the resuscitation chart I had been memorizing for Residency. I had a sinking, unreal feeling in my gut. Something was definitely wrong.

The nurses moved quickly with Natalie, but were unable to stabilize her. They paged the NICU for assistance, but it was quickly decided that Natalie needed to move for more advanced care. They moved her to a cart, allowing Kelly a passing glance as she was taken from the operating room. One of the nurses stopped to talk to me on the way out. She explained that that sometimes babies come out having a hard time to breath. Once she was down in the Neonatal Intensive Care Unit, they would get a better idea of what was going on. I was in shock and was unsure how to respond. Kelly did not say anything. Torn, I decided it was best to follow with Natalie, leaving my wife alone in the operating room.

The NICU was hectic with a large team of nurses and two residents hovering over my newborn child. I would try to explain what the NICU looked like, but honestly I cannot remember anymore. I just remember it had white floors and yellow walls. While the team worked, one physician took me aside and discussed their ideas. He told me that the "differential diagnosis" was sepsis, a lung defect or a heart defect. She was not saturating well and her blood counts had been abnormal. The doctors wanted to rule out sepsis first. Sepsis is a fancy way to say infection and is more common in newborns then a heart or lung defect. My wife was "GBS Positive", which increases the risk of an infection being transferred to the baby as they are born. Kelly had been on antibiotics during labor to prevent this and she had not delivered the baby vaginally, but sepsis was still the most common cause for a new baby to struggle the way Natalie was. The first thing they wanted to do was start IV antibiotics on Natalie. The NICU team told me that they would know more once the specialist came and evaluated her. There was a mild hint that they may need to transport her for more intense care, but they needed to wait until they had further details.

After receiving my "Daddy Bracelet" with "Baby Girl Siewert" and her birth information scribbled on it, I left the NICU to inform my wife of what was going on. The walk seemed to take forever as I moved down the long, brightly lit hallway. I felt awkward and was unsure what to even say once I reached Kelly's room. Watching as they were working on Natalie, I remember not really feeling anything. I felt nothing as the nurses placed the IVs and drew blood. It seems odd, and I wondered, in horror, if I was not "Daddy" material. After finding my wife asleep and alone in a dark recovery room, I struggled with what to do. I knew Kelly was tired from a combination of 2 days of labor, the "major abdominal surgery" and the medications and she needed her rest. While I sat next to her bed struggling with this, I also reflected on how Kelly realty was not an "easy" person to wake In all the years we had been together, one think I had learned was to not wake Kelly up from a sound sleep. She usually would wake angry at the world for disturbing her slumber. With that said, I needed her now and needed her to understand what was going on. I decided it was best to wake her up and get it over with. Surprisingly, she woke up well. I explained to her the best I could where things were with the baby. I probably was speaking to fast, repeating myself too much and was confusing facts as I attempted to relay what was going on, but Kelly just sat in silence, taking it all in. I could tell she was still a bit "out of it' by both her lack of overall response and the zoned out look on her face. While we sat in silence, a nurse came in, asking how she was doing. Kelly nodded, saying she felt fine and denied any real pain. The nurse asked about Natalie and I explained how I was uncertain what was going on. We decided it was best for me to stay with Natalie so we could get immediate updates. I was going to leave but the nurses agreed to bring Kelly down for a quick visit to allow her to see her baby. I thought it may be best for her to get some sleep, but Kelly agreed.

As I walked back to the NICU, Kelly being pushed half-awake in her bed next to me, I started to question things. Was this a dream? It had to be. What if it was her heart? We had completed three different fetal echocardiograms in the past few months that had all came back normal. Did they miss something? How had Natalie developed something so abnormal and it not been seen on imaging? I was convinced that it couldn't be her heart. One thing that was weighing on me was my emotional indifference I had experienced at first. I half expected to have a very strong connection to my first born the moment I laid eyes on her, but that was not the case. Looking back, I don't know if it was shock or if it was normal, but I know that something inside of me seemed very confused about this small new life form that was being worked on so aggressively.

I entered the NICU to see a transport cart next to Natalie's incubator and the doctor that I assumed to be the Neonatologist talking to the mobile team. He was a tall Asian man, middle aged with a stern look on his face. He was wearing light blue scrubs and looked tired. He turned to me as soon as I arrived, letting me know that he felt Natalie likely had a heart defect and needed transported to the children's hospital as soon as possible. I remember how this seemed to knock me off balance and my brain fought it. I explained to him that this simply couldn't be! We had the normal prenatal testing including the echocardiograms. I remember feeling frustrated and a mild panic growing inside. I just wanted him to make sure that it was her heart before we transported her. What if it was something else and we didn't need her to leave? I asked the Neonatologist if they were going to try to identify the defect with an echocardiogram before she left. He quickly refused, almost blowing my concerns off, explaining that it was not their policy. He was very forceful in this denial, lacking all empathy. I realize it was 2:30 am at this point, but I was really surprised by this. I tried to explain where I was coming from, but he was dismissive. "If there was nothing wrong with her heart, why did you have 3 fetal echocardiograms?" he asked sharply. I did not know what to say at first. After a moment, I explained how we had to transfer to different specialists due to my wife and her heart condition. The Neonatologist had heard all he cared to and my concerns were again dismissed.

In retrospect, the reason for my questioning her diagnosis was not trying to disagree with the man. While flustered, I was not rude or belligerent at all. In my time as a medical student in the ICU, we would often try to do things ASAP to get an idea of what we were dealing with in a situation, even if it was not definitive testing. Of course, that was in a rural environment and probably more for the benefit of my education at the time, but I did not understand this back then. I just knew how we practiced in that small town ICU. Now, looking back as a doctor, I can realize what this Physician was trying to do. He just wanted to get my girl the help she needed. His overall lack of empathy to a stunned father is unforgivable as far as I am concerned. I was happy to transfer to another facility.

While all of this was going on, Kelly sat idly in her Hospital bed, still feeling the after effects of the procedure. She was very tired, but voiced her approval for the transfer. She had her heart surgeries at Children's Mercy and they had taken care of her for 18 years. She was comfortable with this decision. I quickly ran out of the NICU to the waiting area to my family. They had been told nothing at this point and were eagerly awaiting to hear if the baby was a boy or a girl. After explaining what I could (it was not much) to my waiting family, I returned to the NICU to go with Natalie. I regret not being able to tell them more at the time, but things were just moving so fast.

When I returned, Kelly was gone and Natalie was being packed into a transport cart. It had machines on the top and below with a plastic container in the middle. Natalie was all wrapped up, oxygen on her nose, arms squeezed in close and a blanket around her. She was fast asleep. It was such a moving thing to see. In all this chaos, she was at peace. I remember a strong urge to take a picture of this. I need that picture. I did not know what would happen when we left and I feared deep down that I may never have the opportunity again. I pulled out my phone and snapped the photo. I smiled, looking down at the photo. As the transport team packed up, the nurse informed me that I could not come with her in the ambulance. It was against policy for me to ride with them. This was my breaking point emotionally. It was as if all of the emotion was being held back by some unforeseen dam and this notification was the first large crack. I lashed out at the ICU manager, complaining about the lack of empathy with the whole situation. I again was explained policy and how I would need to drive. I couldn't believe it, but what choice did I have? I watched, tearful and alone as Natalie was taken away, unsure what the future testing would bring.

CHAPTER 4

THE PINK CASTLE

The ride to the Children's Hospital was not far, only about 4 miles or so from St. Luke's, but the drive was awful. I drove it alone as my Mom wanted to stay bedside with Kelly. Without anyone around to see, I wept openly. It was 4am and the normally busy streets of Downtown Kansas City were empty. I drove quickly, trying to follow my GPS down the winding streets. I somehow managed only to make 1 wrong turn. Children's Mercy Hospital is an irregular-shaped brick complex made up of multiple different buildings that appear almost stuck together. There are multiple entrances, and a roundabout at the center of it. The above ground parking garage is situated to the left of the main complex. The entrance to this parking area was right off the roundabout near the main entrance and was announced by a large blue sign with some sort of colored awning behind it. One had to go through a check-point in order to enter the parking garage. This check-point reminded me of the toll both on the turnpike. There was no attendant on duty at this point of the night. I pushed the little button and was greeted by a nice voice. They asked how they could help and I had no idea how to respond. My voice cracking, I explained that my daughter was being transported to Children's Mercy. Without further comment, the gate opened and I moved my car in. Once through the gate, just past an area of the hospital that seemed to jut out, there was an uncovered area where you could park before entering the main garage. Some of these spots where open. As I pulled into a random parking spot right off the main garage, I received a phone call from my Uncle. I was a mess, trying to explain to him through tears about what had happened. I explained that there were about 10 things I could think of "it being" and only a few are "good". He cut me off, telling me, "Bury that shit down deep. You are a father now. You need to be strong for her and your wife. There will be time to cry and this is not it." I was shocked. The comment struck me as cruel, insensitive and harsh, and for a moment, it made things worse. There was silence on the phone. I did not know how to respond. After a moment that seemed to last forever, I agreed to his wisdom, not sure how to take it and hung up. As I sat in the dark, I pondered those words. Suddenly, it made sense! In a strange way, my Uncle was completely right. I should push my emotion aside and try to deal with what is in front of me. I gave myself a pep talk and forced myself to stop crying. It worked. As I prepared to leave the car and face the news, I looked around for my phone charger. I was sure I had grabbed it, but in the rush I had forgotten. I cursed a little, as my phone was dying, but figured it was just another thing to add to the "worry about it later" list. Somehow, through all of this, I had remembered the stuffed animals I had picked up for Natalie at "Buy Buy Baby". A classic Eeyore and Piglet sat in the car seat next to me. I forgot the charger, but had remembered the stuffed animals. I snagged them up and gave them a tight squeeze, feeling their feather like fuzzy coat against my face. This seemed to help somehow. Emotions again under control and friends in hand, I left my car.

As it turned out, I had not really parked in the correct place. I was in a small parking lot outside the main parking garage, almost like an employee entrance. To enter the hospital, I had to make my way past a small concrete ramp and into a side door. I was confused at first as I entered the building, but soon found myself at the "Star and Moon" elevators which were right past the main elevators for the parking garage. There was a little astronaut poster on the elevator, warning of the possible "ouch" if you didn't watch your fingers. After inspecting the hospital layout on a map near the elevators, I quickly made my way past these and into the main hospital in search of an information desk. The hallway ahead was very colorful and welcoming. There were murals along the walls and the floors. The ceiling had opened up to fill my view with hanging art pieces. It was vibrant and happy. While I would come to admire the extensive attention to detail in this hospital later, for now, I was on a mission. Right past the elevators there was a desk that I hoped would be able to guide me as I was lost and confused on where to go. When they asked how they could help me, my emotions overwhelmed me once again. I tried to explain as best I could what was going on and I needed to find my daughter, but it came out a babbly mess. The receptionist was understanding, handing me a tissue and giving me some time to gather myself instead of pushing. After I calmed down, I explained that my newborn daughter was taken to this hospital and I had no idea where they took her or how to find her. I gave her our name and she was able to find Baby Girl Siewert in the NICU "Bed 38". I was given directions and a map and was sent on my way.

I walked down the main concourse past the rotunda and into another long hallway. I stopped to investigate the map, trying to follow the signs to figure out where the Pink Castle Elevators were. I looked down the long hallway and then to the other hallway on the left. I glanced at the wall to my right and was caught off-guard by a mural on the right side of the long hallway. It was a memorial to children who had passed away at this hospital. It had their pictures, birth date, death date as well as a word from their parents. Uncontrollable thoughts creeped into my mind. I thought of possibility of my daughter being included on this wall. This was incredibly overwhelming to me at that moment in time. My heart started to pick up again and I could see the tears building at the corner of my vision. I had to push the thoughts from my mind and picked up my pace. Above this mural, I noticed an arrow indicated that my destination, the Pink Castle, was down a hallway to the left. I took it, wiping away tears. Down this corridor, I found myself in an opening faced with the chapel, cafeteria and the large elevators. This was the Pink Castle.

The NICU was on the 3rd Floor. I boarded the Pink Castle Elevator and pressed the necessary button. When the elevators opened up, there was a waiting room straight ahead and the entrance to the NICU was to the left beyond it. I quickly made my way to the door and attempted to enter. It was locked. To enter, you had to be buzzed in. I pressed the little button, waited impatiently for several moments, then pressed again. A pleasant voice came over the monitor. I explained my daughter was being admitted and I needed to come in. They allowed me in and I was met at a registration desk. They offered me a smile and gave me paperwork. It explained the NICU policies and rules. Visiting hours for 9:00 am to 9:00 pm with a break at 7:00 pm for shift change. Parents were not considered visitors and could be there whenever they desired. Otherwise, there could only be two visitors at the bedside at any point in time. I also had to sign paperwork stating what information could be given over the phone and who would be allowed to visit without me. At the time, I really didn't care, breezing through all the paperwork and scribbling my name on the last sheet of paper. I was given an orange laminated "parent" badge on a clip that I was required to wear and shown through the next set of doors into the NICU.

The main room of the NICU was very large open area with countless beds. It was about the size of the gym you remember back from your elementary school days. The unit was divided up into "pods" with a walkway creating a path around the room. The pods consisted of 4 "rooms" side by side divided by a blue and purple curtain. There was a wall dividing these rooms from the 4 "rooms" next to them, making it a pod of 8 rooms. Think about a misshapen tic-tac-toe grid. The rooms were not large, no more than 8 foot by 8 foot. Each pod was given a letter. It was dimly lit this time of night. Each room was busy, with monitors, incubators and staff. Looking back, It really was like a honeycomb, each filled with someone's pride and joy. The wall for each cubby had a letter designation and room designation that appeared like children's blocks. The back wall dividing each room was decorated with little makeshift windows as well, making the dividing wall a little less bland. Sadly, many of the rooms were filled with incubators with babies smaller than your hand in them. Parents were nowhere to be seen. I did not notice these details on that first night, instead making my way through the maze of incubators to the "room" number I was given at check in. It was located near the back left corner of the large room. Natalie was there when I arrived, in the incubator in room D-38, just like the receptionist had said she would be.

We were on an end cap near one of the corners of the large hallway. There was the decorative wall that was the back of the room and , the "wall" on the left side of the room was the blue-purple curtain that was used to divide the pods. The other two walls were open to the main hallway. The room was small and rather cramped. There was a small counter along the back was, a blue rocking chair off to the side and of course our incubator. Next to the incubator on the left, between the incubator and the curtain, was a host of machines and the ventilator. The cords and tubes ran from these machines up to the top of the incubator and through a device that almost looked like a plastic Ferris Wheel and then into my daughter. Natalie was laying in the incubator, asleep and intubated. There seemed to be wires everywhere. A thick white blanket was folded over multiple times and squeezed in tight over her arms keeping them tied down. There was another blanket folded down over her legs as well. She had a cloth over her eyes to shield from the light in the unit. She was so calm and peaceful in all this chaos. I placed my hand on the plastic incubator, resting my head on the side and began to cry opening. Besides the fear of the unknown, I was suddenly hit with an unbearable amount of guilt. "I did this!" I said to myself in my head. "This is your fault". I do not know where these feelings or thoughts came from, but they were crushing.

My emotional overflow was interrupted by the nurse assigned to Natalie that day. I cannot remember her name, but she was calm and explained that Natalie was stable. The doctors had already performed the Echocardiogram and would be by soon to discuss the results. She told me that, for now, it was best not to touch Natalie and I could not hold her. She explained all the machines, but the one that struck my immediate interest was the one on the counter above her head. It was connected to Natalie by two hourglass shape patches, not unlike two EKG pads stuck together. She had one on her forehead and another on her lower back. The Nurse explained that it was basically measuring the Oxygen getting to her brain and kidneys. This would tell us how we needed to adjust the ventilator. Natalie was also on a nitrogen machine and prostaglandins as well that were normally used to help a patient with oxygen saturation issues. All of this was very new and confusing to me. I understood enough to know that I wanted that monitor over her head to read "high but not too high" and that her oxygen saturation on the monitor above was very low. I reflected on this as the nurse went back to working at the counter. Natalie's oxygen saturation was reading in the 70's. and, in my limited medical experience, a saturation of 70 meant dying. Yet here we were, no alarms going off and things felt calm. We were sitting and resting without much of a fuss. I decided to forget my ego for a second, walked across the small room and asked the nurse about it. She said that it is perfectly normal at this state for a "heart baby" and told me they were monitoring.

A heart baby? She was the first to say it, at least enough for it to really truly hit me. When we were transported, the doctors worried Natalie had a heart condition. I had been in denial but it seemed that I did indeed have a heart baby. I knew enough about congenital heart disease to know that this wasn't good. My wife was a heart baby, born blue and "almost died". She needed multiple surgeries and had to follow with a cardiology specialist yearly. She had yearly echocardiograms and we had quite a hard time, it seemed, getting someone to take care of the pregnancy. Now, suddenly, it seemed I had brought the same thing onto my child. This only seemed to add to feelings of guilt that was weighing heavily on my soul. I was nowhere near perfect, but Natalie was innocent, and this meant a life of pain, or worse. It also meant a possible life cut short. The very depressing thought of "what is the best case scenario" started creeping into my mind as I stood next near the counter. The nurse interrupted my racing thoughts, asking me if I needed anything else or had any other questions. I shook my head "no", but adding that we would need to see a priest soon. She told me she would reach out to the Chaplin and returned to her work.

I still had Natalie's newest friends with me, sitting off to the side in the blue chair. I looked over at them. She had not had a chance yet to see them. Eeyore and Piglet were supposed to be her first "gifts", so soft, and meant to bring her comfort. I am not sure why, but I felt they were very important, so I made sure to give them a "seat of honor" on the counter behind her incubator. After moving her friends, I returned to the incubator and inspected my new daughter in more detail, trying to memorize every detail. She had so many tubes and wires in and around her. The amount of support she required was something that was hard to get comfortable with. As I stood there, time seem to pass strangely. I had not eaten, drank or slept.

A nurse noticed me teetering on my feet next to the bed and I was shown a small room off the NICU where parents could sleep. I remember laying down, hoping to wake up and it had all been a dream. Sleep came quickly. Oddly, I vividly remember having a dream. During the dream, I was at my mother's house again with my wife. We were in bed and I startled away. I looked over and Kelly was still pregnant! For a fleeting moment, I thought all of it had indeed been a dream. I remember telling Kelly about what had happened and expressing worry that it could still happen. I wanted to be prepared! She was dismissive. I remember being extremely frustrated, wanting to shake the sense into her. I did not get the chance. I awoke soon after in the pitch dark room in the Children's Hospital. My stomach hurt and I was extremely disoriented. Walking around with my hands extended like a blind man, I found my way to the door and opened it, bright lights filling the room. Reality kicked me in the gut.

It was around 9:00 am now. I wandered back to find Natalie in D-38 almost the same as I had left her. They had moved her out of the incubator now and she was resting on a pad in a cold, clear plastic tub that served as a bed. My cell phone was long since dead, so I was unable to contact anyone or check in with my wife. I was not worried about that, instead just feeling the pressure of the moment and fatigue. Instead, I sat in the blue rocking chair that I had pulled up next to the bed. I was back in a daze and my mind started to drift.

I was surprised when suddenly there were other people in my little area. A female Asian Doctor in a long white coat started looking at Natalie in the bed. The rest of the medical team was gathered behind me with a computer on wheels. At the time, they seemed to be discussing another case. I stood up, fumbling over myself with fatigue, and approached the Doctor. She introduced herself, informing me she a Resident and was part of the team here to take care of Natalie. She asked me my babies name, looking down at a sheet a paper she held in her hand as she did. I still felt odd saying it, but I told her that we named her Natalie, but before we could discuss her any further, the attending physician came over. He was middle aged, grey hair and taller than myself. His face had many lines, some around his eyes indicating happiness and one between his eyebrows indicating frustration. He explained that the echocardiogram that was completed before I arrived had shown a defect with Natalie's heart that could be Tetralogy of Fallot or Truncus Arteriosus. They would know more after the heart catheterization that was planned to be completed soon. In the meantime, they would keep her comfortable. He explained to me that she was a "large" baby and this would help her very much. Most children he sees with these conditions were much smaller, so over 7 pounds was a blessing. "We won't have to grow her." He said with a smile. They felt that she was stable and offered to answer any questions I had. I could barely think straight, let alone come up with questions. They assured me they would be around and were looking forward to helping us. I smiled and thanked them and they moved onto the child across they walkway. I could hear them discussing 'Baby Girl Siewert" as they walked toward the next patient on their list.

CHAPTER 5

BABY GIRL SIEWERT

After the doctors left us alone, I went back to sitting in my chair and watching Natalie. I sat there for a moment, watching her chest rise and fall and wondered how the next step would go. I knew that a heart catheterization was not a small thing and had risks, but I felt that we needed the answer. While sitting there, pondering this thought, I noticed the little name cards tapped on the foot of Natalie's bed. There were actually three different little labels. One was a long, rectangular sticker and another larger pink square one below it, both with "Siewert, Bg" written on them. There was also an official hospital ID sticker below these two, also with "Baby Girl Siewert" typed out. I understood the first sticker looking this way, as it was from the transfer from St. Luke's hospital, but the other two were generated at this hospital. I thought to myself that these surely should of said "Natalie" by now. Baby Girl Siewert just felt generic to me and almost insensitive for some reason. I looked over at the folder on the counter, the pages of ID stickers and even the tub with supplies next to the bed. All of them said "Baby Girl Siewert". I distinctly remember at this point getting really upset deep inside. Looking back now, I realize it was such a trivial thing. This is just how she was initially registered at the hospital and it had not changed over, but at the time it seemed like an urgent matter to me. Her name was not "Baby Girl", it was Natalie. Maybe it was the fatigue or stress, but I wanted it changed. I wanted everyone to know her name. I walked over to the nurse and pointed out that Natalie's labels were not up to date. She told me that she knew this, but hospital policy was that they could not change it. It had to be changed in the admitting department. Right now, Natalie was admitted as Baby Girl. She explained, with a smile, that this was common and it usually takes a few days to get straightened out. Once it does, admitting would bring up new stickers. In my frantic state, this was not good enough. For all I knew, my little girl might not live a week and the fact that she had a NAME mattered to me. The nurse seemed understanding of my feelings and instructed me on how to find admitting. They should be able to help. I went to admitting and it became a larger issue then just what the nurse had explained to me. Until Natalie had a social security number, the hospital had to go off of her admitting number as her ID and it was impossible to change a child's name in the system. Did you know that it can take a week or more before a child is generated a social security number?

This was not good enough for me. I was on a mission. I needed to get this process started, otherwise we would be stuck as "Baby Girl Siewert" for the foreseeable future. Natalie's nurse had loaned me a charger earlier and I had been able to get a little juice into the phone before I headed down to admitting. Using this small amount of juice, I called the Social Security office to look for help. I will admit, I was a bit frantic and crazy at this point. While waiting to speak with someone, I took the conversation outside, pacing near the parking garage on the cell phone and practicing the conversation in advance, trying to explain the situation and not coming off as a crazy person. When I reached a person, I was surprised to find out how nice they were about the whole thing. They were very understanding, explaining to me the rules of how the system worked. The assistant on the phone would put in the request for me and it should speed the process along, but she couldn't make any promises. Still frustrated, I thanked them and hung up. For now, that was the best we could do.

When I went back upstairs, the nurse reviewed the "rules" for Natalie. Because she was a heart baby and her oxygen levels were very unstable, we had to be careful with her. We could touch her, but we could not caress her as it would only irritate her. If she became irritated, she would become uncomfortable and then her oxygen levels would drop. We were told that if we wanted to touch her, we could place our hands on her head and feet and add pressure. Holding her was out of the question. Later, I was allowed to place a pacifier in her mouth while she was awake, but I would have to hold my finger in it to keep it steady. She would have a hard time latching with the breathing tube in her mouth. It was during this explanation that we were notified that a heart catheterization had been scheduled. They would be taking Natalie to the catheterization lab soon. I was told it was time to say goodbye, and we would have our answers quickly. I was given instructions on how to find the waiting room, and I had to watch as they took my little girl away from me again. I told her I loved her, and I meant it.

I was told it was going to take some time, so it was likely a good idea to rest or eat. I was hungry, but it was the last thing on my mind. Kelly had no idea what was going on with Natalie. She had been trapped, recovering at the other hospital. I had not seen her yet or spoken to her as my phone was once again dead. I felt silly having used the small amount of juice left in my phone to talk to Social Security instead of talking to my wife. I considered trying to bum another charge, but I decided it would be best to just go back to the St. Luke's. I needed a break for a moment and I hoped leaving the hospital would clear my head. I also needed supplies.

I made my way out of Children's Mercy and down to the car. The parking lot was much busier than it had been the night before. I had to wait in a line to make it through the gated toll booth area. The drive to St. Luke's Hospital was a little less eventful this time. I had brought Eeyore with me, serving as my copilot in the seat next to me. Once I reached St. Luke's, I had a hard time finding the entrance to park, mostly due to lane restrictions and lack of signage. After finding a spot, I snagged my copilot Eeyore and made my way into St. Luke's.

I had no idea where I would find Kelly or what sort of shape she would be in. I knew how rough things had been on my end and could only imagine how she was handling this. I stopped by the gift shop and bought her some flowers with a balloon. My grandparents had shared the story of how my grandfather would always bring my Nana flowers after the birth of each child. A solitary flower for the girls (the first two) and then a large bouquet of roses for "his" boy. It was silly, but funny. I made sure to get a large bouquet. I also picked up a balloon. Kelly hates balloons with flowers, always telling me how it was a waste of money. I figured it may make her smile.

Kelly was in a totally different area of the hospital and I struggled to find her. She had been moved out of the delivery area and was in a generic hospital room. This room was smaller than the room on Labor and Delivery and had a large window. Kelly's bed sat to the left of the entryway and a pull out couch on the right wall next to the bathroom. Kelly sat there, looking out the window with a emesis basin in her lap.

She looked at me when I entered the room with the signs of fatigue and nausea covering her face. "I threw up." She said. Her emotions quickly changed once she noticed the flowers. A small but beautiful smile spread across her face. ".. for me?!" she asked in a cute voice. I made some sarcastic comment about the balloon and walked over and gave her a tight hug. It was one of those hugs that last slightly longer than you would expect, with an extra squeeze at the end. After a moment, after placing

Eeyore, flower bouquet and balloon on the rolling table next to the bed, I positioned myself at the side of her bed, near the window. We sat in silence for a moment, both looking out the large glass windows that dominated the long wall of the room. I did not know how to start, but took a deep breath, and proceeded the best I knew how. I explained what was going on with Natalie and how the doctors were not sure what the next step was. Kelly and I shared some tears, but overall the mood was pretty calm. We had a light hearted conversation about Kelly's mother, who had predicted something would go amiss.

After a bit, I remembered my phone and all the calls that needed to be made. I went and plugged it in with the phone charger while Kelly attempted to eat lunch. My phone immediately blew up with missed messages. I called my Mom, Dad and siblings. My grandparents from Michigan were already in route to try to help however they could. If there was something my grandfather did best, it was always be there for someone when they were in need. One of the more difficult calls was to Kelly's Mom. She excitedly but nervously asked how things were. I explained it was a girl, which she was excited about, but then told her I had bad news. When I said, "something wrong with her heart..", She had screamed "Noooo!". It was long and drawn out and something that still haunts me to this day.

As I sat, phone in hand after the hard call to my mother in law, I finally noticed my hunger. The only food Kelly had left was a package of graham crackers. This did not sound good to me. I looked around the room for snacks. I found what I was looking for in the small fridge. It seemed Kelly had never eaten her "post baby" meal. My wife LOVES Jimmy John's. After eating nothing by mouth for days during the labor process, anything sounded good to her. She was disappointed to find out that the hospital did not offer anything special to new moms, something the hospital in Kirksville was very proud of. If you had a baby in Northeast Regional, you could order a steak dinner. She discovered early Friday that Jimmy John's delivered to St. Luke's, so she had ordered a Turkey Sandwich. Kelly had planned on eating it after delivery. Many things had gone wrong the day before and after delivery and Kelly had never eaten it. In the small fridge by the door, there was the day Old Jimmy John's sandwich. I snatched it up and scarfed it down. It really was not too bad, it was the lettuce that had really suffered.

After spending a little more time with Kelly, I made my way back to the Children's Hospital. After wandering around for a bit, my mother and I found the very bright procedure waiting room back at Children's Mercy. It was in an area of the hospital I had not seen, far beyond the Pink Castle. I sat nervously, my mother at my side and the little blue Eeyore tightly in my clutch and waited to hear the scoop on my daughters condition. I was less afraid of what the diagnosis, being more terrified of what it may mean. A deep part of me was still in denial, hoping that it would all be just something minor that we would laugh off later. A friend from Medical School, Gabe, came by to say hello. His son Derek had been born with a heart defect, Aortic Stenosis, and had undergone several heart surgeries and procedures in this same hospital. His son had had a heart catheterization that same day. It had gone well and Derek was resting. Gabe, who was a veteran at this point of these things, offered some swift stern advice and a strong handshake, all of which I appreciated. After what seemed forever, the doctor called my mother and I to a small room off the waiting room. I remember following him back, heart in my throat as I awaited the news on my daughter.

An image appeared on the screen that showed Natalie's chest cavity. It looked like an x ray. I could see the ribs and her heart shadow. Immediately, I was able to see her heart looked abnormal. It was "boot shaped" as the medical textbooks taught, which is a sign of something called Tetralogy of Fallot. I did not say anything. The doctor began to show me images, showing me how the catheter dye moved through her heart and then did not flow into her lungs as it normally would. Instead, blood was flowing through some unseen little abnormal arteries called MPCA's that were coming off her main arteries, the aorta and intercostal arteries. These arteries, called "collaterals" are not normally found in babies. They are not supposed to exist and yet were the only reason Natalie was alive. He informed me that Natalie had something called Pulmonary Atresia

CHAPTER 6

PULMONARY ATRESIA AND ME

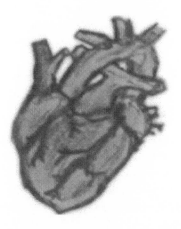

Natalie had a Congenital Heart Defect. We now knew what it was but I was lost. Even having completed medical school, I had never heard of Pulmonary Atresia up to this point in my life. Congenital heart disease affects 1 in 100 newborns. Most heart defects are relatively innocent, requiring little to mild intervention to help a child live a normal life. In fact, most children can make it to adulthood without even knowing they have a heart problem. "Cyanotic" forms of congenital heart disease are much more serious. These babies will be born 'blue" and most will only live weeks to months without help. Pulmonary Atresia is often considered one of the more advanced forms of a common heart defect called Tetralogy of Fallot.

Tetralogy of Fallot is the most common cyanotic congenital heart defect, and it effects roughly 1 in 2000 babies. Commonly, it is made up of 4 defects; Pulmonary artery stenosis, the ventricle septal defect, right ventricular hypertrophy and an overriding aorta. In common terms, there is a large hole in the heart between the two sides and the main valve that takes blood from the heart to the lungs is tight. Blood has a hard time getting into the lungs, so it goes through the hole and out to the body. The blood is never really fully oxygenated, which leads to the low oxygen numbers. Tetralogy of Fallot is associated with several different genetic deformities such as down syndrome but can be found in any child. Pulmonary Atresia is rare and occurs in nearly 1 in 10,000 babies and makes up about 2-3% of the congenital heart disease cases. It is a more severe case of Tetralogy of Fallot,. Due to the large hole in the heart, blood moved through the hole and not into the lungs. The lack of blood flow to the arteries in the lungs causes them to never fully develop. It is uncertain why some children develop Tetralogy of Fallot and others develop Pulmonary Atresia.

When we are taught medicine, we look at charts in text books to teach us what someone looks like on the inside. Once we start dissections, we quickly learn that the dissection guide book is simply that; a guide. Each person has little differences in us that makes us unique. One simply has to look at the way the gallbladder and associated arteries and ducts are arranged to see this randomness. Inside the "Calot's triangle" (Medicine sure loves its buzzwords) there are many of different ways these vessels can be arranged and all of them considered "normal".

Pulmonary Atresia is not an exception to this randomness. All babies with this condition will be born with a completely blocked off pulmonary "trunk", or artery that comes off the right side of the heart and takes blood to the lungs. Other than that, it varies greatly. Some children will be born with completely normal arteries in the lungs. Others can be born with no trace of a pulmonary trunk and lack pulmonary arteries. A doctors ability to treat these babies depends greatly depended on the presence of the pulmonary arteries. A babies chance of survival also depends on the size of these small arteries. Natalie was lucky enough to have pulmonary arteries but they were very small, roughly 1 mm in diameter.

Unlike Tetralogy of Fallot, which tends to be "correctable", many patients with Pulmonary Atresia face a long road ahead. Unfortunately, many patients will not be candidates for complete repair, and will require multiple procedures over their lifetime to provide blood flow to the lungs. The main goal is to increase the pressure on these arteries and stimulate them to grow.

The doctor explained the diagnosis to my mother and I. As treatment is based on what the child's anatomy looks like, he also explained that there are different ways to fix it. He laid out a plan for us with a smile. He made it sound so simple. We would get a shunt placed at some point. This would be a small connection between her Aorta and small Pulmonary Arteries. The hope was that the increased blood flow would help her arteries grow. Then, after a few years, they would put a conduit in place much like the one my wife was given when she was young. This "conduit: was basically and artificial Pulmonary Artery. He explained that it was difficult to predict what was going to happen with her. Right now, the doctors needed to focus on weaning her off her some of the mediations and support and go from there. He told me that she would be back in the NICU after she was stabilized. I heard him, but the thing I was focused on was if it was correctable. I probably asked him 4 times, ".. but you can fix it?!".

After hearing from the doctor, We made our way back to the NICU waiting area to find most of our family waiting. We explained the findings and how we would "just have to see how things go". Most were understanding. While waiting for Natalie to return, I called my Dad with an update. He had been on vacation in Hawaii and had been trying to get earlier flights to come be with us and meet his granddaughter. We had a tearful conversation and I struggled to explain the uncertainty in the air. I wanted to talk more, but had to quickly let him go as Natalie had returned.

My Mother and I went back to see Natalie after she had returned from her catheterization, leaving my friend Gabe, Grandparents and other family members in the waiting room that would soon become our "Headquarters". When we reached bed D-38, Natalie was still asleep, wrapped up and laying on her back. The nurse reminded us of the rules and explained that she needed to lay still. She looked like an angel, laying wrapped up on a green and white polka dot "bed" with the blankets tucked in keeping her snug and warm. I stood over her, again trying to memorize her every detail. My Mom had other work to do. While Kelly and I did not know the sex of the baby before birth, my mother insisted on knowing. She promised not to tell anyone. Around Week 20 or so, during an ultrasound, our Obstetrician in Kirksville wrote a little note to my mother with the sex of the baby. We sealed it up and never looked. While she swears to this day she didn't spill the beans, later I had the feeling many people knew "Natalie' was coming. Since my Mom knew the baby was a girl ahead of time, she had come prepared. "Bubbe" brought out all sorts of goodies and decorations from her purse. She had a package of bows, several dresses, frizzy socks and a large Pink and Black banner that read "Fabulous". The banner was placed over part of Natalie's cart/bed and we put Eeyore and Piglet on the cart with her. The nurse told us was most likely fine and even allowed us to place a small bow on the sticker on Natalie's forehead. After she was done with her work, my mother left and my Nana came in. She went right to Natalie and I remember seeing the tears in her eyes. We spoke about religion and how things happen for a reason, but I couldn't help feeling the guilt and unsteadiness in my belief at that point. Soon, Nana switched out with my grandfather. He came in, and without a word, just hugged me. He hugged me so tight. I could hear the emotion in his breathing. This process continued, one visitor to the next. All exchanging their sorrow on what should of been one of the proudest days of my life.

Before long, it was decided that Kelly needed an update on the situation. We all piled into the cars together and made the way back to St. Luke's. Kelly had been doing much better. One of the doctors from her Obstetrician's office had visited and showed her images, trying to explain how they could have "missed this" with all of the prenatal workup we had done for Natalie. She pointed out to Kelly how on the first Echo did show blood flow through the pulmonary side of her heart and "maybe it was a little borderline" low but it had not been noted by the person reading the images. On follow up imaging, looking now they could see that flow was decreased and actually worsening. This also had not been noticed. They also never notices the hole in Natalie's heart. To Kelly and I, none of that really mattered. Natalie was sick and getting the best care possible. We couldn't really blame them and it is not like knowing ahead of time would have changed much. I remember Kelly's mom seeing things differently. She was already talking lawsuit.

After visiting Kelly, many of us including now my grandparents, went out to dinner at one of the best chicken wing places out there: The Peanut. It was a quaint little dive bar and the decor matched this. We sat at a table right by the front glass of the restaurant. The table had names etched into the surface from past visitors, including my brother Bobby's. It was nice being out of the hospital and somehow separated from all the craziness. Sitting there, laughing, I could almost forget all of the events of the past 24 hours. When we took our seats, I started examining the names, looking for anyone else that I knew. I came across the name "LUCAS" etched out in large block letters right in front of my seat. It took my breath away.

Before delivery, as mentioned before, we did not know the sex of the baby before birth. We had two names picked out. Natalie for a girl and Lucas for a boy. The name etched in front of me was some odd omen. Luckily, the baby was girl, so in reality it mattered little. After a moment, I laughed it off, reflecting how odd and shocking it would have been if Natalie had been a boy. That name could have brought me back to the suffering child in the NICU and ruined the night. Seems the fates had something else in mind. Dinner was uneventful, filled with laughing. It improved my mood immensely.

We finished off the large plate of wings and my grandparents and I decided to go check up on Natalie before they headed off back to my Mom's house in St. Joseph. We went up as a group to find her resting comfortably just as we left her. Shift change had occurred and the new nurse was working on documentation nearby. Her name was Liz. She was middle aged with her dark curly hair pulled back tight in a ponytail. She had dark, tired looking eyes but a kind reassuring smile. She introduced herself

34

to us and asked about the situation. Many of the staff we had encountered this first day had known what was going on, but she was the first to really ask how we had been doing with all of it. She told me that she had reached out to social services for us and they would be getting with me likely the next day. In addition, the priest I had requested had been by, but we had missed him. They left us his card.

It did not take long for me to see the type of nurse Liz was. While a bit cocky and mildly obnoxious, she came off as sincere, caring and funny. We would find in the next few weeks that she was a great advocate to have, making sure things were not getting missed and looking out for us as parents and not just Natalie. She worked different shifts, and I remember to this day the relative disappointment I would have on days that she was off.

Liz reassured us that she would keep a close eye on Natalie and we said our goodbyes. This was very difficult. Personally, I felt torn, wanting to be by my babies side yet needing to check on my wife. While I still felt this deep feelings of guilt towards Natalie and her situation, It was getting compounded by the guilt of not being with Kelly while she recovered. I knew Kelly was sitting alone, in her dark room and that really tore at my heart. I placed my hand on Natalie's side, rubbing her small shoulder and trying to comfort my torn heart. I was not following the rules in regards to "touching". I tended to have a hard time following the "rules" in regards to touching Natalie and what would upset her, and this was one of those times. Liz noticed, but did not see it necessary to interrupt me. I started to cry, feeling so unbelievably torn. My grandparents asked if I wanted to just stay, but I shook my head. I needed to be with Kelly and I felt comfortable knowing a nurse who seemed to really care would be there to watch over Natalie all night. As I walked off, I couldn't help to keep looking back.

After my grandparents dropped me off, I had a hard time finding my way back into St. Luke's. It was late and most of the side entrances were locked. I found myself wandering around the hospital to find an open door. It was very dark out now, but the sky was clear and the moon casted an eerie glow on the campus grounds. The campus was large, well-manicured, well lit near the building itself. While I walked, I reviewed Facebook. I remember how hesitant I was to tell anyone about what was actually going on. I posted the picture I took of Natalie in the incubator, announcing her to the world but left out any details about her heart. I remember reading all of the congratulatory posts, feeling terrible. I didn't feel like I should be congratulated for anything. Only a select few actually knew what was going on and I felt bad for withholding the truth. I wanted to avoid any drama. I put my phone away as I entered into an entrance of St. Luke's that I was unfamiliar with. After some assistance from a hospitality manager, I found my way back to the elevators I had used before and entered the part of the hospital I was more familiar with.

As I had imagined, the room was dark. Lights were on outside, but the thick curtains hid most of it. Kelly appeared to be asleep in bed. Similar to the night before, I wanted to let her sleep. I fought with myself about what to do but decided it was best to wake her. Sitting on the edge of the bed, I told her about how things were going. I explained how the doctors had told me the uncertainty of our diagnosis and how we were going to have to "wait and see". I also explained how we missed the priest.

Kelly started to cry. She had only seen Natalie once, and that had been the night before as she was taken away by the transport team. To me, this seemed like a lifetime ago. I felt terrible. After a good hug, we made plans to talk to the nurses the next day and try to get her a "day pass" to go to the other hospital.

I laid down on the pull out couch in the corner of Kelly's room. Sleep struggled to find me at first. Laying on the pull out, anxious thoughts frequently flooded my brain. After several hours of flopping around, I decided I just could not take it. As quiet as I could, I picked up my phone and left St. Luke's, leaving Kelly to sleep in the dark sad room.

CHAPTER 7

HAVING A HEART BABY

I had a strong sense of deja vu as I navigated the abandoned city streets in the dark towards Children's Mercy. The emotions I was experiencing could not be any more different then the last time I made this trip in the dark. I no longer was faced with the massive uncertainty as I had been just 24 hours ago. In its place, a deep seeded sensation of guilt and grief was taking hold of my heart. I knew now that I had a "heart baby" and that the road ahead was going to be difficult. I tried to be motivated, tried to see it as a challenge, but it was very hard. I tried to tell myself to trust in God and his plan for us, but at that moment it felt very hollow.

As I had made the trip between the two hospitals 4 times now, it was no longer a mystery of where to go. I didn't need the GPS. It was a 10-15 minute drive, ending down Gillham Street. I watched as the Children's Mercy Hospital came closer on the right side, standing out bright in the dark horizon. As I pulled up, I dreaded walking into the hospital and receiving some sort of tragic news. Going through the toll gate was slightly easier this time. After I was greeted by the friendly voice, I explained that my daughter was in the NICU and even provided the bed number. It was quick and painless. Pulling forward into the lot, the parking area straight ahead where I had been parked the night before was now full, forcing me deep into the large parking structure. The garage was divided by many levels, each with a correlating theme. I do not remember specifically where

I parked that night, but I remember Blue Balloon was the level you wanted. It was at the ground level and made it easy to leave. Further down, there was also Red Rocket, Green Train and Yellow Submarine.

After taking the long walk from the parking garage to the Pink Castle Elevators, I checked back into the NICU with the front staff and wrote my name on the ledger. Each patient had a ledger in a book and every time there was a visitor, you would write your name, check-in time and relationship to patient on the current page. We were already partially through the first page. Having signed my name many times, I had been trying to be creative on the title, using "Daddy", "Dad", "Father" and a few others. At this time, I decided on "Pops". I smirked as I inked the name on the paper, then set down the pen and moved into the unit.

The lights had been dimmed throughout the NICU much like the night before. I found Natalie was just as I left her. This was a relief and gave me a sense of relief. Somehow, while lying on the bed at the other hospital, I had convinced myself that in my absence, my little heart baby would crash. Yet here she was, just as I had left her. I did not see the nurse initially, so I settled in, pulling the blue chair over to her bedside. I looked over the bed at the ventilator near the curtain, inspecting the readouts and such. One of the settings on the ventilator is called the FiO2. I knew what that was from my ICU rotations as a student. FiO2 represented the fraction of oxygen in the air being pumped through the ventilator. At that point, Natalie's setting was above what is considered "room air", which meant that she was needing a higher amount of oxygen then normal and was basically breathing more concentrated air. She also still had the device next to the ventilator that provided the Nitrogen. If she was ever going to get off the ventilator, she was going to need to get that FiO2 setting as close to "room air" as possible. Just for the record, the FiO2 for "room air" is about 21%.

There are always alarms in the NICU going off in the background, just like in an adult ICU. The alarms sound different depending on how "bad" the situation is. As a doctor, how close an alarm was to my patient and how loud it was, helped me decide how concerned I needed to be. Some alarms meant that the patients' blood pressure was a little lo, while others meant the patient's heart was not beating. You learned to tell the difference by the way the alarm sounded.

In the NICU with Natalie, things were no different. On the monitor, Natalie's oxygen saturation was at 72%, but still blue, indicating that it was within the set range. Frequently, every 5-10 minutes, it would drop into the 60s and the alarm would sound. It was a quiet "dun... dun.... dun.." type of alarm. Usually no one would come running to this and normally that number would bounce back into the 70s rather quickly. The nurse would come by, look at the baby, and then write something on a piece of paper and move on. It was a very abnormal number to me, but I assumed that it was typical in the care of a "heart baby". But, when Natalie would get upset, her saturation would drop into the 50% range and would alarm. This alarm was different, more of a high pitched "TING! TING! TING!" People would come quickly to check on her, many of these people I had never seen before. In my life before Natalie, I had never really struggled with anxiety. I always thought of myself as a pretty chill guy, but this was changing quickly. Our journey had only just begun, but the inner anxieties were already starting to take hold of me. Those alarms would frequently pull me from daydreams or wake me from sleep, startling me. I would look around in a panic, sure that this time was it. This would be the time that Natalie would not recover and this would be the alarm that damaged her brain. Luckily, she seemed to always bounce back.

Maybe the irritation with the alarms and situation was visible on my face as Liz came by. She asked me jokingly why I was back so soon. I tried to giggle about it, but couldn't. I reluctantly blurted out how I couldn't sleep and the alarms were bothering me. She immediately comforted me, muting Natalie's alarm for the moment. Liz assured me that she and others were keeping a close eye on my little girl and they would let me know if anything came up. She also reminded me that it will be a long journey and I needed to take time for myself and Kelly. She told me she understood my feelings of needing to be here, but if I did not take care of myself, I wouldn't be able to be the support person Natalie needed. She asked how "Mama" was, asking if she would get to come by tomorrow to see Natalie. I shrugged. We discussed this for a bit and Liz expressed her feelings that if Kelly could see Natalie it would likely do them both good. I sure hoped that it would.

Liz was sure to remind me on how to get updates. If I needed to check up on things when I was not at bedside, I could always call and speak with Natalie's nurse and get updates. I thanked her and allowed her to go back to her work. She was responsible for several of our neighbors who we had not yet met. I tried to take her words as comfort, telling myself that Natalie was being watched by experts. Besides, what did I know? I had no experience as a doctor or nurse in the NICU. They dealt with cases like Natalie's every day. I needed to trust them. After telling my little one that I loved her and apologized again, I cuddled up with Eeyore on the purple/blue chair and sleep found me.

CHAPTER 8

MEETING RONALD

It is a funny thing about familiarity. No one would expect someone to CRAVE being stuck in a waiting area at a hospital, but for me, it was my place of solitude and retreat from the bells and alarms in the NICU. The 4 chairs next to the table in the right hand corner of the waiting area had become a sort of Headquarters for our family. Most of the time, it was quite and comforting, the exact opposite of the NICU. During our time in the NICU at Children's Mercy, we were usually one of the first families to arrive in the morning. My grandparents, who were staying with my mother in St. Joseph, would come up around 8-9 and lay out goodies. Coolers, bags of books and puzzles would cover a small table, the floor and several of the chairs. It was a comforting place where we could relax, pray and cry together. Visitors would come and go, but my grandparents were almost always right there. In fact, going through the waiting room whenever they were not in those seats was offsetting, because it felt so wrong without them.

Usually, my grandparents would beat me to the hospital in the morning. On days when I was the first one there in the morning, if someone was ever NEAR our spot, I would feel deep resentment. It was all unfounded and silly, but at the same time, your mind gets filled with odd things in times of deep emotional stress. Those seats became my area for a break. When I was there, I was able to escape all of the beeping and noises and just be me. I didn't have to focus on that darn monitor measuring Natalie's blood flow to her brain, afraid that every time it drops that this was the time she would REALLY be damaged permanently.

On May 31st, the second full day of Natalie's life, I was awoken by alarms sometime early in the AM after shift change. I had fallen asleep in the chair and had not noticed the switch. Liz was gone, replaced by a different nurse. She was standing over the bed, suctioning Natalie's airway. This can be a difficult procedure, placing a floppy tube into her breathing tube, mouth or nose and sucking out any sort of phlegm building in her airway. This was not uncommon, occurring when her saturations were running low. I tried to keep my distance, but it was hard to watch. The resident team returned in that moment and I stood in the background, listening as they reviewed the case. They discussed the results of the catheterization from the day before and what this likely meant for Natalie. The Attending Physician discussed that surgical placement of a "shunt" was necessary for her. After they finished their discussion, they took term examining Natalie, happy with how her lungs sounded. The Attending Physician invited me over to the counter where he stood, sharing some information with me. He felt that placing this shunt in the near future would help Natalie in the long run. He again let me know how "lucky" we are that she is "big" at over 7lbs. Frequently, as he mentioned offhand before, babies need time to "grow" first before they can have surgery and that delay in care leads to an extended stay in the NICU. While there was the benefits of early surgery, he felt we could not proceed until we weaned her down off some of the support. This included the Nitrogen mixer and the prostaglandins. Without weaning, it would make surgery much more dangerous. Over the next few days, our goal would be to get her off the nitrogen and prostaglandins and plan the surgery for roughly June 4th. The doctor asked about breast milk and what the feeding plans were for Natalie. My wife had been instant on breastfeeding, taking classes and had planned on building a strong "breastfeeding relationship" with her baby. I assured the team that Kelly was planning to breastfeed and was likely pumping it and saving it. They asked that we bring it over and store it at the Children's Hospital. They would feed her through an NG tube.

Have you ever seen a baby cry and make no noise? On the second day of her life, Natalie seemed to finally come out from under the anesthesia from the day before and realize that things were not normal. As I stood by her side, she cried and cried, thrashing about, and no sounds came out of her mouth. It was gut wrenching to watch. Her "TING! TING! TING!" alarm was running every 15 minutes or so and it was exhausting emotionally. There was nothing I could do to comfort her. Luckily, after a short while, my grandparents arrived. They gave me a break, taking over "Watch" so I was able to go out to our designated corner of the waiting room. I sat heavily down in the chair and placed my head in my hands, trying to wrap my head around the emotions of the day. Looking for a distraction, I picked up and started reading a book in the downtime.

My Step Father had given me the book to start reading while I had been staying with my parents the weeks leading up to Natalie's birth. He felt it could be helpful as I started Residency, so I had packed it with us. I had not found time to dive into it due to the craziness, but now seemed like a good time to start. "The Richest Man in Babylon" by George Clason is a small book, less than 200 pages and is filled with lessons on what not to do with your money. If one wants to achieve their dreams, according to the book, you have to be successful with money. It stressed saving money and investing wisely. It taught that, while it may seem fun to enjoy the fruits of your labor while you are young, if you "build your mountain of gold first", then you can enjoy as many banquets as you wish when you are older. It also cautions against overstraining to save. It was a semi-dry book, and I was distracted, but the message was a good one. Following these instructions is another issue entirely, and not something that is easy to do.

Digging into the book, I was able to clear my head a little before my grandfather came out and let me know that social work wanted to meet with me at bedside. I went back into the NICU to meet with them. The social worker was a short, plump woman with frizzy orange hair. She seemed excited to meet with me to discuss what sort of things they offer parents and patients at Children's Mercy. Some of what she needed to discuss were more serious in nature though. She had a large white binder with a colorful logo on the front. Inside, it showed some of the different child life activities put in place to help families but also had information in regards to palliative care. Palliative Care focuses on providing relief from the symptoms and stress of a serious illness. The goal is to improve quality of life for both the patient and the family. It is sort of like Hospice, but hospice is reserved for patients with a terminal diagnosis.

The Social worker let me know they would be visiting me later after I had a chance to review the folder to answer any questions. When asked if I needed anything else, I requested again about the priest. She assured me that he would be making rounds and would meet with us. He actually had visited Natalie twice but just missed me. She also asked me where Kelly and I were staying.

At that time, I had basically thought I would be staying with Natalie and I had not really thought too hard about it. She asked about staying on campus, near the hospital. Thinking of what Liz told me about needing rest, I told them that it was likely a good idea to check it out. After a few phone calls, the nice social worker let me know that there was a room available at the local Ronald McDonald House and wanted to know if I was interested. The only experience that I had with the Ronald McDonald Charities at that point was the signs at the McDonald's drive through asking for change. I had no idea what they did or what the house was like. She asked me to take a look at it if I had time and she would "put me on the list". This seem like a good idea so I agreed.

Later that day, I decided to take the walk down the street to the Ronald McDonald House, which was about 1-2 blocks away. To get there on foot, you had to walk down the edge of the hospital campus near a busy Gillham Street to get there. It was the same road I had been taking to get between the two hospitals. I was assured by the nurse that it was not a big deal and many parents walked to the houses. So, after letting my grandparents take the watch, I left through the front entrance of the hospital. It was down on the first floor, past the observatory that I had passed multiple times before.

The day was beautiful, mildly warm with a slight breeze blowing through the air. After crossing the parking lot, I walked through a large metal and brick archway with a metal design on the top. It depicted a sun and there were two stain glass roses on either side. I passed through the metal and brick archway and came to a large cement and metal piano that lined the left side of the sidewalk. It reminded me like the keyboard on the movie BIG. It worked, sort of, playing a note when you stepped on a key. I did not play with it on this first walk down the path. From there, after passing through a large swing set/park, the path met up with Gillham street. Up until this point the hospital grounds had been beautiful. They were well landscaped with bushes and trees as well as random art pieces and even things for kids to play on as they walked. The other side of the street was pure downtown Kansas City filled with large buildings and dark alleyways. While the road was well lit, and they had trees on the right side across from campus, there was nothing beautiful about it. At times, during the night as I would wander back and forth, it could be a scary walk for someone who is not from the city. Cars would fly by.

I followed this street until it met 25th street. On the left near the UMKC dentistry school and you could see the Ronald McDonald houses just around the bend down Cherry street. The lot across the intersection of 25th and Gillham was basically vacant and was set up almost like a little park. There were several trees along the uneven ground with a random bench in the middle. You could see one of the many houses next to this.

Now there were three Ronald McDonald Houses located on Cherry Street; Two fully completed and one under construction. The first house was on the left. I walked passed it slowly, looking up at the large structure. It was classic in appearance, with red brick and green shingles. There was a sign up front indicated it was built in the 1950s. The social worker had told me that this house was full and I would be taking up residence in the other building known as "Longfellow House". She had told me that Longfellow had been newer so this had made it sound more exciting. Looking at it as I approached it on the right, it was definitely newer. It was more modern in appearance, with three large green blocky areas with a metal brown roof and thinner dark brown blocky walkways connecting each of the large green areas to each other. There were many windows. The entrance did not face Cherry street, instead facing the parking lot and garden to the south.

The entrance to this "modern" style structure known as Longfellow was large and made of red brick. The doors themselves were glass and simple. To the right of the door was one of those benches you see at McDonald Restaurants with a Ronald statue sitting there smiling out at nothing. It was made for a photo opportunity for sure.

After a sarcastic salute to Mr. McDonald, I entered the building. For access, there was a button you had to push to the right of the door. I pushed it and was greeted by a kind voice. She invited me in and the doors unlocked with a "clck". Inside, the building was most definitely modern in design with sleek metallic surfaces and quite a bit of glass. The floors were tile and there was a very fancy desk to the left with a mosaic tile pattern .

I was greeted by a middle aged woman. She invited me over to the mosaic desk. They had been waiting for me and had my information in a little binder. We discussed the house, the rules as well as how it was all "free" for families to stay. They did request a "donation" that was recommended for the services. They held game nights, movie nights and usually had catered dinners by local charities and clubs. After reviewing the book, she took me on the tour. She first introduced me to Mr. Bean, a small white dog that lived in the house. She explained how he was there to help comfort and play with families. He had his own dog house in the entry area. From there, we went into the main area of the house. There was a long corridor in the middle of the building with dark tile floors. I remember being attracted to an artificial aquarium diorama inside the wall just past the desk on the left. Just down the hall a large cafeteria and kitchen opened up on the left side. It was large, almost like 4 kitchens put together with multiple ovens, stoves, food prep stations and refrigerators. Near the back was an opening to the pantry which was the same size as the large kitchen. It was filled with almost every type of dry food imaginable. From boxed mac and cheese to Twinkies, everything a family's heart could desire could be found here.

Past this there was a private area with small locked pantries with room numbers on them. There also were more refrigerators, each designated to particular part of the building. Every room had a small area in one of the refrigerators for leftovers. Back in the main hall, there was a large mural of hearts in many shapes and sizes. It really caught my attention. My guide informed me that this was put together by families during the construction of the facility. It was beautiful. She showed me the laundry area off to left of the main stairs as well as the entertainment area and work out room in the basement. She pointed generally at the long hallways of rooms, explaining "quiet time' rules and how we would be assigned on of our own.

After this, we went outside the building, first into that vacant lot I had passed on the corner of 25th and Cherry. There were families now outside, two boys throwing a football back and forth and another sitting on the bench in the middle. The day was beautiful and warm. We shared some small talk as we walked around the other side of the structure and entered into the garden. The garden was large and maintained by the staff. They had large wooden arbors where grape vines grew along and countless other vegetables and fruiting trees spread around the garden. We toured it together before ending back at the check in desk. With a smile, she provided me a Blue wristband that I placed on my left wrist. I was told this was to show that I belonged. They instructed me to be sure to remind my wife to wear hers.

Our room was near the back of the building on the second floor. I walked up the stairs quickly and down the hallway I found there. The room was like a hotel room. There were two large "Memory foam" beds in the room on the wall to the right. In regards to other furniture, an older wooden dresser with a very small TV was on the wall to the left across from the beds. There was a large wooden shelf along the near wall by the door, with cubbies and areas to hang clothes. The bathroom was to the left, closed off by a sliding door. The bathroom was spacious and the counter had multiple donated hotel soaps and shampoos. On the edge of the first bed there was a "Ronald McDonald House" branded diaper bag, brown and white zig zags with big pockets. Next to it, there was a hand Knit blanket and small Robin stuffed animal awaited on the foot of the bed for us. On Top of the blanket, next to the bird was a message, signifying its significance. Another family who had struggled as we were had donated the items and hoped it would bring us joy. I sat down on the bed, sinking into the foam and picked up the bird. It was a run of the mill "TY" beanie baby robin. Reflecting on how hard things were right now and how someone thought of us and our struggles, it made me tear up. I decided to leave things as they were, placing the bird back down for Kelly to hopefully find later.

This was my first experience of the Ronald McDonald House Charities and I came away amazed. It was like a family friendly hotel. It was clean and the staff was so friendly. In a time like this, in the haze of all the change and sorrow, they were here to help make our day just a little bit easier.

After getting settled in the room, I made my way back to check on Natalie. It was on the way back I was really able to appreciate the outside of the hospital. After cutting through the grassy area of the empty lot at 25th and Gillham, I took the sidewalk back towards Children's Mercy past the park and piano and under the archway. As I approached, warm sun at my back and the sounds of birds in the trees, I was able to appreciate all the work that was put in to try and keep the hospital fun for children. The main entryway was very similar to a park in design with many small trees and different pieces of art spread throughout. There was a roundabout between myself and the front door with a small animated clock tower in the middle. The base of the small clock tower was made of thin metal supports with a ball in the center. The top was pointed with circus animals poking out below. The parking garage entrance with the toll booth was to the left with the fancy blue and yellow metal awning. The main entryway itself it the hospital was a two story large glass building that could be seen in the distance, a large round stained glass window above the double doors.

Inside the hospital was very colorful and fun. Right away, I noticed a purple information desk and the "lightning elevators" behind it. I had walked past it multiple times in my rush to the Pink Castle Elevators, but never really took note until now. It was obvious that the designers had done their best to make this place childlike. Everything had a fun name or color. Wanting to pass the time, I decided to explore a little. I took a look around the entryway as well as several of the main hallways. The floor was purple with large fish designs spread around. There was an atrium with odd sculptures hanging to the right as well as an abandoned piano. If one took the path to the right, which I did, you first enter a very large room that was circular in dimensions. Above your head you would see what appeared to be a dome of the night sky, almost like a observatory. I stood for a while, looking up at the artificial stars. Every once in a while, a streak would cross it, simulating a falling star.

CHAPTER 9
GUILT AND CONFESSIONS

When I returned to the floor, things were just as I had left them. I had to "tag" my grandfather out and found my grandmother sitting in the purplish chair by Natalie's bed. The small room had always seemed so crowded with all of the pumps and ventilators. She was reading a book. I approached Natalie, who was asleep, and admired her. She was a little puffier in the face, but otherwise similar to how I left her. I tried to make sense of the ventilator settings, but it was gibberish. I walked over and gave my Nana a hug.

She told me nothing had changed since I was out and about. Some people came by but she had not seen the priest as of yet. She did notice our neighbor and pointed him out to me. You could see the little guy behind the ventilators sitting in a swing. He was just rocking back and forth quickly, not a care in the world. I had not noticed him earlier, either because he was so silent or I was distracted. His name was Skyler. We would find out later, through the grapevine, that he overall was doing really good. At this point he had a cleft palate and was just awaiting procedures before he could escape. Our nurse, the same one from that morning was also taking care of Skyler, working at his desk. When she saw us, she came over and explained that they were having a hard time weaning the nitrogen and oxygen concentration on Natalie's ventilator and that was worrisome.

My phone vibrated in my pocket. I thanked the nurse for the update and checked the message. It was from Kelly and She had been granted the "day pass". She needed me to come pick her up. As I drove the now familiar path to St. Luke's, butterflies appeared in my stomach and decided to flap around. I don't know if I was nervous, excited or a mixture of both. I just wanted Kelly to be with her baby. I knew how important it was for that relationship to be established. We had planned on allowing Natalie to rest on Kelly after birth and breastfeed right away, but you know what they say about the best laid plans: They often go awry. Hospitals don't normally grant "day passes" to patients to leave while still admitted, but this was a special circumstance. Equipped with an abdominal binder and wheelchair, I rolled Kelly out of her room and out of the hospital. She had a hard time getting into the RAV4 even with my help.

Silence filled the air during the on the short drive to the other hospital. I did not know if Kelly was angry with me or just sad and, truthfully, I didn't really want to find out. It is in my nature just to assume something is my fault. I thought giving her space was likely best. I dropped Kelly off at the main entrance, bringing out a wheelchair for her before I parked the car. Kelly had not been to Children's Mercy in years and it was likely a surreal experience for her. After I parked the car and made my way through the maze of the hospital, I met up with her and pushed her to the Pink Castle. As soon as we came off the elevators, Nana jumped up from her chair, letting us know the priest was there waiting for us.

The Priest, whose name I cannot recall anymore, was older, likely in his 60's, with thinning white hair, a white beard and glasses. He wore all black, but it was not the traditional black garb of a priest. Normally, Priests wear black slacks and a button up black shirt and a color. This was more like a Black Tracksuit. He introduced himself and explained how he had been stopping by daily and just kept missing us. He discussed how he was praying for her and had blessed Natalie as well. Kelly asked about baptism in the hospital. She had been baptized in this same hospital when she was a child in distress. After we spoke and asked about baptism, we asked if he could do confessions for us.

He agreed. I decided to go first. I was being crushed by guilt and I just had to tell someone. The priest and I met in the room off the NICU I had slept in on that first day. The priest sat in a small chair off to the side and I sat on the bed. Normally, I was someone who did not like to sit face to face during confession, but on that day it didn't matter. I just wanted help. Before the priest could say anything, I voiced my apologies for lack of procedure. Beyond "forgive me father for I have sinned", I could not remember any of the "set things" you are supposed to say. The priest dismissed this, stating that it was the least of his worries. I then spoke quickly, almost unable to control myself. My words came out quickly, painting a picture of absolute guilt and questioning. Questioning my faith, my life and especially my fatherhood. I expressed my emotional detachment and indifference at times and wondered out loud what kind of father that makes me. I was careful to explain the questions I was feeling about faith, explaining that I never had asked God "Why Me?", or even being angry at God for allowing this to happen to us. To be honest, I think I had faith that things would work out, but it was just so hard to see the light at the end of the tunnel. He responded calmly to me, explaining that this was not uncommon and not a sin. None of it was my fault. He told me to focus on my family and being the best support person I could be. Somehow, simple as it was, this seemed to help.

As I left the room, tagging Kelly to go in next, I tried to consider what the priest had said. While it did not help loosen knot in my gut that had been tightening over the past few days, it did speak to the guilt. I walked into Natalie's room, looking over the little one. I went over what he said again in my head, promising myself to double down on my efforts and really trying to serve the rest of my family in this, especially my wife. I needed to not feel sorry for myself and just trust in the Lord that things would work out. One way or another, it would work out as intended.

CHAPTER 10

DAY TO DAY

I can remember very clearly waking up nearly every morning during these first few months in a fit of anxiety. I could not WAIT to find out how Natalie was and what had happened overnight. She always seemed to be "stable" during the day and then take step back at night. I would dress and brush my teeth as quickly as possible and head out. I would often leave before Kelly even woke up and would make my way to the hospital. Sometimes, trying to ease the queasiness in my stomach, I would call ahead of time. Frequently, I would find my Nana there, watching over my baby girl until I could get there.

On the morning of June 1st, I had left just as the sun was coming up over the city. Shift change was at 7am, and I had arrived on the floor just as Liz was getting off. I always appreciated her input and felt she was a real advocate for Natalie. Overall, she was about the same as we had left her. They had tried to wean off some of the nitrogen, but she had not done well, requiring "deep suctioning". When I came in, she was laying on her side, propped up with a small rolled up burp rag. It was nice to see her from a different angle, but It was beginning to be a trend. The words "stable" but "didn't do well" was starting to seem like the nursing staff and team of doctors favorite words.

We had many visitors over the next few days. Old High School friends, medical school friends, and friends of the family all came out to show support. It was really nice and definitely thoughtful, but ended up being a little overwhelming to me. I was processing so much with Natalie, it almost felt like a constant parade of friendly faces where there to shake my hand, hug me and cry with me and then move on. I was repeating the same story over and over again either in person or on the phone and it was exhausting. What really helped me was getting out of the hospital. At least when I "escaped" I could sort of feel like my normal self and not focus on my daughter's situation constantly. I was able to enjoy dinner with my college roommate Barkley at Applebee's one day. I will never forget how he criticized me for not getting a "Grown Up" Beer when I ordered a short instead of a Tall one. The waitress played in, even bring my drink in a kids meal cup. I was also able to head off to the Plaza in Kansas City for dinner with Zach, one of my best friends from Medical School. He had driven in from Oklahoma. He showed me a GOFUNDME account he had set up for us to help. It was amazing. While I really appreciated all of the support everyone brought us over those first few days, it is the times people pulled me from my new "routine" that really sticks with me to this day.

On June 3rd, the words the doctors were using suddenly changed. As Natalie was unable to be weaned, they started talking seriously about surgery. One of her doctors felt that if they increased blood flow to her lungs through a shunt she would do better. This made me nervous. I knew we had discussed surgery during June, but that was if we weaned. I was told earlier that performing surgery without weaning was dangerous. The doctors seemed dismissive about this risk, feeling confidently the "risk was outweighed by benefits". I had no choice but to go with their recommendations, but it was a scary thing.

Upon Liz's insistence, Kelly was able to hold Natalie. With the upcoming surgery looming, she felt it was worth the risk. It was not as simple of a process as it would seem. Natalie had tubes and wires everywhere and most of them could be dislodged by the slightest bump. It took three nurses to do move the baby. With Kelly sitting on the blue chair, they lifted the green and white polka dot bed Natalie was on and placed it on Kelly's lap. It was not "holding" her, as it was more just supporting her little bed, but it was something. Kelly cried and so did I. The waiting room was full with supporters of Baby Girl Siewert, anxious to see her and give support for the upcoming trials. One of my mentor was an Anesthesia doctor name Charles. He and his wife Sue came up, catering the dinner for everyone. Sue brought her niece Tiffany with her. Tiffany also suffered from Tetralogy of Fallot. In her case, it was not found right away and had drastic consequences. Medical care has advanced significantly in the last few decades, especially in the diagnosis and treatment congenital heart disease. Where Tiffany would have never left the hospital with current screening tests, back then she went home and suffered from the low oxygen levels. It caused damages that she still struggles with to this day. She was nonverbal. I can remember looking at her and think that, even with all the struggles she had to live with, praying that we could at least get to that point. I prayed for life. Sometimes, during the first few weeks, I felt like we may never get out of the hospital. It felt like we may never make progress and I feared never getting better. I felt that even if she ended up having severe side effects from treatment, anything was worth it. Anything to give me time with my little one.

CHAPTER 11

ORIGINAL SIN

Besides the upcoming surgery, some of our visitors were there for the baptism. After enjoying the meal and spending some time in fellowship with our visitors, many of our family members were allowed back to bedside for the baptism. Kelly and I are Catholic and normally children are baptized in a large ceremony in the church sometime during the first year of life. We believe that it is important for the child as it symbolizes marking them as a member of the church community and washing them of original sin. It is also important for the family and parents as we affirm our dedication to raising them a Christian and in the church. With the possibility of open heart surgery the next day, the church made arrangements to have a ceremony at the bedside.

When I reached Natalie, I noticed that the nurses had dressed Natalie one of the dresses my mother had bought for her the day she was born. The beautiful white dress was elegant, frizzy and perfect. Underneath, she had a white onesie. She also was wearing a white hat with a white bow attached and little white booties. Natalie was asleep.

The Priest was wearing what appeared to be the same black slacks and black windbreaker from a few days prior. He stood, waiting near the foot of the bed as the family came in. While the NICU was pretty strict about the number of visitors, they allowed an exception on this day. Some family members had traveled quite a distance to be here for us, including my half-brother Zach. My grandparents were there as was my mother. My Brother Tyler and Sister Stephanie were chosen as godparents. For such a normally joyous event, the mood was somber and overall pretty sad.

After saying a few words and instructions, the priest instructed us to take up our positions near Natalie. The first thing we had to do is make room. Her ventilator and nitrogen mixer was pushed from the the side of her bed back a few feet, invading our neighbor Skyler's space. He didn't complain. Since her heart catheterization, Natalie had at least 4 additional monitors attached to the right of her bed on a pole. It was moved closer to the counter near the head of her bed. The small table to her right, which held the pump for her tube feeds, was left in place.

Kelly and I stood to Natalie's right, crying silently. I had wrapped left arm around Kelly and she held my right hand in both of her hands, squeezing tight. Tyler and Stephanie stood at the end of her bed, both holding light pressure on Natalie's feet. The remaining family gathered in around.

The Priest pulled out a small book and began reading from it. It had the general outline of what was to follow and I could see the things he was supposed to say were written in red. He asked us what the purpose of this meeting was and we responded "Baptism" as instructed before. We proceeded through the procedure, which was pretty typical for a Catholic Baptism in words but not in surrounding. We renounced Sin and promised to raise her in the faith.

With that said, the priest produced a small vial of holy water and blessed Natalie. He then produced oils, first rubbing it on her forehead just above the monitor sticker as he read out loud from his book. He also had us pull down the front of her dress to rub a small amount on her chest. Natalie slept through the whole procedure. Tears flowed freely from everyone in the small cramped room.

After the procedure, we thanked the Priest. He offered us his congratulation and prayers. I can say that it felt good knowing that, if something did happen, she would be taken up immediately and all the suffering she had already endured would end. Per the schedule, Kelly had leave right after the procedure to go pump. The NICU staff allowed our visitors to stay at bedside for some time. We spent time a while longer visiting and I watched over our Angel who was fast asleep.

Kelly was planning for discharge the next day from St. Luke's, hopefully before Natalie's surgery which was set for the second case of the day at Children's Mercy. Later that night, after everyone had left, we both went back to her hospital to spend some time together. I wheeled Kelly down to the cafeteria at St. Luke's Hospital, with plans for a quick dinner. It was a very large and recently updated. There were quite a few options for what to eat. They even had a health food and sushi stand. Unfortunately, by the time we had said goodbye to our guests and made it back over, much of those choices were gone and the small shops were closed. Choosing between a bland hamburger and Pizza after eating in the hospital for a week becomes a difficult choice as everything starts to taste the same. After picking out some food, Kelly and I sat eating dinner in silence, not really discussing what was going to happen the next morning. I had broken down and posted the situation on Facebook earlier in the day and had quite an outpouring of support. It was hard to keep the cat in the bag at this point anyway as so many people now knew of our struggles. At dinner, instead of talking, I posted about the upcoming surgery and asked for prayers. I asked that we would pray that not only would Natalie improve, but also that she would be deemed a "surgical candidate" so we could finally proceed.

After finishing dinner, we decided to explore the campus of the hospital. With everything going on, we had not spent much time together since Natalie's birth. Kelly was my best friend and we were both dealing with the surprise and "tragedy" in different ways. I pushed Kelly in her wheelchair around the outside of St. Luke's Hospital in the dark, exploring areas that we had only seen from her window. It was a pretty campus, but pretty dark in some areas. It was nice to get away together and to spend some time "rebonding" in the dark.

Back on the night of Natalie's birth, my Uncle had given me advice on how to deal with my emotions throughout all this. It was harsh but actually had been very helpful. His call had come out of left field. He was the last person I expected to call at 4am. Sometimes, the best advice can come from unexpected sources. While I was pushing Kelly back towards one of the hospital entrances, my phone vibrated, letting know I had a notification. I have never been one to let a message or email sit. I don't know if it is my ADHD or just the idea in my head that someone is trying to contact me, but I usually respond very quickly. I pulled up the Facebook message soon after I had received it. It was a surprise to say the least. I had received a message from an old girlfriend from 7th grade. Someone I hadn't talked to in about 8 years or so. One may ask why we were friends on Facebook and I would likely chalk that up to my habit of accepting anyone who I have ever "known" as a friend on Facebook. Heck, I still have classmates from my college classes as friends on there who I can barely remember. My old ex-girlfriend had seen my struggles in update posts about Natalie. In her life, she had lived through some tragedy herself, including the loss of her mother and father. She wanted to reach out to me to help. Her advice was to remind me of a simple truth. "It is not your job to fix her. Your Job is to Love her." It was simple, obvious, and profound. Somehow, either with the guilt or shock, I had been focused on how to get this right. I felt that I was a failure to her because she sat in a hospital bed on a ventilator. None of that was true. I should be focusing on being there for her to the best of my ability. That is what a father's job is. It seems simple, but it was something I had overlooked. I literally felt a weight coming off my shoulders after thinking on it, much like I had after confession and I let go the "guilt". That phrase became my mantra for the next few weeks. I placed it on my home screen so, even in times of stress, I would see that and it was extremely helpful.

CHAPTER 12

JUST DO YOUR JOB

On June 4th. I woke up with the sun coming in the window at the Longfellow House. Something felt "right" that morning. We finally had a "plan" and while it was a scary one, It was nice to have one. For almost a week, we had just been "watching and waiting" and that was getting old. I made my bed up, which was not normal for me, and made an extra effort to clean up my room at the Ronald McDonald House before taking my daily walk in the early morning sun to see my baby. Besides, Kelly had not yet seen our room, and I wanted to make the best impression for the Ronald McDonald House as I could. My initial plan had been to check on Natalie, then go pick up Kelly after she was discharged and we would be together for the surgery. In the 5 days since Natalie's birth, I had been much more concerned with Natalie than my wife. This was something in the back of my mind. While it makes sense, someone had to be there for Natalie, I was starting to feel some resentment. I felt bad for leaving Kelly behind all the time while I was dealing with the situations and making all the decisions. Having her by my side would make this easier.

I moved quickly down the walk, coming up on the Hospital with a smile on my face. This was going to be the day. While they had never said 100% surgery was officially scheduled for that day, they had "tentatively scheduled it". I was new to this situation and I did not fully understand that sometimes "tentative" plans can change quickly. As I made it to the floor, I was anticipating finding Natalie off the oxygen and prostaglandins and ready to go. As I moved to her room, I did not need anyone to tell me that things were not improved.

Natalie was basically just as she had been for every morning of the last 3 days. She still had both the ventilator and the nitrogen mixer next to her bed. She was stable, comfortably sleeping with the machine breathing regularly for her and her saturation stuck at 72%. I was mildly concerned. I looked around for the night nurse looking for answers, but the room was empty besides Natalie and myself. It seemed I had taken too long to getting ready that morning cleaning the room, and the staff was going through the checkout process for during shift change.

After shift change, Natalie's nurse came in saying hello, introduced herself and acted as if everything was normal. It was just another day. I asked her what the plan was. Natalie was supposed to go to surgery. She looked at me with surprise. "Oh! I thought you knew!" she replied, explaining it had been canceled. Natalie had a rough night and was just coming out of it. She pointing to the monitor. While the current saturation is on there in big teal letters, if you looked closely on the side, you could see the a record of the "alarms" recorded on the side. Looking at all those small red letters, my heart sank. It was as if every 5 minutes she has been alarming, last occurring at 6:15, shortly before I came in. I looked at the nurse, unsure what to say. Luckily, the team came by.

Much like the nurse, the doctors were relatively calm and spoke to me in a firm "matter of fact" method. A wean was attempted again, but Natalie was just not doing well with it. When they had cut back the support, she would alarm almost constantly. They couldn't tell me what this "meant", but they knew surgery would be too high risk if she went in on the current level of support. The initial plan had been to cancel the surgery for June 4th and "re-evaluate" in several days. Once she was "optimized", then they would proceed.

Hopeless is not the right word. It was more of a deep disappointment. One couldn't help but wonder what it meant and other darker thoughts. They had assured us that they would constantly be reevaluating, but until she was able to be taken off some of the medications, it was not worth the risk. I tried to give myself reassurance, but my mind kept going back to the alarm monitor and all of her alarms overnight. I wondered to myself, "What if she never is 'optimized'?"

I shook it off. This was not the worst thing that could happen. The worst would be coming in and she was suddenly on bypass or something. I could deal with a little delay. Focusing on that positive, I decided to pull my mood up and try to be as positive as possible. We had an entire support team coming that day, so I had to make calls. Most people asked the same questions, and I responded with simple, reassuring answers.

Kelly was set to be discharged around noon that day. After leaving Natalie with the steady hands of my grandparents, I went over to St. Luke's to break Kelly out. It went quicker than I had anticipated and, once out of the hospital, we made our way back to our new home at the Ronald McDonald House. We decided that it was probably best to get checked into the Ronald McDonald House before going to Children's Mercy. We parked as close to the door as possible for Kelly and made our way in. Luckily, they had a wheelchair available for a short tour. Kelly was given a bracelet to match my own and I was able to show her the room.

One thing that was coming abundantly clear by this point was that people take information very seriously. Most people do not like to find out second hand from ANYONE about updates, taking it as a personal insult if I do not tell them personally. I have always been a passive person and usually try very hard keep the peace in most of my relationships. As we made our way back to Children's Mercy, someone informed me that I had hurt some feelings by posting to Facebook and not notifying "someone' of the change in plans. When I was told that "someone" was irritated I did not call them personally, it was my turn to be offended. I probably overreacted, but outsiders had no idea how difficult this was and how stressed I had become. They also didn't seem to comprehend how hard it can be going over the story over and over again. I ended up taking the high road and simply apologizing, but it is something that still comes up to this day. Later, I created a Facebook group for updates and it helps.

With Kelly out of the hospital and ready to help me with Natalie. After a short visit, Kelly went out to the lactation room to pump and I took over watch. Posting myself up on the blue chair, I was able to bring up a Hockey game on the iPad. Over the last month or so, I had little to do with my time besides "Clash of Clans", Farmtown, and hockey. Following Hockey during the playoffs can be challenging at times even with the simplest of circumstances. While games are usually exciting and intense, they also drag endlessly into the night and early morning hours due to the way overtime works in the playoffs. While normally that would be a problem, when you are in an endless time loop stuck at the hospital, any distraction is helpful and welcomed. Either way, I had been following closely and was "invested" at this point. At this point of the playoffs, things were starting to wind down. The season had basically ended with a bust. my Red Wings falling to the Bruins early on. I had hoped that San Jose would break though, but they had been taken out early as well.

I always had assumed that brainwashing was important when it came to children and sports teams. How would Natalie learn to love hockey if I didn't show it to her early and often? They are not born little Red Wing fans after all. While my team had been knocked out of the playoffs, the final round had just started. On this night, the Los Angeles Kings were playing the New York Rangers in Game 1 of the Stanley Cup Finals. I propped up the iPad on the stand usually designated for her tube feed pump and placed it near her bed. While I cannot say she enjoyed it, or even reacted, in time she would. I remember many times over the next few years where, while in the PICU or generic hospital room we would stay up late watching games together. What else was there to do to pass the time? The good news is that it totally worked. Natalie loves watching hockey and pointing out "the Goalies". She even wanted to be a Goalie for a short while. It only took one hit to the face with a puck to change that dream. Did I mention I am a wonderful father.

CHAPTER 13

GROWING A BABY

It is funny how quickly a person can get used to something. The roller coaster of emotion from the pending surgery and excitement of Kelly's discharge, things suddenly fell into a "routine". The routine involved me waking up before Kelly, rushing over to the hospital, visiting with Natalie and awaiting to be relieved by either my wife or my grandparents. The rest of the day would be spent in the waiting room, chapel or walking the grounds of the hospital. Initially, the plan seemed to be "surgery could be any day", but her overall lack of improvement seemed to dampen that excitement after the first few days. The story seemed to remain the same, "Trying to wean", "trying to grow" or a mixture of both. We made some progress here and there, and tried to celebrate small victories. Natalie was starting to take feeds regularly though the OG tube that was in her mouth, which was a good thing. Some things were harder, especially since Natalie was also becoming more aware or her soundings. She was not exactly a fan of being stuck, isolated in the bed with many of the discomforts that made up her life. For me, things begin to blur in my memory, but some things stick out.

Up until now in this story, Natalie probably comes off as a silent protagonist/hero. She is born and I have given updates on her status but not much about "her". We could not even "hold" her. As mentioned before, we were allowed to have her large foam mattress set on our lap, but it all felt disconnected. This is probably because, up until now, she was more or less a "thing". Sure, that sounds terrible to say, but she never really "looked at you", made noises and couldn't move or be held. After about one week, things started to change.

One day, later that week, I came in as I normally did and in a nervous rush. My anxiety, which would later become something I had to learn to deal with, was just starting to take route. The fear of the unknown was the worst. After signing in at the front desk with another interesting name, I found Natalie as I normally did. She was laying on her back in the bed with a white and pink blanket over her face. I asked the nurse how the night was and was told the same old "she did ok'. When looking back now, a verse of a song rings out in my head, "Every Day is Exactly the Same."

One day, As I pulled the book from my back pocket and sat down in the chair next to Natalie, it seemed like a typical day. I expected to read the book, ignore the alarms and await the team of doctors to come by with updates. As I looked around the room, checking Natalie's statistics, I almost jumped out in surprise. Natalie was awake, her steel blue eyes looking out from under the small blanket, focusing over at me. It was shocking to say the least. I leaned over, wanting to make sure she saw me. Somehow, I could tell that she did see me. It was like she was studying my face. Her hand was right there, so I placed my finger in it. She grasped it tightly.

While all of this was likely just random and even a reflex, sitting there with her hand around my finger and her eyes locked on mine, I felt a connection. Whatever feelings I had of guilt or inadequacy of a father before moment melted away. I was overcome with excitement. I smiled and spoke to her quietly but intently. I told her how much I loved her and how proud I was. I didn't really know what to say besides that, so I sat in silence. I don't know what I expected, I had never had a baby before, but I sat in silence for a short while, listening to her ventilator doing and watching her. She slowly slipped back off to sleep and I leaned back, appreciating that her Oxygen seemed to be a little bit better. Deep down, I felt like I had "helped" somehow and felt proud.

While it was exciting that Natalie was finally being awake and more aware, it brought on a new problem; crying. Babies Cry. It is a fact of life, but most of them are not on a ventilator. It is an odd thing to see a child cry while intubated. Physically, she would be freaking out, flailing her arms and turning purple, but no sound would come out. While on a ventilator, a baby can cry all they want and you would hear little to no change in the routine sound we had grown used to. It was disturbing. We found out pretty quickly that Natalie liked to use the pacifier. They are designed to pacify the infant after all. It seemed to really help during her "fits" of crying, but it was not easy to use. As Natalie was intubated, the tube interfered with the round base of the pacifier. It made it very hard for her to not only suck but even have it in her mouth.

As the cliché as it is, desperate times do call for desperate measures and something had to be done. I could not take the constant alarms and Natalie was not going to do well for long as long as she was constantly crying. The solution we came up with had two parts. First, Liz cut a large chunk out of the side of the pacifier with her bandage scissors. This allowed the pacifier to at least fit into her mouth. With the tube though, she couldn't produce enough suction to keep it there. This is where the second part of the solution came in. We had to hold the pacifier in her mouth with our hand. I usually used my pinky finger to do so and Natalie would chew and attempt to suck on it. This worked like a dream, but the moment the pacifier would fall out of her mouth she would start to cry. This would drop her saturation and her little monitor above her head monitoring her perfusion to her brain would alarm. To keep Natalie 'stable at goal" we would sit for hours holding this thing. Arms would ache, and then go numb. I felt terribly guilty, focusing on my own discomfort instead of how as was actually "helping her for once".

Natalie had genetic testing completed by the specialist during this first few weeks. Pulmonary Atresia is associated with a few genetic "syndromes" including something called "DiGeorge Syndrome". As the Geneticist told us, finding out a genetic cause is important to know for many reasons. First, if a child has a "syndrome" then and it is found, it can let doctors know what other possible abnormalities to watch out for. For example, a person with Down Syndrome has an increased risk for heart defects. If you know a child has Down Syndrome, you know to watch out for that. In addition, identifying genetic disorders it also can help with future research. Natalie was negative for the "DiGeorge Mutation", but was positive for a genetic mutation change found in something called "Charge Syndrome". Charge Syndrome is associated with heart defects, but also slow of growth, deafness, vision issues and mental retardation. That said, most present with the eye abnormalities and nose abnormalities. It was felt that Natalie did not meet criteria for this "syndrome" which was felt a blessing. They also compared Natalie's Genetics to Kelly's. As they both have "conotruncal" defects (malformations in the arteries off the heart), if a genetic link was found it could predict the possibility of future children with heart defects. Looking at both of their DNA, they did not find a link. This was good news. It meant that Natalie's mutations were likely random and she did not inherit them from my wife. They placed our risk of having another "heart baby" at 5%. That is still a scary number, but we have had two children since then and both are healthy.

CHAPTER 14

PUMPING AND ME

Words cannot express my shock at how difficult feeding a baby could be. I always assumed it was just something natural that occurred and was "not that big of deal". Every picture you see of a breastfeeding mother seems to be a Kodak moment, Mom smiling down at her baby who might as well be laughing. It is magical! I assumed it would not be that easy. I had not had any real experience with newborns during medical school and I had quite a bit to learn. I know now how difficult breast feeding in general can be. In a perfectly normal situation, it can be a difficult, frustrating and painful process and nothing about our situation was normal.

Natalie could not breast feed at first as she was intubated. After several days, the doctors recommended feeding through a tube placed in her stomach. Natalie could have been given formula, but Kelly did not want this. She was excited to breastfeed her baby and was excited about the health benefits that came with it. So, in order to keep her "supply", Kelly had to use a mechanical pump until Natalie was well enough to learn to breastfeed on her own.

Something changes in a breastfeeding mothers mind that makes her milk and her milk supply one of the most important things in their world. I do not know if it is something that is normal or if it had to do with our "situation" but my wife was totally consumed. She kept a detailed diary, and would become defensive if anything came close to messing with her schedule. She would refuse to eat, go on walks, go to bed, go see a movie or do anything that would delay her next scheduled pump. I realize that a baby has to eat and being the sole nutrition for your child is a very big deal. I just never expected it to totally consume a person as it did my wife. All that semi-sarcastic crud aside, I firmly supported Kelly breastfeeding. It really is better for kids and she was a real trooper putting in all the effort required with little in return.

The routine would take Kelly from us for about 40 to 60 minutes. She would gather her pumping parts and then take them to the small lactation room. She would pump for about 20 minutes and then pour the milk into containers. She would clean her parts in the little pink tub and then come back to us. Every two to three hours she would have to disappear to go pump. While I had my routine of early visits, reading stories, watching hockey, etc, Kelly had a schedule entirely of her own. It was like this, around the clock, day in and day out. As Natalie struggled for some time, this kept up for months on end. To make matters more stressful, Natalie was not eating much at this point, so she was given small cylindrical bottles to fill, place a name tag on them with the time and date and then they were taken off to the freezer at RMC.

CHAPTER 15

HALLELUJAH + LATE NIGHT HOCKEY

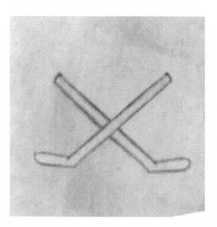

As the days turned to weeks, things settled into a routine. Kelly, myself and my grandparents maintained the "watch" and manned our little corner in the NICU waiting room. The weekends always seemed to lead to a steep increase in visitors, which was both a good and bad thing. It was good to have new conversation and It was always great to allow others to see my baby girl, but it was frustrating to have to explain the same results and uncertainty over and over. At this point, we were stuck in a purgatory of waiting. Waiting on a wean that may or may not occur.

The priest had recommended the week before that we attend mass. He felt it would be good for Kelly and I. Luckily, the church was within walking distance down Gillham road, about a block further than the Ronald McDonald House. The Church was named "Our Lady of Sorrows" which I could not help but find ironic. I had encouraged Kelly to come with me, telling her that it was not far and she could make it by foot. She was making progress with walking after her surgery, but it was still difficult for her. The church itself was a beautiful building, made of dark brick. Itr had two large bell towers and a large circular stained glass window on the the front that reminded me of the Notre Dame Cathedral. Inside, the church was very long, with a vaulted ceiling and dark wooden pews. The altar was very fancy, surrounded by columns topped with angels. The backdrop was a light blue.

I don't remember much of the mass, instead staying on my knees most of the time and praying for redemption. My mind was flooded with the images of my newborn daughter crying, but no sound coming out. It was something no father should have to see. I lamented with guilt over the whole thing, allowing my feelings to poor out through my tears. I never asked God why, but I begged for it to go away or for the suffering to be passed onto me. After the mass ended, I went to the prayer desk and placed a request for my daughter. I also picked up a small "thumb rosary" which I have carried with me to this day on my keychain.

Looking back now, the last thing I want is for it to "go away". While we have suffered, each in our own way, Natalie has brought so much joy to my world. I don't know how "It is all worth it" comes across, but it is totally worth it. Nothing has brought me more joy and more pain in my life than my Daughter.

Later that day, Kelly and I were able to get away, going to Hooters to enjoy dinner with my brother and his wife. In between discussing the Stanley Cup Finals, munching on fantastic wings and watching monster trucks, Tyler handed me a gift. It was from my Uncle and was unexpected.

Now let me tell you about my Uncle. He has always been a bit of an oddball. He is loud, obnoxious, and always seemed to enjoy a good time. He had different views in regards to sports teams and he frequently enjoyed rubbing in how his teams were superior. So, when Tyler handed me this gift, and I noticed the writing on the box that said "Steelers and Sparty Gear to follow", I expected the worst. I was pleasantly surprised to find a Detroit Red Wings onesie. My Uncle would also be the one to pull that kind of joke.

That night, the movie Shrek was being shown in the basement of the Ronald McDonald House. Kelly and I came in halfway through the movie and most of the children had already gone to bed. The song "Hallelujah" near the end of the movie stuck in my mind as we made our way to the room after the movie was ended. There was something about "... it's a cold and it's a broken Hallelujah" seemed to echo some of my feelings as of late. During that first week I remember wanting to sing Natalie nursery rhymes for comfort as those days stretched on, but oddly enough, could not remember any of them clearly enough to feel good singing them out loud. After that movie, "Hallelujah" became the song of choice during those long hours of the watch.

Over the next week, not much changed. There is a saying that I picked up from a Stephen King book that I reflected on during my early morning walk to see Natalie. "Same Shit. Different Day" It seemed to be pretty appropriate for our current situation.

We constantly seemed to be waiting for word on surgery but later be told we cannot proceed unless we could wean her more. Sitting in silence was always difficult, especially when Natalie was upset. While I couldn't remember those old nursery rhymes, I did pick up the lyrics to "Hallelujah" as well as a few songs I had heard from the church choir the day before. I decided to start with those. Those who know me may or may not know that I am a singer. I don't know where I picked it up, most likely from my father. I remember when we were young, my brother and I would visit him on the weekends. He would belt out Oak Ridge Boys like he was part of the band. He would also ad lib songs to fit his purpose. Deep down, I loved to sing. I would do it in the shower, mowing the lawn or driving, but never in public. I was always worried about what others would think. Somehow, in the halls of Children's Mercy NICU, I no longer cared. I just wanted to try to connect with my little girl. I would sing frequently and felt it helped.

Natalie was given little white mittens with frogs on them to prevent scratching and grabbing of tubes. As she was more awake, she was getting a little more "grabby". To combat this, she was given a small brown bear blanket. Known as "Colin's Sugar Bear" in memory of a baby who had passed in the NICU, the bear was basically a small square brown blanket with a teddy bear's head on it. The Sugar Bear was meant to comfort babies in the NICU. Natalie's bear looked like all the others except had a bow on it thanks to her "Bubbe". During that week, we would take turns hold her in the afternoon on her pad, cuddling the best we could.

Somewhere along the last 13 years Kelly and I had been together, we came up with a nonverbal way to remind the other one of our feelings. I would squeeze Kelly's with three quick squeezes, sending the message "I Love You". Kelly would squeeze back two to three times for "Love you too" or "You Too". During our first weeks together, I tried to "teach" Natalie this same thing. I knew that the three squeezes I was giving her foot or hand likely meant nothing to her and possibly made things worse, but something inside just needed to tell her constantly she was loved. At night, I would stay late, reading her my books or watching Hockey "together".

Things were not always uneventful in our immediate surrounding in the NICU. Thankfully, I was not in the NICU at the time our neighbor across the path from us "coded". I was out in the NICU waiting area, manning our corner, when my grandmother came out wide eyed. She told me that alarms had gone off on the monitor for the baby across from us. A Code blue had been called and people came out of the woodwork to help the visibly blue child. My grandmother had been asked to step out, so she had quickly left the area and came to me. It made me feel good that so much support existed if we ever needed it, but it was truly terrifying.

Another thing that bothered me at the time the overall lack of visitors for some of our neighbors. There were many incredibly small premature babies there, being "grown". Our closest neighbor, Skyler, rarely had visitors. I remember vividly overhearing one day how he was on the surgery schedule for his cleft lip but his parents never came in to give consent. It was unbelievable and a bit infuriating. We couldn't get surgery to fix our baby and this kid's parents couldn't be bothered to help theirs. I realize now that knew nothing of them, and it is not my place to judge them, but I cannot help my interpretation of the situation at the time. Sitting and staring in the NICU for a long time does odd things to your mind.

One never forgets the "sounds" that surround you in an NICU or ICU. There is documentation in adults admitted to ICU coming down with "ICU Dementia" brought on by the strange environments and constant tingling or beeping. To this day, four years later, I still can distinctly remember the sounds that constantly surrounded us in the NICU. As I mentioned earlier, there were always beeps and pings from the vital sign monitors, both Natalie's and our near neighbors. There are different kinds of alarms, some more of a "hey look at this" and others "OH NO SOMETHING is wrong". You can tell by the change in pitch and elevation in tone. It is hard to describe. I remember, sitting there reading or daydreaming, constantly hearing Natalie's vent which was constantly going in the background. One of our neighbors was an "alarmer" as well. That same visitor also had a mobile that was constantly playing. It had four different songs, the first one being a Mozart piece, the "Piano Concerta 21 in c major". In Demo mode, it would switch between the 4 available songs. While three of the songs were soothing, one of them was a very upbeat piano tune that I always found unnerving. It also had ladybugs on the mobile portion that constantly rattled back and forth. At first, I found this constant "tick click tick" thing annoying, but it became a noise we were used to and found comforting before our time in the NICU was done. I remember searching the internet desperately to find one of our own. Kelly thought Natalie may be used to it and wanted to make sure we had our own to take home with us.

It was during that first week that my Dad was able to make it back from Hawaii. I remember he was not only excited to meet his granddaughter but also show her what he brought. I remember smiling as he showed her a Hello Kitty Box carved from wood he had found. He also brought out a very colorful dress he had gotten her. I had to guard my feelings on this, as I felt in y mind that she would likely never get to wear it. Not due to the bright colors, but I felt we would never escape or get to the point of wearing any dress.

CHAPTER 16

... IT DOESN'T MEAN WE HAVE TO

In Natalie's third week of life, things were staying "stable" but not improving for Natalie. This was both good and bad. She was not doing well enough for her first surgery, but not doing poorly enough to rush anything. During my last week there, during the middle of the day, her doctors called a "meeting", pulling Kelly and I into a conference room near the front of the NICU.

The room rectangular, with a large rectangular grey table in the middle. There were 4 doctors on the other side of the table and chairs for Kelly and I on the side near the door. We held hands as we walk in, squeezing tightly before releasing and taking our seats. The head doctor, one of the NICU attending doctors started off the meeting letting us know the "goal" of this meeting. He wanted to review the case and to at least think about what we may want to do from here. We had been trying to wean and had not made much progress.

There was concern about how small her pulmonary arteries were. While the doctors felt, as a team, improving blood flow would hopefully help them get bigger, if they could not get her off nitrogen and prostaglandins, they were less sure about her outcome after the surgery. We had discussed "ECMO" in the past. ECMO was a type of bypass that a baby could go on temporarily to give their heart or lungs a break. While it sounds simple, it is very difficult and very risky. In the past, we had briefly discussed how, that if Natalie crashed during a wean, they would use ECMO to figure out what to do next. At this meeting, they suggested that we may need to rethink this. This shocked me. Why wouldn't we put Natalie on support and try to help her if she needed it. Trying to remain calm, I immediately questioned just that. "Just because we can do something, doesn't me we should. We don't think that, if it came to that, it would extend her life." It was hard to hear, but I did my best to listen to the rest of the plan, which included increasing feeds and trying to wean.

I think of this point similar to how someone must feel when they hear the word "cancer" come out of their doctors mouth. You try to focus but suddenly things become jumbled. The Doctors tried to be reassuring. "Hopefully she will improve with growing a little and we would not even have to worry about ECMO" they had said, but I was losing focus. I know that they were just wanting to talk "worst case scenario" but it was absolutely terrifying. Kelly started to cry, and they offered words of encouragement and hope. They said, "maybe things will change and we can schedule surgery "early" next week." We had heard something similar now for days and I was uncertain anymore if they actually meant it or not. As the meeting ended, one of the other doctors told us Palliative Care would be meeting with us soon.

A short while later, Palliative Care called us to a small room off to the side of the waiting room to the NICU. They provided another version of the "palliation" binder, similar to the one I had received the first day Natalie had been admitted. The social worker introduced herself and discussed what palliation and hospice does. Typically, they are consulted when options are either exhausted or families have decided against intervention. If any person has a life expectancy that is less than 6 months, typically Palliative Care and Hospice can help. They can help arrange for home care, medications and supplies. In Natalie's case, they would make it possible for us to "take her home" and "keep her comfortable". She then asked us about arrangements and if we had thought about it yet. She was very kind in tone, and I know she meant well, but the conversation quickly became a very difficult for both sides. I was semi-defiant, explaining that we didn't need that yet. I felt that, while the meeting before had not gone "well", there was still hope. This meeting felt quite the opposite, talking about death and planning for a funeral. The palliative care nurse was calm, placing her hand on mine. She told me that she knew that feeling, but it will help later, god forbid something does go wrong, to be prepared. I was dismissive again. She then proceeded to give me the name of some local places, commenting that some have very beautiful caskets in children's sizes. I don't remember what happened for the rest of this discussion. The talk of baby caskets, much like hearing your child should be made comfortable, is greatly disturbing.

While I sat, unable to really speak a rational thought, Kelly leaned in closer and was listening intently. Somehow, she was able to focus and She wanted to know everything she could. She knew that, in the insanity of such a moment of your child dying, knowing and planning in advance could really be valuable. Looking back now, I know that I "needed" to have this conversation. If things haven't worked out, we needed the information kept in the book the social worker offered us. It not only contained information to help us move forward, but also contained information about arrangements and group support afterwards.

The hospice conversation pushed me over the edge. I could not "bury" the fear and pain building up inside as I had before. I excused myself from the group in the waiting area and walked around the corner. I called my brother Tyler, crying. I relayed the message I had received from the meeting the best I could. I remember relaying that, there was many things we could do, but none of it "may not make a difference." I also mentioned the "baby casket" conversation. I was hopeless and started crying. Tyler's response was strong, loud and defiant. "She had made it this far., RIGHT?!" he had said. "How can they know?! How can you just give up. Don't you DARE give up." At the time, I remember feeling that he was being naive. These Doctor's see these things day in and day out. If anyone knew what was coming, they did. Tyler continued to press me. "God has a purpose for her!" he said, sounding so confident. He told me he would come by later and we would talk more. I hung up the phone and walked around the corner back to the waiting room. Kelly had spoken to my grandparents, I could tell by the look of their faces. It was the familiar face of someone who had been crying. We came together, there in our little corner, and held hands as a group. We said a prayer. It was simple. Please watch over our girl and help her get through this.

I went down to the chapel across the hall from the Pink Castle elevators. They had a small garden connected to the small room and I laid out on one of the wooden benches and cried harder than I had since the first night.

The next day I was set to Fly back to Toledo for the start of Residency Orientation. I had been coordinating with my Residency Coordinator, who had assured me that It was not "required" and that we could even put off starting residency into July if necessary. I did not want this. I had a strong sense of "duty" and, deep down, I did not want to fail in this. I had never been very confident in myself and the last thing I wanted was to be a liability.

CHAPTER 17

KANGAROO CARE AND GOODBYES

That night, Kelly and I were surprised when Liz asked if we wanted to hold the baby. She did not mean hold a foam pad. She was going to let us really hold the baby. I was terrified. I am a worrier about these kind of things and I knew it was going to be an inconvenience. I was worried how "safe" it would be. Liz assured me she would be right there. Kelly was very excited.

Kelly was allowed to hold her baby for the first time without the pad on June 14th, 16 days after Natalie was born. The whole process was quite the ordeal. Kelly sat in the big blueish chair, eagerly awaiting Natalie. Liz had to get assistance moving the baby as there were so many wires and tubes. We had to be extra careful with her breathing tube as if it became dislodged it would be an emergency. Liz had her take off her shirt and hold the baby "Skin to Skin" as it was supposed to do on Natalie's birthdate help them bond. It is called "Kangaroo Care". They placed Natalie on Kelly's chest and wrapped them both in a blanket. Chest to chest, it was magical to see. The nursing staff pulled the curtain and we sat there, as alone as one can get in the NICU. I will never forget sitting there watching as Kelly cried over her baby. Natalie could not make a sound due to the tube, but one could appreciate how important this was. She did not cry. They asked if I wanted to hold her and I declined. I knew this was likely stressful on Natalie and did not want to make things worse. All the stress of uncertainty had been very hard on us the last few day and the fear of how poorly Natalie seemed to be coping was first in my mind. Kangaroo Care was a welcomed distraction.

The next day was Father's Day. It started like most of the days we had in the NICU. I was at Natalie's side early in the morning, long before Kelly was awake. As a new father and one caught in the twilight zone of the past two weeks, I had not realizing that it was Father's Fay. Later, Kelly came in with a large smile on her face. She held in her hand some gifts for me that she had picked up at the gift shop. The first was a lime green envelope, "Daddy" written on the outside in chicken scratch. Obviously someone was trying to make it look like Natalie wrote it, which was funny to me and did bring a smile to my face. Looking at the envelope I remember thinking that the name "Daddy" did not apply to me. Not yet. To me, "Dad" was my father. I didn't say anything, just smiling and opening it. Inside there was a card with an outdoor theme with a compass and a Father and son raccoon working outdoors. Looking at it, It was less a card and more a certificate, bestowing me the title of "World's Greatest Daddy". I had a complex set of emotion as I looked at the card. I was grateful and touched, but it almost felt artificial for some reason. Like we were pretending to be a happy family and that I was a "great Dad". Looking back now, I can see what a strong person it takes to sit idle by your child's bed, watching her suffer and continuing to do it day after day. It can break even the strongest of people, but back then, it just felt like what I was supposed to be doing.

Kelly also gave me a fabric book. The book was titled "I Love My Daddy" and walked through the reasons a child would love their father. It was mostly about all the things he "does". "He feeds me things I like. He holds me tight and reads me my favorite books at night." While I could not do most of the things in the book, I could definitely do the last part if given the chance. I remember thinking it was too bad the book didn't include watching hockey with her at night. I was pretty good at that. As the day went on, the clock loomed large over my head. I knew I had to leave relatively soon and found myself counting down the minutes. When it was the absolute last minute, after kissing Natalie's forehead and hugging my wife, I went to the airport and caught a plane to our new life. Alone.

CHAPTER 18

EMPTY HANDED

In self-reflection on the plane ride to Toledo, I thought about the idea of being a father. I remember feeling like I had not yet "earned that title". The NICU had given me a card for Father's Day which I held in my hands and inspected. It was a pink piece of construction paper with my daughters hand print on it. They had added googly eyes and drew a hook with the title "Hooked on Daddy". It was cheesy but also wonderful. They had also given me a cup that was safely tucked away in my bag above me. It read; "Dad. Son's first Hero. Daughters first love". It was very kind of them, but I hardly felt like I deserves such recognition. I felt that I had been so lucky to have the privilege of calling Natalie my daughter and no matter how this thing turns out, I knew nothing would change that. I just didn't know what I did to deserve such recognition.

After landing at the Detroit Airport, my Dad picked me up and drove me home to our new house in Toledo. I had been there just over a month ago and it stood there, well lit, and empty. I knew it would be hard coming home alone. Before the birth the plan had been to come home as a family, but here I stood in front of the house, empty handed and alone. I stood outside the front door for an extended moment, looking up at the house, trying to gather my courage to go inside. My Dad, who was still in the driveway, asked If I needed help getting in. I yelled back that I was ok, but his interruption was what I needed to move on. I unlocked the door and went inside.

Inside the house the initially was a small entryway with slate tile floors. Just through the entryway, the large living room right off and the stairs to the second level to the left. The house was clean and a dim light was cast by a lamp off to the right. After all this time away, the house smelled foreign and deep inside I felt that inner sense of "wrong" building inside my chest. I dropped my bags inside the entryway and took the wooden stairs to the left up to the second level. I had not made up my mind yet on what I wanted to do but I remember making a conscious decision to avoid the nursery, even pointing to the closed door and saying "Nope" out loud as I passed to go to my room.

I was so tired, likely from the lack of sleep and turbulent emotion of the past few days. The most important business at hand was to start to prepare for a busy first day of residency orientation the next day. Sleep seemed like the best thing to do first. After grabbing some clothes from the bedroom, I went to freshen up in the bathroom. The shower was nice and the steamy warm air helped me feel a little more at ease. After finishing up in the bathroom, I started to make my way towards my room. The nursery was right outside the bathroom and the large white door that was closed. There was little ceramic tag hanging from the doorknob of the nursery caught that my eye as I passed, "Celebrate" it read. The plaque caught me by surprise and sort of took my breath away. I was trying to ignore what was going on in Kansas City and just deal with the problems at hand, but It seemed I could not escape it. I fought the odd inner urge to go into the room, knowing that the feeling of regret, guilt, pain and hopelessness would certainly follow. Instead, I told the door "no!" out loud once more, moved down to my room and, after speaking with Kelly for a short while on the phone, went to bed. I remember a dream that night in regards to residency. It was very vivid and odd, but involved meeting up with my new teachers and visiting one of my brothers in the hospital. He was in the hospital, in a diaper, being treated with electric shock therapy. The dream was nonsense, as dreams can be and I had no idea what it meant. It may have been a reflection about my nerves and how confused I was about what was to come.

The first day of Residency started with a meet and greet breakfast at the newly completed Family Medicine Center. I met the new staff as well as my new fellow Interns. I had met most of the people with the residency, including the attending physicians, residents and support staff, but the interns were all new. I had received the email several months back from the program when we had all "matched" to the WW Knight Family Medicine Residency Program and had reviewed the faces. I had not known any of them from my interview and tour dates and was very nervous that day about how we would meld. These people would be on the front lines with me and I just prayed I could relate.

Luckily, the WW Knight class of 2017 seemed top notch. They were friendly and inviting. Even as nervous as I was, it seemed I had been very blessed in the people I was starting this journey with. After this was over, we met with Christine Miller to go over policy and procedure. We were given clearance for computers as well as pictures taken for our badges.

After this was done, we spent some time in clinic shadowing and then were released for the day. Several of the senior residents decided to take the "TERNS" out, meeting at Maumee Bay Brewing Company for dinner and a beer. I ordered a "Ghost Pepper Burger" as well as a Habanero based beer. It was not nearly as hot as one would expect and, overall, it was a pretty cool thing to do. Having good fellowship is always good for the soul.

After dinner, I made my way back to the empty house. I wanted to go upstairs and lay down, but something inside drew me to the nursery. I walked up the stairs and my eyes caught the "celebrate" sign on the doorknob. It is like something inside me took over the controls at that point. I couldn't stop. I walked over, and felt the cold door knob on my hand. I turned it, almost instinctively, opened the door and went in. Nothing compared to the emotional turmoil I walked in on. Not the discussion of palliative care, nor the talk of baby coffins had been as difficult, emotionally, as walking into the warm, sunlight nursery alone.

As I walked in, I remember my guts immediately tightening up inside me. Light poured in through the window across from the door. The room still smelled of fresh paint, put up a month ago by a happy daddy to be and his ever helpful grandfather. The dresser/changing table was on the right. Above it, we had hung a "Pooh Themed" set of cards that read "Baby". The crib was on the left, as was the rocking chair. The walls, yellow and green, had different large classic 'Pooh" character stickers spread throughout the room. I walked in and my hand barely grazing the top of the crib. After a moment, I felt like I couldn't breathe. I sat into the rocker and tried to deal with the tightness in my chest. The feelings I feared, regret, guilt, pain and hopelessness, all came on strong. I started balling openly, tears rolling down my face and I found myself moaning in agony.

Our lives had been so "perfect". We had done everything like we were supposed to. How could this of happened to us? I again wondered if all of this was real. I found myself asking "What if Natalie never made it home" out loud in a mumbly messy voice. I think, in my heart-of-hearts, I feared that that was exactly what was going to happen. Something would happen and she would pass. The thought about taking down all of the nursery decorations was too much, leading to more crying. After a moment, pulled up my phone and reached out to Kelly.

Kelly was able to talk me down. My grandmother was with Natalie and Kelly was pumping. Things were the same with Natalie. It seemed that she would be good during the day and then not so good at night. No plans had been made about surgery. Kelly had never seen the nursery either, so I tried to describe it, taking pictures to send her later. There was long periods of silence in the conversation, interrupted occasionally by the sound of her pump, but that wasn't a bad thing. Words could not fix what was going on in our lives, but we were in this together as a team, and we would deal with it as a team. Kelly asked about my first day and I calmly explained that things had gone really well. Taking a moment to discuss something besides impending doom did seem to help. After the conversation ended, I sat on the floor in the Nursery for some time reflecting on my feelings. During my crying fit I had found Pooh and Tigger, the other two members of Natalie's group of "friends", and I held them close as I thought out loud and cried. Pooh had made a good tear rag. As the sun started to set through the window, my stomach reminded me that I was in fact starving. I grabbed up Pooh and Tigger and made my way down stairs for dinner.

PART II

The Winding Road Home

CHAPTER 19

FIX YOU

There are some things in life you will never forget. Some memories in this book are fuzzy. Using pictures, Facebook and emails I had sent to Natalie, I had to slowly piece all of these things together into a coherent memory. The events of June 19th will always be crystal clear in my memory, both because of the gravity of the events of the day, but also because of the large swing in emotion.

I woke up that next day in a slightly better mood, ready for my second day of orientation. I called the Children's hospital to check in on my baby girl. It was a bit of a process to get information. I would call the main line and ask for the nurse of bed D-38. Sometimes you would get the right nurse, but other times you would get one from a pod Nearby. The nurse would ask for a "verification number" before they would provide any details. That morning, after using the number written on my orange wrist band for verification, I was able to speak to her nurse about updates. I was relieved to find out nothing "bad" had happened while I slept. Natalie was doing about the same. This was the typical morning and there was nothing alarming told to me during this call. It was "SSDD" as Stephen King would say. In Toledo I was now on eastern time so Kelly would still be sleeping at the Ronald McDonald House. She was spending much of every night either at Natalie's side or pumping, so sleeping in a little was no worry. I knew it was best to let her sleep and figured we would catch up at lunch.

Day 2 of orientation consisted of computer training for the residency as well as several more hours of shadowing. Computer training was scheduled for 4 hours that morning at a generic office building off campus. I met my fellow interns at the random building on executive parkway and found the designated random room deep inside. The class was for training on the Toledo Hospital Electronic Medical Record as well as the separate system used in the clinic.

Now, in medical school, I struggled greatly at times sitting in class. I would usually attend lecture, but I was "distractible". I can be terribly scatterbrained at times and I don't always do well sitting in one spot for too long, especially if I do not find the topic engaging. It is also hard for me to just go to a class and "learn". Instead of sitting for a long time, working through 'theoretical' situations" and learning what buttons to click, I do better trying to use the system on the fly. This was only the first of four days of computer training. As I drove to the random building, I was really worried how hard that morning was going to be.

Luckily, my fellow residents were amazing, cracking jokes and making the morning entertaining and keeping my mind away from the uncertainty still looming in Kansas City. After the training was "complete", I jumped in my car and headed back towards clinic down Lewis Road. While on my way back to the residency clinic, I stopped at a Circle K on Lewis Avenue just off Alexis to fill up on Gas. Just as I placed the pump into the tank, my phone rang.

"Is this Natalie's Dad?" It was a Missouri number. I had no idea who or what this could be. I told them that I was Natalie's father. "Natalie had a hard time overnight. The team has decided that she is simply not going to tolerate a wean. We want to go ahead with the surgery and we are not confident she will do well. Do you want us to cancel the surgery for tomorrow?"

Cancel? They knew I was out of town and wanted me to be there for the surgery. I took too long to reply. "Hello?" They asked, making sure I had heard them. I walked out to the front of the car, leaning against it. "No… I will be there" I responded, trying to stay calm. "Are you sure? I…" I responded calmly, trying to make sure I understood what was said. I tried to keep my suddenly racing thoughts at the back of my mind. "I will be there." They agreed and let me know it would be the second case of the day. They hung up.

My first reaction was to call my residency coordinator Chris Miller. "They called and want to know about surgery tomorrow… " I said in a tizzy. "They don't think it will go…". She cut me off, telling me to go. I started asking about orientation, and she cut me off again, telling me she would take care of it. I hung up the phone, finished pumping the gas and headed back to my house, mind racing.

I was surprised by their assumption. There was no way I would NOT be there for a procedure, especially if it was a semi-emergency. *She may not do well.* The words rattled through my mind as I packed my bag. I had spoken to my Dad who was back at work in Findlay. He lived about one hour to the south and said he could give me a ride to the airport. I had originally planned on flying back to Kansas City that weekend. Luckily, Delta was able to adjust my reservation. I made an arrangement for a flight going out that night at 9pm.

My Dad picked me up and we drove to the airport in silence, each in our own thoughts. I tried to keep cool, cracking several jokes, but most of them came off stale. Once we parked, I noticed that my Dad had a bag as well. He had made arrangements and was coming with me. It was a very nice surprise and lifted my mood greatly. Not being alone with my thoughts was an uplifting idea.

We made our way through the airport quickly and reached our gate with plenty of time to waste. Even with my Dad near, I could feel my emotions fighting to break free once again. I tried to hide them. I had done so well in the recent past, pushing things under the surface and keeping a fake smile on my face. I tried to play it tough, but the idea of my daughters mortality in the balance was simply too hard. I placed my iPod earphones in my ears, hoping to simply overwhelm my brain with something other than Natalie.

We had some time before the flight, so I decided to stand in line for a coke from one of the food vendors. It was dark outside and I was growing tired and knew it would be hard to make it through the flight and to the hospital without a little caffeine. As I stood there listening to my iPod, "Fix You" by Coldplay started up. The song starts up first with the sounds of waves, followed by a nice piano introduction, the breaks into the first verse in a somber, beautiful voice.

The words, especially the ones about trying to fix "you", struck hard right at my core, destroying any remaining strength I had left. It was like the song perfectly described what I was feeling. I took an unsteady step backward and my back hit the terminal wall. I leaned into it, placing my face in my hand and started sobbed loudly, slowly lowering myself to floor. In an instant, My Dad was there. He wrapped his arms around me tightly as we sat together on the terminal floor. He didn't say anything, he didn't need to. We cried.

My Dad and I arrived in Kansas City, late that night. I was doing a little better emotionally. A good cry can do that for you.

Now, I am a pretty short guy, measuring in at 5'5" on my best day. This brings quite a few disadvantages in life. While getting off the plane, I was reminded of on of the few benefits of being short. As I stood in the aisle, One of the overhead doors flew open on the side, just kicking my hat. The man in front of me looked at me wide eyed, but I smiled and waved it off, laughing almost. It reminded me of a conversation I had with my best friends about my height.

In medical school, I was given the nicknamed "baby bear". During a long study break, My friends and I came up with some real benefits for being vertically challenged. For instance, if Velociraptors ever attacked the school, I could be easily placed in the air vents in the ceiling. My vertically gifted friends would be dino food. As I stood in the line to leave the plane, I was reminded of that conversation and laughed literally out loud. I probably looked like a crazy person, eyes red from crying and laughing, but It was a nice momentary reprieve from the grim thoughts that had been dominating my mind for most of the plane ride.

My Dad and I rushed to the Children's hospital, anxious to see Natalie. I remember the sensation of having a large rock sitting in the pit of my stomach as I looked out the passenger window at the KC skyline. Arriving at night, much of the parking garage was open and we were able to park in the Blue Balloon right next to my grandparents car in the handicap slots. I recognized their car by the big Michigan State Spartans Magnet on the back.

When we arrived onto the floor, Kelly was holding Natalie for "Kangaroo time". My Dad excused himself. Kelly looked up at me, tears in her eyes and a smile on her face. I could tell she was happy to see me, but the weight of the moment was really pushing down on her. My Mother was there. After a short while, Kelly offered to let someone else hold her. Being the "thoughtful;" person that I can be, I wanted to make sure my Mother had the chance, so she was next. I tend to just want other people to be happy. That is what makes me feel fulfilled and in that moment, I wanted my Mom to hold her. I cannot say I was not oddly jealous, but at the same time, I was being selfless. I'll never forget the look in my mother's eyes as she looked at me, holding my only child. The emotions on her face were so complex; joy, pain and fear.

After a bit, it was to be my turn. I was unsure if I should even have a turn, as Natalie had already been through so much that day. Liz told me not to be silly. "Hold your baby" she said. I just didn't want to be an inconvenience. I was told it was my turn for Kangaroo Kare. It felt odd to me, wondering why I needed to take my shirt off, but I was assured that it would help Natalie. I remember feeling uncomfortable sitting in the chair without my shirt waiting for the baby to be handed to me. As they held her above me, I remember feeling so nervous. I had held a baby before, but never MY baby. I remember how warm she was as they pressed her against my chest and tucked her in. I was terrified I would drop her or hurt her somehow. I could feel her little chest moving in and out. It was a miracle. I actually started tearing up, not something I am embarrassed of. I normally was not a person to cry, but I tears were presenting themselves very frequently over the past month. I felt like a crying veteran. I held Natalie for some time and she seemed to do well in my little cocoon of blankets. It was such a terrific experience and I probably would have not held her if it was not for our Nurse Liz. This also was our last night in the NICU.

CHAPTER 20

TO THE PICU

Oddly enough, I do not remember much about the day from Natalie's first surgery. I remember waking in the day of the 18th almost mentally surprised I was back in Kansas City and the routine that I had just left. I had woken up the day before in my bed in Toledo and here I was back at Ronald McDonald House. I made my way to the NICU to find Natalie "orange". She had a special bath earlier in the night to prepare her for surgery. Holding Kelly tightly in my arms, I remember how helpless it felt as they took Natalie away. " We will take good care of her." they said. The words from the day before, "She may not do well" rang in my head once again. We had not been able to wean her. Was this really the best thing to do? All I could do is trust the guy upstairs. I decided not to worry, instead throw prayers to God. I had been begging him for a "shot" at life and this seemed to be it. It was finally here and I was not going to allow certain questions to dampen the mood. As we left our room D-38 for the last time, I grabbed Eeyore off the counter. He was now my procedure buddy and expert tear absorber. I kissed Kelly's forehead and we joined our support team out in the waiting room.

We were given directions to the Ronald McDonald "Family Room". It was a family area located inside the hospital just off to the right off of a main hallway. While anyone who's child is receiving care at the hospital can visit this family room, a select number of small rooms were also available to stay overnight. The staff later educated us that the rooms were reserved the families of the hospitals most serious patients. Sometimes, if a child is undergoing major surgery, bone marrow transfusions or just very ill, these families needed to be close. In times like that, families can't take even out of the hospital for fear of something happening and they not be there. The family area also served as an area for parents to rest from the noises and anxiety that comes with having a child in the ICU.

There was a large mural along the wall near the entrance to the family room. It depicted a several different animals living in the city. It was heavily stylistic and the animals all had large goofy smiles on their faces. The entryway to the room had a fake window similar to the window in our NICU room and a large door. Once inside, there was a check in area to the right and then the room opened before you. The area was well lit, clean and felt very modern. The floors were hardwood and very shiny. Large glass windows dominated the far side of the room to add in ambient light. On the left, there was a very large kitchen with the largest refrigerator I ever seen. To the right, across from the kitchen was a a small lounging area with a large Television and couches. There was also a seating area near the back far wall and even access to an outdoor patio. Hidden on the right were two doors off to the side that lead to a hallway where there small rooms where families could stay.

By the time we made it from waiting room to check in, the staff was serving pizza out of the fancy kitchen. Much like the Ronald McDonald House proper, this mini House had volunteers who would sponsor meals. It was very busy, with a line snaking into the lounge area. We were given a tour by a volunteer and shown to a room that had just been freed up for us for Natalie's surgery. Down the back hall, there was a laundry area and a communal bathroom for all the rooms to share. I do not remember much about the room, except that the room itself was seemed small and "brown" to me.

After the tour, we went into the main area. I wondered how I had not known of this place before now. I noticed a stash of what appeared to be bottles of Bar-B-Que and cards on a shelf to the side. I walked over to see that it was in fact a bottle of Bar-B-Que. Picking it up, It was a special Bar-B-Que created for Father's Day. It was a brand I had not yet seen, "World's Best Dad". I found it kind of funny. I snatched up a bottle and hid it in my room, intent on giving it to my father at some point. He was the "World's Best Dad" after all.

After snagging some pizza, we took up waiting in the strange, foreign land of the PICU waiting area with the rest of the family. Looking around the waiting area, the room was a little bit more friendly than the NICU. It was actually quite a bit larger than the NICU waiting area, and there we even different "rooms" that divided the large space. There were colorful chairs spread throughout, similar to the NICU waiting area. There were designated play areas with a small house structures and toys meant to help siblings past the time. We found a semi-isolated section off to the side, divided with walls on three sides, and set up camp. It was odd, not being in our designate corner in the NICU waiting area. I had grown so comfortable in that Corner on the third floor. This are felt so foreign that it was hard to settle in emotionally. Some of the chairs in our back corner actually pulled out into beds. I picked out a green one in the corner and pulled it out, setting up almost a lounger. Studying the area around us, I noticed Books and magazines were kept in odd cubby shelves on the wall. I picked up a copy of a book I recognized, as I had read it before during childhood, and flipped through it to pass the time.

Hours later, we were notified that Natalie had made it through surgery and had done well. She was still unconscious but we could come see her in the PICU. I remember walking quickly in the direction of the PICU in silence with Kelly's hand tightly held in mind. As we made our way there, the worst of things came to my mind. I said a silent prayer, thanking the Lord for allowing Natalie to make it this far and prayed for the strength for what was sure to came next. I was a doctor, and I had seen patients when they come out of cardiac surgery. They rarely looked "good". Usually, they are puffy and there are wires and tubes coming out of everywhere. Once they wake up, they usually struggle with breathing and pain. I feared what Natalie would look like afterwards and how I would deal with it.

At check in, we were given orange "parent" tags to clip to our shirt. The PICU was quite different from the NICU in many ways. Unlike the large room filled with cubbies in the NICU, the PICU was one large hallway with isolated rooms on each side in a large semicircle. Each room had large glass doors that could be closed. Natalie's room was on the right side halfway down the long hallway. Her room was much bigger than her NICU room and Her bed was positioned in the middle. Natalie was bundled up in the small bed with 3 different blankets covering her. As predicted, she was taking quite a bit of support to stay alive. Next to her, there were two IV poles filled with monitor and pumps filling Natalie's IV with all sorts of medications and fluids. Some of these mediations I knew, such as norepinephrine, others I did not. One thing that I remember noticing right away was Natalie's oxygen saturation. That bright teal "92" on the monitor hanging from the wall was stunning. 92 percent was higher than I had ever seen it for her. It was almost impossibly high. I wondered if it I was reading the monitor right. Sometimes, different monitors have different settings and you can be fooled. Deep down in my soul, suddenly I felt a like a large weight had been lifted off of my shoulders. 'Was she fixed?" I wondered to myself as I approached the bed.

My optimism of Natalie's situation was dulled a little after we spoke to the attending physician. He first told us that we should be proud as Natalie was exceeding all of their expectations. They did not know how she was doing so well with the way her arteries looked, but she was making excellent progress. He did warn us though, telling us that we did not want her oxygen to be as high as they were. It seemed odd to me and I asked for him to clarify. He explained that with Natalie's lungs were not used to that much blood flow up until now, the increased flow could cause an "injury" to her lungs. It could lead to her lungs being overloaded and lead to respiratory failure. They would keep an eye on things and, if things seemed to worsen, they would give Lasix to help get the fluids out of her lungs. I remember not really understanding how finally getting blood into her lungs could be a bad thing, but nodding anyway. I really just wanting Natalie's lungs to get as much flow as it could so we could get "better". I was so overjoyed that she seemed to be doing so WELL. It had been a while since anyone had used that term. WELL. It felt good. Maybe there was hope after all.

After things settled down, we were able to "move in" to Natalie's room and get to know her nurse. Once she was unwrapped, I could see the extent of her surgery and what they had "done" to her. She was pale, puffy even and had a large tan bandage over her chest. This was covering the incision. There were tubes coming out every which way, with a large tube coming out from below the large bandage that was draining her chest. She had a larger IV tube coming out of the side of neck and her left hand had a large pad on it to keep the IV there safe and secure. I remember I tried to lighten the mood, making a joke to Kelly about how it seemed Natalie was already in training to be a goalie. She gave me a sarcastic "Yeah..." in response.

The "rules" in the PICU were a little different from the NICU. We were allowed up to 4 visitors at one time not including parents, as parents were considered "Part of the team". Visitation hours were similar and no visitors were allowed after 9. They also asked for visitors to avoid shift change. We were able to invite family members back for a short time after we settled in. It was nice allowing other to see her. I remember distinctly asking family to avoid pictures that first da. The last thing I wanted was pictures of my daughter plastered all over Facebook in this shape. Most visitors listened. We spent the remained of the day in fellowship together, praying, reflecting and making jokes about Natalie's "hockey pad".

Things moved quickly in the PICU. Nurses were not only competent but seemed to be very caring in regards to my baby and her wellbeing. While normally, rules dictate that nothing be left in a baby's "crib", our nurse allowed Natalie's "friends" to stay with her after she stabilized. This included Eeyore, Piglet, Colin's Sugar Bear and a ballerina mouse given to us by a medical school friend Sean Sturm.

After the crowd of visitors died down, Kelly and I spent time just looking at our little heart warrior. She was resting comfortably and her alarms had slowed to next to none. We had placed her sugar bear over her face to allow her to rest. The lights were so bright. I would sing to her constantly, mostly the "Hallelujah" song that I could not get out of my head.

CHAPTER 21

SOMETHING TO CELEBRATE

I was at Natalie's bedside early the next morning. I could not sleep well in the Ronald McDonald room inside the hospital. I came to her room in the PICU to find Natalie wise awake with dark eyes open wide as she calmly looked around the room. I was excited, moving quickly over to her side to say hello. I felt a little bad that I had not with her when she opened her eyes, but, emotionally, I was more than spent. I used that to justify the situation. Her nurse was there and spoke to me while I talked to Natalie, my face hovering in front of hers. She told my that things had gone well overnight and we would have to wait until the team of doctors came by to know the plan for the day. I was excited. "Going Well" was not terminology we had heard much of.

In the PICU, you could tell when the Attending and their team of Residents was coming. You would hear them, the group of 10-15, moving down the halls. They would go room to room and having open discussions about the "cases" in the hallway. I would always get anxious when I would see them lined up in front of one of our neighbor's door, wondering what sort of news they would lay on me this time. When it was our turn, they would stand in the doorway, filling in most of the front part of our room. The youngest member of the staff, be it student, intern or resident, would present the case out loud to the attending, rattling off lab values and ventilator settings. After the presentation, the attending doctor would grill them about the plan, asking questions about medications, as well as a few "what ifs" scenarios. I would watch as the student or interns face as they struggled with the questions. You could tell how nervous they were. I had been in that situation many times already in my career and knew I had quite of bit of this to look forward to. It was the best way to learn. After the "pimping" (as it is called) ended, the team would address us, explaining things in "normal-speak" and let us know the plan for the day.

As a doctor, I usually was able to follow along with the presentation. I didn't always know what is going on, especially at this part in my training, so I tried not to think too much into one thing or another. I tried to soak in all I could about their thoughts and listening to the plan in detail. Most of the time, I did not tell anyone I was a physician, as I did not want to be treated differently. Even with my knowledge, the situation was confusing and I do not know how a non-medically trained parent stood a chance following some of the things these doctors said. Some of the terms they would use were hard for ME to understand, which could be frustrating. Kelly usually just nodded and would say "ok", with a blank look on her face. Ask her about what the doctors had said and she would usually not be able to recall many details.

On 6/19, the team consisting of a cardiologist told us they were impressed how well Natalie was doing. They were able to finally wean her some of her "respiratory" support, something we had been trying to do and failing at for the past two weeks. Overnight, they had been able to stop her prostaglandins and her ventilator was only using "room air". Their plan was to start to wean the nitrogen.

I felt so much pride, looking over at my baby and knowing that she was finally improving. Hope started to bloom inside my heart. Had all that worrying been for nothing? Was there a chance Natalie may yet still see the nursery I had prepared for her. I tried to temper these sudden expectations and thoughts. "Natalie is only 1 day post operation. So much could happen in the meantime. Hold your horses" I told myself. After the team left, I posted to Facebook the good news. I took a photo to go with it, showing Natalie wide awake, dark eyes blazing with life.

That night, we celebrated. The whole family went to a restaurant at the plaza called Buca di Beppo. Most of the family came, including my Mom and Dad, stepmom, and siblings. The restaurant is a "family style" Italian themed eatery, located mostly underground in "brick" tunnels at the Plaza in Kansas City. The walls are covered in odd photos of people and statues, some of them silly and some of them very serious. One of the cooler features of this specific restaurant is "the kitchen table" where you literally eat in the kitchen while the chefs prepare meals. You get to watch all of the drama that unfolds and they show you other customers dishes as they make their way out to the other guests. The Kitchen Table was not available, nor was the "Pope Room, so we sat near the back of the restaurant at a large rectangular table with a red checkerboard tablecloth.

We laughed and feasted for several hours on the three large platters we had ordered as well as enjoyed an adult beverage or two. For the first time in a while, spirits were high. Just when we thought we were done, my wife spoke up that she wanted desert. Most members of the party groaned as their stomachs were just too full for that. Laughing, I brought up a lesson from my anatomy classes. The stomach has this small pouch near the top, called the "fundus", and, at least on that night, I brought up that there is technically ALWAYS room for desert. This brought on more laughter and an agreement to order more.

Much like their main dishes, the desserts at Buca are also huge. Kelly ordered some sort of brownie sundae. When it came out, it was in a martini glass larger than her head. Even I was unsure if there was enough room in the "fundus" for all that sugary goodness. Kelly proved me wrong, dominating that desert.

CHAPTER 22

ROAD TO RECOVERY

It is amazing what good news can do for ones "mental health". I remember waking the next day, now back at our room in the Longfellow House, and not being overwhelmed with the usual anxiety I had in the morning. I was excited, ready to tackle the day. Natalie was resting comfortably when I entered her room. I was glad she was not awake looking for me when I walked in. She still had the tube in place in her mouth with her sugar bear over her eyes.

Soon, the team of doctors came by. Kelly was there by this point and they informed us that Natalie was completely "off support". She had been weaned off of the nitrogen and, while still intubated, she was breathing room air. They had planned to "sprint" her today and if it works, they would pull the chest tubes and exudate.

Breathing, while simple, can be quite a complex process. It can be hard to understand the physiology behind it sometimes, but when a person breathes, their diaphragm lowers and pulls air into the lungs. A ventilator works a little differently, blowing air into your lungs. As this is a different process, sometimes patients can have a hard time breathing once a ventilator is shut off. It is almost as if your lungs get "lazy" from not having to work. "Sprinting" is a common term used in respiratory medicine and is done to test if someone can breathe on their own before the tube is removed. Sprinting is a setting on the ventilator where the vent no longer initiates the breath. Instead, the patient's lungs start to pull for air and then the ventilator supports it, pushing air into the lungs.

If someone is intubated and the tube is taken out and the patient is not "ready" it can be a medical emergency and require 're-intubation" or worse. There is always the chance someone cannot pass a "sprint" and that can be a serious problem as well. Since Natalie had been intubated, she had not had to breath on her own for about 3 weeks. The doctors were worried her lungs may be lazy and what trouble that could bring. They were going to Sprint her with the ventilator for an extended period of time to test her lungs. If she did well with this, they felt that that she likely would be able to breath on her own and could be extubated.

Natalie did very well with the sprint the nurses began to start the process to extubate. The first thing was the removal of her chest tube. Now, I have never had a chest tube, but from what I do know they are no fun. I have helped put them in and I have assisted with pulling one once. The look on that patient's face when we pulled it was one of pure agony. When they came in to remove Natalie's chest tube, I remember how nervous I had been. First, the nurse removed the large tan square patch that was covering her chest incision. I remember being curious, so I watched closely, holding her pacifier in her mouth to keep her calm. The incision in the middle of her chest was from just below her collar bone to the top of her belly and was not nearly as sickening as I thought it was going to look. It was "well approximated' as surgeons like to say and it was not really leaking anything. The chest tube was sticking out from the bottom. I was relieved it was not worse than that. Still, somewhere inside myself felt terrible and nauseated.

My thoughts drifted in that moment to my wife. Kelly told me about times people would make fun of her scar. It was not a happy memory. I looked down at my daughter's chest, which was now "scarred", just like her mother. I was feeling pity, but quickly fought it off. Without that scar, Natalie wouldn't be where we were. She would not have made all this progress and we would still be in the NICU talking little baby caskets. That thought straightened up my mind and allowed me the courage for what was next.

Taking out a chest tube is a good thing overall. I have been told in the past they are very uncomfortable and a patient cannot usually go home with one in place. Technically speaking, removing a chest tube is not very hard to do. Using scissors, you clip the stitches holding the tube in place then pull hard on the tube. It usually slides ride out. After the patient settles down, you have to watch for possible side effects of the procedure. Doctors will order x-rays to make sure the lungs does not deflate. If is a fairly routine procedure in the "post open heart surgery" world.

There was nothing routine or easy for me helping with the removal of Natalie's chest tube. The look on her face when they pulled it was pure shock and horror. She immediately started flailing, screaming silently and "fighting the vent". Her saturation levels dropped back into the 60s and, suddenly, it was like being back in the NICU, watching my daughter crash. She wouldn't let me put the pacifier in her mouth. I leaned over, kissing her forehead above the brain monitor, trying to shush her and offer loving words.

After a few moments, she started to settle down but the situation did not get easier on Natalie. After confirming she could "sprint", the doctors decided extubation was next. This should of been something I was excited about, but somehow the drama from the chest tube had me worried about things changing too quickly. The Resident asked us to step outside while they pulled her breathing tube and stabilized her. I think that if the chest tube was not so hard on me emotionally, I may have asked to stay, but I did not fight their wishes at this point. Kelly and I went out to the waiting area near the PICU and awaited the call to come back.

When we did came back after about 30 minutes, we could hear Natalie crying from the hall. I was very nervous, but Kelly seemed excited. "The mute button is officially off" she said as we walked back through the door. I had not heard Natalie cry since the day she was born, all of a month ago. While her crying was not loud, nothing like when she was born, it was something that one never forgets. The noise was very hoarse. Kelly had described it well, commenting on how it sounded close to the noise my cat makes when he chokes on a hairball. Even with crying, she seemed to be "compensating well". She was breathing on her own and holding her saturations in the 70s to low 80s.

After a tough day, Kelly and I reflected as we sat in Natalie's room on the progress we had made. Both tubes were out and Natalie was coasting on her own. It was something we had considered impossible only a week ago. Natalie could now cry, at first very hoarse, but as time went on, it came on. Growing stronger and stronger, It was something we were always very cautious with. When she would cry, her oxygen would drop and alarms would sound. It was both excellent and panic inducing. Luckily, Natalie seemed to love her pacifier again. She would take it and could hold it in her mouth, helping her calm down and keep her oxygen levels "stable".

CHAPTER 23

ESCAPE TO SUTHERLAND

I woke up on Sunday the 22nd with mixed feelings. I had to fly back to Toledo that night to get bank into orientation. Residency was starting up soon and I was very nervous. Things had been going so well with Natalie all of a sudden, but there was always that fear of the "unknown". The last time I had left town, it ended with me running back, anxious for surgery. What if something happened while I was gone? Kelly and I walked to the hospital together and was surprised to see how well she was doing off the ventilator. After extubation, a large nasal cannula with a huge sticker that covered half her face was put on. Initially, they used high flow and even some pressure, but overnight they were able to wean support. When we arrived and spoke with the team, they allowed us to hold her.

It was like holding her for the first time. Instead of this stiff, unconscious thing I had held before the surgery, Natalie was able to move around freely and to look at you while she sucked on her pacifier. I could kiss her, squeeze her or even caress her lovingly and nothing would happen. In the past, this would have been caused her to get irritated and lead to her saturation levels tanking as well as alarms, but no longer. She seemed to enjoy it. It was magical, holding Natalie, hearing her make noises and watching as she cracked a smile at me. I think every parent feels that way when they see their baby, but there was a time when I was uncertain I would ever be able to see or do any of these things with Natalie. It only made it that much more magical for me. Tyler, Tracy and Stephanie all paid us a visit that afternoon, all taking their turns with her. The mood was so up as we shared laughs, stories and even dared to plan on the future. We were able to take photos, including our first "Family Photo" with Natalie, Kelly and Myself.

That night, I flew back to Toledo again, hoping to get more orientation under my belt. Unlike last time, I was filled with hope. Suddenly, it seemed like that, sooner or later, I would get to bring my family home. I arrived home in a good mood and the dark cloud hanging over our new house seemed to be gone. From there, Every morning before work I had a simple routine to deal with any anxiety that did flair up. I would wake up, get dressed, and on the way to the hospital, call Children's Mercy to check on Natalie. They would ask me for her "code" which was printed on one of my wrist bands that I continued to wear. I would hear how well she was doing and any updates planned for that day. It was hard not being there, not looking at the now wide awake face of my baby girl and holding her close, but sometimes duty calls.

To try to stay connected to Kelly and my baby, I called on modern technology for a solution. The solution was "FaceTime". I had received an iPad from work and was able to FaceTime with Kelly. We would FaceTime multiple times a day. Often, Kelly would hold the iPad over Natalie, allowing me to talk to her. She was growing up before my eyes, fidgeting around and becoming more alert.

For the last weekend in June, with the help from the funds raised on our GOFUNDME, I was able to fly back to Kansas City for Natalie's 1st Month Birthday Party. To an outsider, it may seem odd have a celebration of a "month" birthday, but when we had been through so much, it made perfect sense. Heck, there were times when we were unsure if Natalie would even reach 1-month of age. My mom picked me up from the airport and the mood was high. On the way to the hospital, I reflected on the past month. With everything is going well, it was hard to believe how sick Natalie had been and how scary things had been just 10 days ago. It was like a bad dream and one I was happy to be done with. Heck, on the iPad that morning Natalie had smiled at me. What more could a father ask for?

By this time, Natalie had been moved to a normal recovery bed in a different location at Children's Mercy hospital. The Sutherland Tower was more of a "general ward" area of the hospital, with many small generic hospital rooms. There were some play areas near the nurses station as well as a puppet house. When I reached her new room, Natalie was fast asleep. She was in a large crib, larger than a toddler bed, wrapped up in a blanket like a burrito. I laughed when I saw her there, asking Kelly how much extra we were paying for the "King size crib". Attached to the crib was the

Yellow and White Green frog musical mobile I recognized from our neighbor at the NICU. Kelly had requested it come with us from the NICU and they had found her one.

I walked over and stood over my little one, happy to see her with my own eyes again. Natalie was wrapped up in her blanket, or "Nata-rito" as we called it, with a large pink bow on her head. She had a yellow feeding tube in her left nostril and a bandage on her left cheek holding it in place . She held her teal pacifier in her mouth. She was growing quite attached to and I was fine with that. Anything that made her happy at this point was good as far as I was concerned. Underneath the wrap, she was wearing a pale green onesie with a large pink bow in the middle of the chest and pink ruffles around the waist. Even Natalie's socks added to the outfit, matching the pale green of her onesie. Kelly had outdone herself, all dressed up for her birthday and was quite proud of herself.

Kelly was excited to show it to me her work, getting Natalie out of her bed and unwrapping her. It woke her up, but she was only mildly upset. As we sat there, together with our One Month old baby before us, I started to cry. After what seemed like a lifetime together, suddenly Kelly had been spending quite a bit of time apart. While we had been using FaceTime, that can only go so far. I was so happy to be there, with my family, and finally happy. When I initially left for training in Toledo, the doctors made it clear that we may never get to see Natalie extubated. We may never leave the NICU. We f had eared we would never get to celebrate simple things like "birthdays" and yet here we were. It was almost like being a "normal" family with a "normal" baby. Thinking back, it was so great that we had come that far and, while we still had a long way to go, things felt pretty damn great.

I asked Kelly what the doctors had to say about Natalie's progress. Deep down, I was excited about the details at this point and wanted to know whatever I could. Kelly was, as usual, vague about things. There was some concern about Natalie's blood pressure and kidney function. There was a discussion about getting an ultrasound of her kidneys soon, but otherwise things were trending well. The doctors even dared to use the magic word we thought we would never hear, bringing up DISCHARGE that morning. Before we could leave though, they first had to figure out feeding. Kelly was trying to breastfeed and Natalie was having a hard time gaining weight. Personally, all things considered, it seemed like a good problem to have. Worrying about whether Natalie was eating or not seemed like NOT that big of a deal compared with the fear from recent heart surgery!

Later that night, we had the party! Most of the family came to our small room to celebrate. We picked up an Ice Cream Cake from Baskin Robbins, which was the family tradition for all celebrations. Natalie's cake was pretty complicated, designed to look like a pail of sand. The pail was blue, made of chocolate cake and ice cream and filled with graham cracker sand . On top, there were several animals created with frosting, including a small red crab, a smiling yellow starfish, green turtle and a pink octopus. There was a small pink "card" on the side, "1 Month" written out in blue icing. It was delicious! Natalie seemed entertained by her guest. We discussed upcoming discharge and at the end of the night things felt better than they ever had.

CHAPTER 24

RESIDENCY SUCKS

In case you don't know, Residency is really tough. Medical school itself is pretty hard in its own right. I've heard it compared to trying to drink water from a fire hydrant. While this seems really silly, it is actually pretty close to being true. As a medical student, you find yourself constantly just trying to keep head above water while an endless flow of information is flooded your way. Once you finally get done, you feel almost bulletproof, confident in what you know and clues what you do not. You walk into Residency this way, sort of in an odd spot. You are in this grey zone of "being a doctor" but not yet able to practice on your own. You realize quickly that you have no idea what you are doing. All of that "book smarts" that you had spent years memorizing doesn't mean jack in the real world with real people depending on you. The only way to learn and improve is through experience and repetition. That is where Residency comes in.

Through restrictions from the governing bodies, the hours you are allowed to work during residency is capped. We are limited to 80 hours per week on average. You have to log the hours you work on a tracker online. It is supposed to be for safety sake. Years ago, residents had no such restriction, working 120-130 hours a week. Residents would work 2-3 days straight and then go home for a short break only to go back on shift that night, If you are interested in a good satire on this, I would highly recommend the book "The House of God'. I want to warn you ahead of time, it is a bit crude but is an interesting illustration into the mindset of a resident.

After Natalie's Birthday party, I had to get ready to leave Kansas City for good. Residency was due to start the next week and I had to get home and get ready. One thing I had to do before we left was say goodbye to Liz, our NICU Nurse. She had gone out of her way multiple times making her day harder to make ours better. We met with her down in the NICU, exchanged a hug and thanks. Kelly and I also had a meeting and discussed how things were going with Natalie's team of doctors before I left. They felt she was doing pretty good and may get discharged in a week or so. This was an exciting thought, something I did not anticipate. The plane ride back to Toledo was uneventful.

I started my Residency on July 1st with one month of General Surgery rounds. On my first day I remember being extremely nervous. Walking to the hospital at 6am on that first day, I had little idea of where to go or even who I would meet. The "team" met on the 9th floor in the "PA Lounge" at the top of the "old building" at Toledo Hospital. The team consisted of two senior surgery residents, myself and several Physician Assistants. We also had rotating medical students who would come and go as the month progress. I introduced myself and everyone seemed nice enough, My nerves washed away as we started to "run the list". "Running the List" is the term used to describe when we walked through the listed patients under the care of our attending and discussed each case. We discussed the Operating Room schedule as well as who would see what patient. I was to keep an eye on what Operations I wanted to help with and we would divide that up amongst the residents. We would also be assigned a certain number of patients who were recovering that needed to be seen. I was given 4 patients and planned on getting "in" on an appendectomy later that day. Otherwise, I was given a pager to answer for both questions and consults. Even though this was Surgery Rounds, It felt very similar to the hospital medicine I had worked on as a student, so it was nice to feel familiar. I left thinking, "eh.. This doesn't seem so bad."

It was not too bad. I had a rough Idea what to do and the Attending Physicians were very nice to me. The Surgery residents though we're not as lax. Surgery Residency in general is tough, lasting 5 years, plus fellowship if you want to specialize. While many specialties follow the rules in regards to hour restrictions I mentioned earlier very closely, others specialties see it as more of a "suggestion" and residents will simply lie on their logs to avoid investigation into their residency programs. In general, Surgery is one of those specialties who may or may not want you to lie on your timesheet. Duty hours were nothing they were worried about. One would be encouraged to be dishonest if it came down to it. I remember getting so much flak from my Senior because I had taken July 4th off as a vacation day.

It was nothing I had planned. I found out that first week that the clinic was closed on that day. I asked my coordinator if I was supposed to work, and she told me, "As long as you are not on Inpatient work, you can probably just take the day." I was super excited. It turns out that there are only a limited amount of rotations you can take time off on during first year and we are encouraged to take time during General Surgery.

As I explained to the team at rounds Wednesday morning that I was going to out Friday I received quite a bit of push back. How DARE I not be at the hospital one day for a holiday? My Senior Surgery Resident couldn't believe I had been given the day off and asked me to provide the email from our attending "proving" he had approved it. Luckily, my program always fought for us and made sure we were not abused and that our education came first.

Part of the surgery rotation was assisting in a set number of specific types of surgeries. You had to take part in three colectomies, 2 appendectomies, 4 gall bladders, and several others. Once these were done, you could almost just focus on the hospital portion which most of us Family Doctors preferred. We would spend our afternoon doing consults from the ER. There was a saying on surgery, "When in doubt, cut it out" and it seemed, most consults, this ended up being the solution.

On that first Tuesday, the first surgery on the docket was a gallbladder removal procedure and it was one I needed. I volunteered to be second assist for this at morning rounds. Scrubbing in for my first case was more difficult that I had anticipated. While we had trained on making ourselves "Sterile" in school, there was always the fear of screwing up. The first step, was removing the wrist bands. It was an emotional thing for me. Natalie was still in the hospital and I still "needed" them, but I could not go into surgery with them on. Placing my education first, I cut them with bandage scissors in the OR prep area and placed them in my back pocket and simply moved on. You get all clean and then walk into the operating room, hands in the air dripping with water, and over to the surgical tech. They help you gown up and you are good to go. It is a whole process but once you do it many times, it comes second nature. At first, I was terrified. I kept telling myself "Don't touch anything!" and "Don't Lock your knees!" while I watched in pure excitement as the surgeon performed the laparoscopic procedure. We made several small holes and filled the abdomen and filling it with air. My job at this point is holding things, which can be tiring. They used a camera and went in using tools on long rods that were specially designed for this procedure. It went rather quickly and soon the patient was being wheeled to his recover, minus 1 gallbladder. It was pretty amazing to see.

Later that night back at home, I cried as I sat in the nursery with the cut ID bands in my hand. I don't know if it was from what the bands represented or due to some sort of inner sense of failure for "removing them", but it was emotional for me. I was feeling much better the next day. If I could not wear the bands, I would keep them on me at all times.

Back in Kansas City, Natalie slowly but surely improved. I was tempted to fly back that weekend of July 4th but decided against it. I had just left that past Sunday and the funds from the GOFUNDME would only go that far. I was less nervous by now as Natalie had been doing so well. The biggest issue was eating and weight gain. Kelly rarely left Natalie's room, focusing on her perceived duty of needing to be the full time caregiver. She would order all her meals from the hospital itself. The Nursing staff showed her how to insert a NG tube and push feeds to try to get calories into Natalie. It was not fun, but it was a mean to getting out of the hospital and getting home.

Discharge became a real possibility. Once "Discharge Planning" had started for Natalie, Children's Mercy wanted to make sure we had close follow up. They wanted to know who would be seeing Natalie" within the week". This was actually a complex question and Kelly and I had no idea. Before residency started, I had asked our residency coordinator about local pediatricians. I had just moved to the Toledo and had little time to do much of anything let alone research doctors. She quickly recommended a local private pediatrician named Gary Gladieux. She reported that he was her children's pediatrician when they were younger and he was "wonderful". I trusted Chris completely as she had been insanely supportive during the past month, so the recommendation she provided carried great weight to me. During the first week of residency, I looked up the number to his office and tried to call to get an appointment. They were scheduling almost a month out, which was not going to work for Natalie. She needed to be seen within the next few days after discharge secondary to feeding difficulties and the recent blood in her stools or the doctors would not discharge her. I explained to Dr. Gladieux's staff how complicated Natalie's case was and how she needed to get in. I also wanted to make sure that Dr. Gladieux felt comfortable with her condition. They told me they would speak with the doctor and get back with us.

Later that day, Dr. Gladieux called me himself. He started the conversation pretty serious, introducing himself and asking me "What's up". I had given his name to Children's Mercy and He had been getting quite a bit of documentation and paperwork coming in on Natalie, who he had not yet met or accepted. There was paperwork to inform him of the hospitalization and ask for signatures for home care.

One thing patients in general do not understand is how homecare works and the amount of paperwork it requires. In order for you to have a visiting nurse or an oxygen machine at home, a doctor has to fill out paperwork. You have to have documentation on "medical necessity and part of that "requires" a face to face visit and documentation as to "why" you need these services. We were in a tough spot as Dr. Gladieux hadn't even seen Natalie and was not comfortable with just signing paperwork. Panic set in on my mind. I needed this doctor. I explained my situation quickly, explaining how I was a new Resident at Toledo Hospital and had just moved to town. I explained how Natalie was still in Kansas City and our need to get established. We needed these orders from a doctor or they would not discharge us from Children's Mercy. He asked about a cardiology and I explained how Natalie would be seeing her new Pediatric Cardiologist as soon as she gets to town.

Dr. Gladieux was more than accommodating. He told me OFCOURSE he would take care of the paperwork. He did request that we get her in to meet him in the next week. He would take of setting up our home care and supplies and his office would call me. He also gave me his personal cell phone number, telling me that I can call or text him any time of day. He laughed, saying, "The only time I will not answer is if I am in the shower or out on the tractor mowing the lawn". It came off very genuine. I felt he must really care. Initially, I assumed he reacted the way he did because I was a physician, but as I worked with him later in life, both as a parent and later as resident, I learned that he was everything a real doctor should be. He would bend over backwards for his patients when they were in need. He was an old school doctor, still visiting the hospital to see newborns as well as take care of his patients who were admitted to the hospital. Reflecting on him now, I feel like he has a real love for his patients. He knows what is going on in his kids' lives and has been known to donate his time and energy to things that matter to them. It takes a special person to do all of this and it is something that most of us as doctors simply no longer do.

Duty Hours aside and concern for safety aside, I do feel that a new Doctor needs the heavy workload to really figure out how things work. Education and experience was the most important thing for myself and the other new doctors starting at our clinic in Toledo. I've heard it said that "90% of the way you practice in Residency is how you will practice afterwards" and If you don't "see it" during that time, you will not recognize it when you are done. We had many rotations that first year with the idea to build that exposure. While hour intensive, the rotations were good for growing our minds and helping us become better doctors. I loved my residency program. I felt they honestly cared about me as a person and was extremely blessed being allowed to train under them. We did tend to have quite a good time. About halfway through Residency, I came up with a perfect metaphor for it, as a joke. Residency is sort of like prison sentence without parole. As long as you put in your time and behave, things will work out, but you have to "pay your dues". While it was just a joke, it does seem to be pretty accurate.

CHAPTER 25

LIBERATION

Natalie was discharged from Children's Mercy Hospital and into the outside world on July 6th with plans to stay in the area for the next few days and then make the trip to Toledo. My Mom helped Kelly pack up the room at the Longfellow House and get Natalie fitted into a special car seat she had purchased for us. Kelly's Dad picked up our "tab" at Ronald McDonald House and, before the week was out, they made their way to my Moms house in St. Joe. Natalie continued to struggle with gaining weight and was discharged home with an NG tube. Kelly had to manage the tube, using pumped milk and pushing down the tube. Luckily, she was not in short supply of milk. While at the hospital, Kelly had pumped so much milk that the staff actual asked her to stop saving it. Upon discharge, Kelly collected the boxes upon boxes of frozen milk back to my Mom's house. She was able to defrost it and use it to feed Natalie while they worked on breastfeeding. It took some of the stress out of the process.

Kelly tried to keep things normal, brining Natalie around with her. She would hold Natalie close, wrapped in grey and white wrap she had bought. I remember using FaceTime with them frequently during this time. I was lonely at home alone and very excited to see how Natalie responded to the world. I needed to be a part of my daughter's life and this was it. On the iPad screen, Natalie's small head could barely be seen poking out from the wrap Kelly would keep her in on her chest. Her dark bright eyes were very focused, looking out of the wrap as the world passed her by, the NG tube she had been discharged with hanging out the front of the wrap.

While Natalie initially was doing well outside the hospital, things were not exactly easy or "normal". Feeding continued to be an issue, forcing Kelly to push pumped breast milk through her NG tube. To make things more difficult, Natalie couldn't cry. We knew from our time in the hospital that when Natalie cried, her saturations would drop. We were not discharged with any sort of way of monitoring her oxygen and whenever she would start up, it would make most of us nervous. The last thing we wanted was to end up back in the hospital. My mom never seemed to be too nervous. She would scoop Natalie up, tapping her rear pretty quickly and rocking her singing ABCs. I remember, watching on the iPad, wondering if it was ok to hit a baby like that. Either way, it worked.

Things started to settle in and we made plans for Kelly and my Mom to drive to Toledo soon. One night, Kelly and Natalie went to my brother's house for a visit. Besides her and the baby, it was my Mom, my brother, sister in law Tracy and her sister. It was just meant to be a calm hang out with Natalie before they made the trip to Toledo.

Kelly was changing Natalie's diaper and noticed that there was blood in it. Her first instinct was to not tell anyone. They had just left the hospital and Kelly really did not want to go back. She shook the thought away. She had to find out if blood like this was normal or not. She asked Stacy, who had twins of her own, and Stacy assured her it was not normal. The baby seemed fine, but this blood as not. Natalie had just had heart surgery and Kelly could not afford to be "conservative" on this. Kelly started to panic and went to my Mom. Speaking calmly, she suggested that they would take Natalie to the hospital to get checked out and it would all work out.

They decided to take the 60 minute drive to go back to Children's Mercy in Kansas City, visiting the ER there. Natalie was just discharged from there and they hoped that, since they would have all the records, the Doctors there would know her and know what to do. The Doctors checked Natalie, appreciating that she seemed calm and not in pain. She had another stool there, which was also bloody. After some time, the doctors returned and assured Kelly that it was likely nothing, "Maybe it is just from the NG tube" they had said. It was frustrating for Kelly that it took quite a long drive and time to come to that conclusion, but it was nice to not have to stay. Plan had been to keep an eye on it and get established in Ann Arbor after the move.

One week after discharge, Kelly, Natalie and the Bubbe made the trip to Toledo. They almost made it in one day, but had to stop on Lima, Ohio.

Natalie had "enough" by that point and was screaming her head off.
 Luckily, a little time out of the car seat seemed to do it. They arrived on
July 12, just as I finishing my second week of my surgery rotation.

In my down time from residency, I had deep cleaned the house and
prepped the Nursery for the new arrival. It was like bringing your newborn
home and I was a mixture of excited and nervous. I wanted everything to
be perfect. Waiting for Natalie, attached to her crib was a very familiar
looking yellow and white mobile. I had found on EBay, identical to the one
in the NICU. Well, almost. This one had animals hanging down on strings
that was absent from the one in the NICU. The hospital had removed the
animals from their version of it as it made it more difficult to clean. I was
very proud of myself and my find.

When they arrived, I could tell that it must of been a hard trip. Both
Kelly and my Mom looked beat. Natalie was asleep, dressed in a pink and
green tu-tu. Kelly was quite happy with how I had decorated the house and
cried when she saw the nursery. Natalie settled right in, able to sleep in her
crib right away. .

PART III

Setting Things Straight

CHAPTER 26

A STRANGE CASE OF NEC

On Monday July 14th, during my afternoon surgery clinic, I received an unexpected call from Kelly. She was very upset and almost frantic, speaking very quickly through tears.

Natalie had an appointment to get established with her new Cardiologist in Ann Arbor at the University of Michigan "Motts Children's Hospital". She had met Dr. Sara Gelehrter and they had reviewed what had happened in Natalie's life so far. When asked about how things had gone since discharge, Kelly had to her new doctor about the blood stools Natalie was having during the last few weeks. She explained that the ER in Kansas City had told her it was nothing to worry about and had sent her home.

Dr. Gelehrter was not convinced about this diagnosis and ordered some testing. Natalie had to have an X Ray as well as blood work. Holding a baby still for imaging is never easy, but Kelly had completed the tests and returned to the Cardio clinic. Dr. Gelehrter returned, fellow at her said and explained that the X Ray had showed "tram tracking" of her intestines. This was "pathognomonic" for something called Necrotizing Enterocolitis or NEC. Basically, NEC is caused by decreased blood flow through the gut and the intestines start "dying". All of us have normal bacteria in our guy, but in NEC, the bacteria start digesting the bowel wall.
This causes little air pockets in the wall of the intestines that can be seen on X-ray. Dr. Gelehrter was very concern and wanted to admit Natalie

immediately, start her on IV antibiotics and she wouldn't be allowed to eat. She may even need surgery to remove parts of her bowel.

Kelly did not tell me that last part. I was able to come up with that conclusion myself. I had heard of NEC before, but it is usually seen in premature babies, not 1 month old babies. I didn't know what to say to Kelly. I remember hanging up the phone and walking into my Attending's office, almost at a loss for words. He already knew about Natalie and her heart, as I had explained it to him over a cholecystectomy the week before. He was extremely empathetic and, without me even having to ask, released me from clinic to drive to Ann Arbor, which was an hour north.

It was pretty disheartening. To think, just over the weekend I had gotten my family back, and here we were running to the hospital again. So much had happened in Natalie's first 6 weeks of life, and yet it suddenly seemed more suffering was on the horizon. I went to the house, packed up Kelly some cloths, Natalie's "friends" and the Music Mobile. On the drive to Ann Arbor, I couldn't help but wonder about "treatment". Thoughts of more surgeries, colostomy bags and more scars crossed through my mind on the long, straight drive up Highway 23. I tried to stay calm. By the time I reached Ann Arbor, Natalie was already tucked into a room on the 11th floor.

If you asked me to describe Children's Mercy in Kansas City, I would use words such as bright, very colorful and fun. The hospital has amazing tile work on the floor with large murals, paintings and sculptures covering the walls and ceilings throughout. It is obvious the designers tried to hide what the structure really is: A Hospital. Children's Mercy looks like it was designed by a child and I am ok with that. Mott's is the opposite of this and I remember being a little bit put off by the aesthetics of the hospital when I arrived. Mott's is very sterile and modern in design with large curved glass and metal walls. It looks like an art museum. The parking garages, which you have to pay to park at, are arranged just by level and color, without any mention of balloons, rockets or trains. There is artwork and sculptures lining the walls, but they are pretty plain in design, dull in color and made with multiple different fabrics with little lights hanging down from the ceiling to keep the bright. There is a robot statue inside the entryway made up of all sorts of different metal things as well as a Spiderman hanging from the ceiling. Motts looks like it was designed by an adult, trying to make something that looks childish. It is almost as if Motts was designed for the teenage patients. The building itself is 12 stories tall and stands tall amongst the surrounding buildings. As soon as you walk in, a security "greater" welcomes you, asked if you have been sick and where you are going. Everyone is given a visitor sticker and you are given directions on where to go.

While aesthetically the hospital may not be as appealing to what I was used to, they do take their clinics and specialties very seriously. At Mott's, the entire 11th floor is for "Heart Babies". Comprised of the clinic, surgical recovery room, multiple echocardiogram rooms and the Inpatient wing, it is very specialized. There are 64 rooms on 11 West where patients stay long term. After stepping off the elevator, you are greeted at another welcome desk. This one has some mosaic tiling work on it and even has little tiles made by patients who were in the hospital when they were building.
Behind the desk sat a woman in a blue blazer. She directed me to my right, through a set of double security doors. This lead to the inpatient rooms and lead my closer to finding my family.

While the hospital is more or less 'sterile" in appearance, 11W is pretty colorful. The floors are bright white in color with long sections of different colors. The walls are bright in color with multiple winding hallways. The hall is lined with patients rooms along the outside. The main wall between the hallway and room is glass with a large wooden Door. There is a curtain for privacy. Each door has the patient's name, cut out in construction paper, arching across it. Natalie was in one of the rooms right across the hall from the nurses desks and the play area. Inside, Natalie was in Kelly's arms as she sat in a large bluish purple rocking chair near the back of the room. The room was large, much larger than the room at Children's Mercy, with a tall grey crib in the middle. On the right, there was a countertop, a small fridge, large flat screen television and a pad to help control it. There was also a private bathroom in the corner as well as an orange pull out couch just below the large window. The window looks out over the nearby Ronald McDonald House and a cemetery.

When I arrived, I was able to meet with Natalie's new heart doctor. She had stayed late so she could meet with me to discuss the case. This seemed odd to me, but I would come to learn that Dr. Gelehrter frequently made time for us outside of clinic. Dr. Gelehrter is a middle aged female, average height and build with a large smile and dark reddish brown hair. She is soft spoke and comes off as very empathetic and understanding. She had completed her residency and fellowship at the University of Medicine and was board certified in pediatric cardiology. As mentioned before, the plan she laid forward to me had been simple. Bowel rest, antibiotics and observe. She had hoped that things may improve on their own but they had to watch for worsening infection. Natalie did not look sick, but she could get very very sick very quickly. Dr. Gelehrter was on for inpatient that week as well, so she was going to be following the cases and would let us know if anything changes.

It is hard to not let a baby eat. They do not understand 'why they cannot eat" and react the only way they know how. It doesn't matter what you put through the IV in their arm, fluids or nutrition, it does not help that burning hunger they feel in their stomach. Kelly struggled as well. Sitting there, holding the baby as she screamed, it was clear Natalie wanted to breastfeed and there was little Kelly could do. Seeing her frustration, I took the baby from her in my arms and tried to cuddle her. I hoped that she did not associate me with feeds and maybe it would help.

Holding Natalie, I felt so bad for her. She would start crying, which would drop her oxygen levels and trip the alarming on the monitor. I tried to help, trying to force her Pacifier in her mouth and sing to her. She was hungry, but all she was allowed was the pacifier and Vancomycin. My Grandparents appeared shortly after our doctor left. The look on their face said enough. They had been in Missouri for over a month, daily watching over my daughter, and we had thought we were through the woods. We explained the situation. My grandmother had obtained a small swing from a garage sale recently and she thought may be helpful.

As I drove home that night, I thought about how hard the upcoming weeks would be. As my car made its way down the highway back to our empty house I cried openly. I prayed out loud, begging for relief from this constant struggle. I was able to calm down after I crossed into Ohio and took the exit for 475. When I pulled up to the house on the end of Lambert Street, I again started to cry. The house was dark, with not a single light on. Sitting in the driveway, I had this feeling of hopelessness. I tried to talk myself down. Natalie was getting good care and she was in the right place. I slowly regained my composure and chucked to myself with the realization that I was becoming a good "crier". I went into the house and turned on every light on the first floor. I also moved quickly in and out of Natalie's room, turning on her nightlight. I never wanted to come up on a dark house alone again. I was tired of the way it set me off. At Least with these lights on, I could pretend I was coming home to my loving family. Sitting at the end of my bed, fatigue hit me. I had surgery rounds in the morning and really needed to try to sleep. After I quick shower and a quick check up call to Kelly, I went to my bed. As I sank into bed, I laughed to myself, saying out loud, "Well.. at least the crying won't wake me up."

CHAPTER 27

RETURN OF MR. MCDONALD

The next day, Kelly met with child life as well as social work. They had an opening at the Ann Arbor Ronald McDonald House which was nearby and wanted to know if she was interested. It would offer a place to sleep as well as provide meals. At first, Kelly was not interested. She thanked them but told the Social worker that she planned on just staying on the pull out in the room with Natalie. Besides, Kelly did not need meals as "breastfeeding mothers" are allowed to order meals for free at Mott's.

I was a bit upset with her when she explained this to me between cases. ".... what about me?!" I asked, a bit surprised she only thought of herself. She seemed surprised as well, admitting that she had not thought of that. I encouraged her to get registered so I would have a place to sleep and eat as well when I visited over the weekend. I did not want to spend the time running back and forth everyday if I did not have to. Luckily, the room at the Ronald McDonald house was still available. After work, I made my way back up to Ann Arbor to check it out.

Much like the hospital itself, the Ronald McDonald House in Ann Arbor was vastly different from what we were used to. In Kansas City, there is a large presence of the Ronald McDonald charities. As I described earlier, there are three houses and the very nice house inside the hospital. It is well supported and well kept. While there is a "waiting list", but as they have 3 houses most families have access right away.

The Ronald McDonald House in Ann Arbor is much closer to the actual hospital. You could see it from our hospital window. The walk was a very short distance, across the street and down a sidewalk with large trees on each side. A dorm was on the right and a parking lot on the left. The house was across the next small street. On the outside, he house comes off almost like an old church without a bell tower. It is constructed with light bricks and has a dark roof with multiple peaks. There are not many windows and it almost reminds me of a castle. There is a small, winding sidewalk off of the street, but the main entrance was near the middle of the structure hidden from the street by a brick wall. bushes and trees.

Inside, there is an office space on the right with half glass walls that reminded me of a pharmacy. Straight ahead you can see the stairs to the left and the dining area straight ahead. Past the office on the right is a play area and another "lounging" area with a large piano. Past the dining area was the kitchen in the far left corner of the main floor of the house. It was recently updated when I first visited and had nice appliance with long counters. The floors were made of wood and reflected the bright light from above. There was a coffee maker inside the dining space that had a large stash of McDonalds Coffee Cups. This made me smile. McDonalds probably makes these for less than a cent with all the coffee they sell. I thought to myself, "If you have them, why not use them."

Across from the "office". there was both an elevator and stairs to the basement and upper levels where most of the bedrooms were located. Coming off the elevator in the basement, the laundry facilities was just off to the left. From there, one could see the lounges to the right as well as several long, dark hallways that reminded me almost of some sort of hidden passage in a dungeon. It was dimly lit and made me feel claustrophobic. There were two large lounge area with old leather couches, rocking chairs and shelves with random books, VHS tapes and games. They were also well furnished with sports memorabilia.

The bedrooms were pretty depressing overall. They seemed very dated, coming off as very "grey" with greyish blue carpet and light grey walls. Each room had a two single beds with a small closet and a dresser. Bathrooms were shared between two rooms. While most rooms did have a window, in the basement level earth covered the bottom half of the window.

As I walked to the lobby and met with the staff, I reflected on the house and what I had seen in Kansas City. While the house at Children's Mercy was very colorful, well lit and vibrant, this house seemed dark, dingy and dated. It was also pretty empty. I do not know if it was the house itself, or just our general mood with recent events, but it came off very depressing. It was just so empty and quiet. I tried to shrug off my initial perception and focus on the task at hand. All I was worried about was having a place to rest my head. While the house was not as "new" as the one we lived in at Children's Mercy, the people were just as caring and kind. They were very empathetic and came off as cheerful. You could tell they enjoyed their jobs. A guide showed me around the house and gave me a key to the room in the basement. We went over the "rules" of the house and, while it was pretty straightforward, I was a bit surprised with one of them. While the house in Kansas City asked for a donation to stay, this house had a chore list. From cleaning the kitchen, taking out trash, to vacuuming, we would be assigned a chore daily to help with the house. This seemed reasonable to me, but Kelly was not enthused. "I should be with my sick child, not taking out trash!" She exclaimed to me. I just encouraged her and told her I would handle the chores when I was around.

Natalie handled the treatment "well" for the next few days. She cried less and less it seemed which made everyone's life easier. My grandparents visited frequently and I came up whenever I could. Natalie's stools cleared up after a few days, but the doctors wanted to complete two weeks of treatment. About 4 days into this, when it appeared apparent that Natalie would not be able to eat for a few weeks, Natalie was started on IV nutrition, which made Kelly happier. The doctors always had been so worried about Natalie's weight in the past so the idea of "starving her" did not sit well with Kelly. I was able to come back that Friday night a few days later and spend the weekend with Kelly and Natalie. She completed her treatment and we were able to escape back to Toledo on July 27th.

CHAPTER 28

LESSONS IN PARENTING

Starting my second month of Residency, my spirits were high as my family was finally home. Kelly and Natalie worked on getting acclimated to living outside the hospital and I was getting into the groove of being a new doctor. Natalie slowly was able to start taking more and more with breastfeeding. While nothing was "normal" in our lives, Kelly and I did our best to try and make it feel that way.

During this time as a young father, I learned several important "lessons" on proper ways to take care of children. First, I learned the importance of wiping "front to back" when cleaning up a diaper. As a male, it never occurred to me that there was a 'way" you were supposed to wipe. I was very quickly taught otherwise. Both my wife and my mother jumped all over me one day as I was changing a Diaper in the living room. Comments like "Aren't you a Doctor?!" and "Have you ever changed a diaper before" were thrown at me in angry voices. I was confused and, honestly pretty embarrassed of the situation. It is not exactly something taught in medical school. While it is kind of obvious if you think about it, how was I to know there was a proper direction?

Another lesson I learned involved NG tube management. I luckily never had to put the thing into place with Natalie, but I learned that it was to always make sure the little pink stopper is in place on the NG tube after a feed. If left open, not only would stomach contents leak out and soak everything, but sometimes all the formula you put in there will also leak out. It was disgusting and very frustrating. I can remember the absolute frustration when you would pick Natalie up and she would be soaked. You would think she must of wet herself only to see the little pink stopper hanging off. Later, it became harder as the stoppers would wear out, forcing me to tape the little thing on. While she only used the NG tube for a relatively short time for those first few months, later, this lesson was one that would keep giving later on in Natalie's life. Proper NG Tube management is paramount if you want clean cloths.

This next lesson was quite a terrifying one to learn. Natalie had not been home from the hospital 1 week into August when I attempted to cut her nails. I had a set of "cute" little nail clippers someone had given us as a baby gift. They were small, cute and had a yellow handle with a little duck. Natalie was a little squirmy as I held her on my lap trying to trim her nails which had been snagging on things. I had accomplished the task with one of her hands and went for the thumb on the other when Natalie moved. I was not paying enough attention obviously, clipping down and taking off a little chunk of thumb near the tip. I looked at it, wide eyed, knowing I had messed up. Natalie let out the loudest scream I had ever heard. For a kid who had gone through pain before, you would think a little cut would not be that big of a deal, but she acted like I killed her. She failed around and the started bleeding SO much. She was taking an aspirin from the doctors and this only makes bleeding worse. I felt like the absolute worst person in the world as I held a rag on the bleeding thumb as hard as I could. Just as I had just about given up hope and take Natalie to the hospital, the bleeding from the small cut stopped. It had taken almost 45 minutes and I had seriously thought we were going back to the hospital. What a silly reason to get admitted.

Speaking of nails, I also learned to never put your babies hand in your mouth. I know it sounds obvious and even gross, but I would pretend to eat Natalie's hands while playing. She would laugh and coo so loud. It was hilarious to her which made me feel good. What I didn't know was how sharp those little fingernails could be. She scraped the roof of my mouth hard with her middle finger during playtime. It was my turn to cry out and bleed. It was extremely painful. Safe to say, I did not do that again for a while. At least not until Lucas was born. An the final lesion: always lock the bathroom door. This one is self-explanatory.

Well into August, Natalie had not made that "establish care" appointment with Dr. Gladieux we had scheduled when she left Kansas City. She had been admitted and was stuck at Motts for the three weeks. Luckily, we were able to make the rescheduled appointment in the second week of August. Dr. Gladieux's clinic was located about 15 minutes down

475 in Maumee in a small two story office building. It was pretty typical office, with a "sick" and "well" waiting area and character themed rooms. Dr. Gladieux walked in the room with a wide smile on his face, eager to meet us. He was probably in his late 50s, but came off as if had the energy of a young man. He was welcoming, mildly goody, and very energetic, spunky even. Most importantly, he was passionate about your child. Everything you want your pediatrician to be. His first words to us were, "Now who is this girl I have read so much about".

In general, Dr. Gladieux carried himself well and confident with that "Been there.. Seen that" aura. He never seemed to get worked up no matter the complexity. This was really refreshing. Besides our specialists, most doctors we had seen up to this point come at us in a "near panic" look in their eyes. Over time, Dr. Gladieux would tell us how we were "one of his favorite families" and would ask Natalie if he could take her home with him. Natalie would giggle and cry out No. It was really special. Later, he would ask Natalie if she could say "Baby Brother", leading to nervous looks between Kelly and myself. Going to see him was never nerve racking.

At this initial visit, he seemed to be well versed in what was going on up in Ann Arbor. He encouraged Kelly to work on breastfeeding, gave us some "anticipatory guidance", and asked for close follow up.

At work, things were difficult but moving smoothly. My August rotation was also based in the hospital, working on Inpatient Medicine. The "Inpatient" rotation involved taking care of patients who are sick in the hospital. We had the rotation four times our first year, 30 days each and it routinely had some of the longest hours of any of the rotations during residency. The shift is from 7am to 7pm with a 16 hour shift on the weekend. It is intense, taking care of both adults and children in the ICU and on the floors. We would treat everything from pneumonia, sepsis, heart attacks, strokes, diabetic ketoacidosis to severe bronchiolitis.

Our patients were spread all over the hospital, and as a new resident, I did not understand the complicated layout of Toledo Hospital. The Hospital was made up of two buildings and you could only cross over to the other side on floors 1,2,5 and then on 7 you could crossover but you would end up on floor 8 on the other building. I frequently found myself walking all over the large complex trying to figure out where specific rooms were located and get my patients seen on time before we would round.

As I wandered the halls, going room to room to see patients, I found myself avoiding the third and fifth floor at Toledo Hospital. In July I had spent quite a bit of time on the second floor as the operating rooms were located there. Now on inpatient, I tended to go down to the second floor to cross over most of the time. I knew it was inconvenient, always going down to "2" to cross over, but I did not want to get lost. My Senior Resident could not help but tease me, but little did they know I had other, personal reasons for avoiding floors 3 and 5.

Floor 3 was Labor and Delivery and babies freaked the heck out of me. It was not babies themselves, more the deliveries that scared me. I had very little experience in medical school. In rural Missouri, pregnant ladies did not tend to want male students to help with much of anything. I was terrified I would walk onto that floor and someone would call out for help. I knew it was something I would have to "get over". I had a rotation on Labor and Deliver coming in October, but I had hoped I could just avoid the floor until then.

The 5th floor was the pediatric ward. While very different from the floor in Ann Arbor, it brought back many tough emotions that I tried to keep buried at the lowest level of my conscious. Right off the elevators was a large sign advertising the Ronald McDonald house. It was just too painful to track that path unless absolutely necessary. For obvious reasons, I avoided this floor like the plague. When rounding with the team, I would play it tough. I would fool around and tell jokes to try to keep the idea that I was suffering hidden.

CHAPTER 29

APPEARANCES CAN BE DECEIVING

The optimism that came early August did not last long. My work kept me away frequently and this was difficult on all of us. Natalie and Kelly spent much of the next few months in and out of the hospital. It became almost a sick routine. Any time Natalie would get sedated for a procedure, she would end up with blood stools and "NEC". The doctors would then make her NPO (nothing by mouth) for 2 weeks with IV antibiotics, just like the first admission in July. Overall, Natalie handled it well, maintaining weight on IV nutrition. I would come stay with her on the weekends, finding her sitting in her swing chair on top of her crib rocking out to "sprout". It was funny to see, but Natalie loved it.

By the time September rolled around, Natalie was very much growing into a person and not just a slug. Gone were the days of endlessly sitting by her bed and holding her hand while she sat and stared at the ceiling. She was developing a personality all her own. Natalie CRAVED attention, wanting to touch and play with everything. Everything she grabbed went to her mouth. She would laugh so much, watching everything with her big brown eyes. She still had chubby cheeks and a very small tuft of brownish blond hair. For someone who had been through so much, she seemed to be very quick to smile and laughed. She did not really move much, usually content to sit where you left her and play with whatever was in reach.

We had become very used to "hospital life" by this point. Kelly basically lived at the hospital in Ann Arbor, always at Natalie's side. I, meanwhile, became used to coming home to an empty house and weekends visiting my family. During the day, Kelly and Natalie would take walks around the large hospital campus or go to the play areas. One time, after getting permission to finally take Natalie outside on the concourses to enjoy some of the beautiful fall weather, Kelly accidently set off the "child abduction" sensor. Alarms went off overhead. After clearing that little mistake up, Natalie finally made it out on one of the outside to enjoy the crisp fall air.

The one thing that Motts really excelled at, besides communication and care, was the view. The' hospital is near the college campus, which is heavily wooded near the outskirts. There is a large cemetery nearby as well. We didn't think much of it at first, towering over the town in our 11th floor suite, but when the fall started to creep up on us, the trees began to change. We had never seen anything like it. The colors blend together in a beautiful mixture of orange, yellow and reds with an occasional purple and both Kelly and I loved it. I would spend hours looking out over the rainbow of color, mesmerized. We both vowed to each other to be buried in the cemetery.

After being home for a week, Natalie was set to have her next procedure on October 16th. Her Cardiologist Dr. Gelehrter had called upon one of the interventional Cardiologists to assist. Dr. Martin Bocks was in charge of handling Natalie's case. He was middle aged and pretty tall with dark thick wavy hair. He spoke in a mildly nasal voice. He came off as cool and confident. His plan was to go in and access the situation. I was nervous, but prayed that we would be making some sort of progress.

The hardest part about a heart catheterization is when you have to say goodbye to your baby as the nurses take her back for the procedure. Your head is filled with not only concern and even that wonder if you will see your baby again, but also the fear of something going serious the wrong.

The time waiting is not so bad. Usually we rushed to get to appointments so the initial time after we send Natalie off is spent getting a snack or resting for moment. After watching them take Natalie for the procedure, Kelly and I settled into waiting. We were experts by now at waiting and passing the time. We set up shop in the waiting room, watching the latest episode of Walking Dead that we had missed.

Now we did not just pack up entertainment for ourselves. While working on pediatric inpatient oncology ward, I observed many children and families going through unbelievable situations. It has been some of the hardest things I have observed. I noticed though that the families always seemed to always come prepared. They would have their DVD players, coloring books, stuffed animals, and even decorations for their hospital room brought from home. Their parents did absolutely everything they could to bring even the slightest bit of normalcy in a very abnormal situation. I took mental notes on this.

It was right around this time in Natalie's life that I realized that packing a bag is a good thing, just in case we needed to be admitted. We had been to Ann Arbor several times by now and even with something as an echocardiogram we would end up staying in the hospital. Having a bag ready to go meant one last thing to worry about when things hit the fan.

When packing, I was sure to try to grab anything that may come in handy during a possible hospital stay. There were lots of things besides just cloths that were needed to pass the time and keep a hungry baby distracted. Usually I packed things like Natalie's mobile from Children's Mercy, her sound machine from her crib, her swing, her "friends" and even a small fan to help her keep cool. Natalie never did well in the heat. At some point we had even purchased a portable, just in case Natalie's favorite movie was not on the "Get Well Network" at Motts. I tried to have whatever Natalie may need close at hand. It was a hassle, and maybe silly, but it is what we did and it gave us one less thing to worry about.

After the procedure, Dr. Bocks called us into the little meeting room right off the procedure waiting area on the 11th floor. Natalie handled the procedure well, but the procedure showed that her arteries had not grown enough to complete a full repair. They had found a collateral artery off on the right side of her main artery as well. To me, this sounded like a good thing, but he assured me that it could cause problems later. She was not making the progress we had hoped and Dr. Bocks felt that Natalie would likely need to have another surgery before the end December. That surgery would be to place a "conduit" from her heart to her lungs and "patch" open her pulmonary arteries. The surgeon would also take out the shunt that was keeping her alive. It would be considered another palliative procedure for now, but hopefully the increased blood flow would help her arteries grow. From there, he planned to repeat her heart catheter in march to figure out how things looked out in the lungs. Dr. Bocks was unsure if we would stay overnight, that night, but he hoped Natalie would wake up "well". Discharge would depend on how she recovered.

I was actually not surprised by the overall plan. Way back at Children's Mercy, on the first day of Natalie's life, the surgeon there told us this was the likely approach. Dr. Bocks did not seem as confident as that surgeon was in regards to a "full repair" but he had assured me that we would handle it, no matter what came next. The "increased blood flow will help them grow" statement was becoming a familiar hypothesis as well. That was the same thing I had been told with the shunt. Sadly, it had not made a difference. Maybe this conduit would.

Overall, Kelly and I were happy with the results and having a rough "plan" in place. We thanked Dr. Bocks and then went back out to the waiting area. We tried to explain what the doctor had told us to our family. No one likes the idea of another surgery, so I tried to reassuring to my grandparents and parents.

A short while later, were told that Natalie was ready for visitors. They took Kelly and I to the small surgery prep and recovery area right off the main ward on the same floor. It was though two locked doors and had 6 rooms. Two on the right when you come in, two more on the left just passed a small nurses station as well as two more down the hall. The main 4 rooms were separated by a cloth divider. The rooms down the hall looked to be more likely for isolation with glass doors. Much of my attention was immediately drawn to the large windows on the right side of the room across from the nurses station. Natalie was in room 4, which was located just past the nurses station. When we came in, she was awake, but not really "there". She was lucid, but had her eyes open, focused on the television hanging from the ceiling above her bed. She looked sad and very tired.

The second hardest part of a heart cauterization comes once your child wakes up. Part of the instructions, besides watching for worsening blue lips or alarms on the monitor, include lying flat for 4 hours. This is to prevent damage to the surgical site and bleeding. Do you know how hard it is to have a baby lay flat for 4 hours? Your baby is crying from the pain, reaching out for you and you cannot even hold her to comfort her. When Natalie was older, we were able to mitigate this time with Troll Movies, My Little Pony, Bomb Pops and apple juice, but when Natalie was 5 months old, all we had was pacifier and calm words.

Natalie ALWAYS seemed to do worse after heart catheterization. Her saturation percent would hover in the mid 60s and would become worse when she cried. It was nerve racking, watching that number hover around the "alarm point". It brought back tough memories from Children's Mercy from all those times they tried to wean support. That said, after this procedure she seemed to tolerate the whole "wake up" pretty well. After a few hours, they allowed Kelly to hold her, making sure she kept her legs straight. I walked over to the window and just took in the view. You could see for miles and the brightly colored trees covering almost the entire landscape was breathtaking.

After several hours, while Natalie was doing well, the doctors wanted to move her to an Inpatient room just to observe for several more hours. Kelly and I were a little bummed as we thought we were going to escape, but we understood our doctors caution. We had just tasted freedom for 10 days, and the last thing we wanted to be in the hospital again. Better safe than sorry. Natalie's numbers started to recover and soon, she was back to her normal self. Suddenly, about 6 hours after her procedure, I felt her bear down while I was holding her close. It was not very abnormal and Natalie did not seem in pain, so while there were butterflies in my stomach, I tried not to get too anxious.

I usually did not change her diaper right away in these situations. Better to let her finish then to change multiple diapers. So I sat there watching Sprout and waiting for her to finish. While I was sitting there, after a few moments, I noticed a very funny smell. Yes, I realize she had a dirty diaper, but it was not that smell. It was a very specific smell, one I do not want to try to describe to you, but it was something I was familiar with. It was the smell of digesting blood. I did not say anything to Kelly, instead taking Natalie to the bed and laying her on the yellow blanket and gathered supplies. I knew what I would find before I even took the diaper. I took a deep breath and proceed to remove the soiled diaper. My fears were confirmed moments later when I found bloody stool. I cursed under my breath in frustration. I was not angry, just upset and frustrated. Kelly noticed my frustration and walked over. The sinking feeling you get in your guts when something goes terribly wrong was quickly back. I hit the button on the controller near the bed for the nurse.

After a short while, I called my dad and let him know the situation. When times are tough, my Dad always seems to be the one I reach out to first. We had already spoken about the Cath results and last he knew things were fine. I explained the blood in stool and how we were going to restart treatment again. Natalie's x-ray did not show the pneumatosis and she was acting fine, but the doctors still wanted to go for the treatment. The Doctors had explained that sometimes you may not see the" tram tracking" in the intestine walls at first. I remember saying these words to my Dad with almost zero emotion, the advice "bury that shit deep" echoed in my mind. My Dad's voice, while calm, was more concerned, but I explained that it was a "wait and see" sort of thing. He told me he would make it up for the weekend and to keep him informed. I excused myself from the room as the nurses started Natalie's IV fluids and went to the bathroom down the hall for a good cry. I made sure to wipe my face once I was done so no one would notice.

CHAPTER 30

CARVING OUT MEMORIES

So there we were, stuck in the hospital with another round of IV antibiotics and no food for 2 weeks. I had lost count at this point in my memory how often this seemed to happen, but I think it was "Round 4". While it was quite upsetting at first, the emotion and frustration passed quickly and we fell into the "hospital routine" once again; No food, Vancomycin, and SPROUT. Kelly wanted to make sure things were done "right" and pushed to have the TPN started early this time instead of 5 days into the hospital stay. The doctors initially pushed back, explaining how the body usually doesn't need IV nutrition this early. They also pointed out the risks. Kelly pointed to Natalie's growth chart and they reluctantly agreed and started IV nutrition on the day of admission. Our Hospital room was one we had stayed in before so things were familiar. Luckily, we were also right across from the Child Life play area. This was becoming one of Natalie's favorite past time.

Mott's, for all of my "complaining" about aesthetics before, really performed well in the child life department. Every day they hold some sort of activity for children. There is Pizza and moving night on Thursdays, Cupcake therapy on Wednesdays and other weekly activities to pass the time. There are multiple "Activity Centers" at the hospital that allow children to run and play as well as interact with crafts and books. They also invite guests dressed as Disney Princesses to put on performances. The playroom on 11 West was about 20 feet by 20 feet with a kitchen to the right and a play area to the left. There were some couches, a sandbox filled with rice as well as a bookshelf and lots of toys. They also had art projects and other activities laid out for families to do in the downtime. The child life "experts" had an office here and were the ones responsible for making up the colorful construction paper "Names" that go on the patient's door. I wondered at times how it was not a violation of some privacy act, announcing to world who was inside the hospital room, but I think the kids seem to enjoy it. To this day, Natalie has one of those construction paper "NAT"'s on her bedroom door at home.

From a young age, Natalie LOVED going in this room. WE would spend hours crawling around on the floor and playing with things. We made quite a mess multiple times with the sand box filled with rice. You could even take several toys back to your room to play with there. Natalie loved singing toys and ended up with two of those crib "soothers" on her crib in her room before the first week was up. The days were lazy, full of just simple checkups while we sat and waited for the treatment to end. It was not always pleasant though. Frequently, nurses would come in during the middle of the night for blood work just as Natalie would be falling asleep. After the draw, Natalie would struggle to get back to sleep forcing Kelly to try to comfort her for hours after that, spending the night rocking her. Medical students would come in around 5 am sometimes, waking Kelly and asking questions. Safe to say, she was not a fan of them either.

It was not all bad. Kelly and Natalie would play games and activities too. After the first week of treatment, Natalie's bloody stools were gone and we were allowed to wander the hospital grounds. One afternoon, Kelly took Natalie to the gift shop to waste some time. Mott's has two gift shops. One is on the main floor just outside the elevators and near the "baby cafeteria". It is called the carousel and is shaped as such with a rounded outside wall with large windows showing off the new wares inside. They were "seasonal" items usually on display, changing often as the weather did this time of year. Inside the door to the shop there was a large pillar in the middle that had large cubby holes around it filled to the brim with stuffed animals. From small cup size animals to animals the size of a dog, the choices were endless. The shop sold candy, Michigan apparel and even toys and coloring books for older kids. On the far left wall of the shop, behind the counter, was supplies for parents who were staying in the hospital as well as "baby" stuff. At this time of year, Halloween was big. The shop carried small decorations as well as simple costumes. Kelly decided that playing dress up at gift shop would be a fun way to waste time and get some smiles. They spent 30 minutes trying on different hats. The best one was a small orange witch hat with black spider webs and a big orange bow.

Natalie seemed to really enjoy this. They also had a feather bow and a large big pink boa. Natalie almost disappeared when Kelly wrapped in that. This made for a very cute picture as well. While looking around the baby stuff, Kelly also found what ended up being Natalie's best friend for the next few months: Puppy Pacie.

Puppy Pacie was a wubbanub, which is a brand of small stuffed animals that have a pacifier attached to their face. Up until now, Natalie just had a pacifier on a zebra string. Kelly felt that having something to cuddle would be nice, so she picked it up. Puppy Pacie was actually a small grey bear with bright lime green, orange and blue spots. I have no idea how it became "Puppy Pacie" but that was its name and it stuck. Kelly told me later that she thought it was a dog until she looked it up on the internet later and found out the truth. Personally, it looks like a bear. Natalie did not like it at first, mostly due to the strong rubber smell that it had initially, but quickly became inseparable from her little grey friend, holding it close and sucking on it. She would not go to bed without it and, as she couldn't eat, it offered a small; bit of comfort in a time of little comfort.

We tried to make our hospital room a fun environment. We purchased Halloween decorations from the gift shop and decked out our room. We also would try to keep some of the scarier things in the hospital fun. For instance, for the past few months Natalie had an IV pole following us around. While she really couldn't talk,, I knew the constant beeping and alarms the pole gave off bothered her. It definitely bothered me. Trying to be creative, I dubbed the IV pole and pumps as a "robot". Beeping sounds are terrifying to a child and annoying to an adult when they come from machines controlling nutrition, pain control and electrolytes. They are not at scary when they are coming from your Robot Companion. It was not such a big deal having to plug in the Robot or bring the Robot to the playroom. Robots need to have fun too! Kelly would also sing her songs whenever Natalie had to have blood draws or other "ouchies". She would sing the ABCs to try to comfort her as it was the first thing that came to mind. Later, Kelly figured out that Natalie was attributing the song to something bad happening, crying whenever we sang it back at home. This was tough on Kelly as she felt she had almost conditioned Natalie to fear that song. It took quite a bit of training to fix that.

Natalie also was becoming an expert at Facetime. Her and I would Facetime at least every night and usually during my lunch break at work as well. Natalie seemed keenly interested in the screen and, to me, it looked like she was looking right at me. She responded with my goofy voice with huge smiles and her high pitched giggles. It almost did not matter how hard things were at work, seeing that smiling face would make every day the best day ever. We had a routine as a family and things seemed to be going according to plan.

Near the end of October, things suddenly changed. We had completed two weeks of our treatment plan and normally this is when we start talking discharge. On 10/29 Natalie had another bloody stool. This was different from the past and seemed to come out of the blue. This was the first time it happened spontaneously and not after a procedure. This forced our doctors to consider alternative diagnosis as opposed to NEC. The idea of some sort of colitis or "Milk protein allergy" was thrown around by the resident team during Rounds in the morning.

To try to test the diagnosis, the Team decided to cut Natalie off completely from breast milk, forcing Kelly to "pump and dump". Instead of making her "nothing by mouth", Natalie was started something called Elecare. It is an "elemental" formula made up of digested proteins. It is supposed to be simpler and easier to digest. Natalie hated it and, while I never tasted it, it smelled terrible. Natalie continued to act like a "normal" happy baby throughout all of this.

Personally, work was really starting to weigh me down. I was on the Obstetrics Inpatient rotation for the month of October on the Labor and Delivery Floor. This service really took the "average" part of work hour restrictions to heart, pushing you to 100-110 hours for two weeks of the month and then 60 hours for the next two weeks. As long as it averaged 80 hours a week, they felt it was "good to go". I was terribly lonely, working very long hours in Toledo, while Natalie and Kelly stayed in Ann Arbor.

There was a hidden benefit of being away. When I would visit the hospital, I found that I tend to focus on all the little things in Natalie's life a little too much. I would jump at every little coughing fit, tense up at every dirty diaper, and my nerves would go to a crazy level every time a doctor gave us a visit. While I missed them being away, I found that I did not have to deal with the moment to moment anxieties when I was in Toledo. They just seemed to fuel my ever worsening anxiety, so I am thankful that I had a healthy distraction during this time.

Even with the worsening fatigue associated with my rotation, I still loved it. It turned out that I was really good at delivery babies. It was a magical experience and I was churning out the "deliveries". The hard part was getting there at 6 am to round on the new mothers. It was thankless work, almost cookie cutter in nature. You would ask the same questions to every patient. Are you cramping? How is the Bleeding? Are you getting around? Have you had a bowel movement? How is the Baby? Answers were typically the same. It amazed me how fast people recovered in general from the delivery. Towards the end I even created generic notes for each post-partum day where all I needed to do was fill in the blanks. It was kind of lazy but it worked well and allowed me to see 10-20 patients in the 1 hour between arriving to the hospital and the start of rounds with an attending physician.

Scheduling wise, the hard part of the month was upfront hours wise. I grinded through this with my head down, working hard and often. The schedule was 12-13 hour days and mine called for 19 days straight. I struggled at times, both with work hours and the testing that is required this time of year for residents. I felt I needed to be strong, keeping my struggles to myself, and continued pushing myself to the limit. It was hard to focus at times and I found myself sitting in empty patient rooms at time either dozing off or crying, depending on the day.

The good news was that time seemed to passed quickly. Before I knew it, I was finishing my third week on and I was happy to be able to spend some much needed time off on the weekends with my girls in Ann Arbor during the end of the month.

With the blood stools and the new "Elecare" plan, Natalie seemed to be stable and her stools went back to normal. The doctors were hopeful that Natalie had some sort of allergy and the complex formula was the answer. Kelly was told to follow a "dairy free diet" and we were going to just wait to see if things improved. Plans for discharge were placed on hold and we were stuck in the hospital though for the foreseeable future.

During the holidays, Child Life really takes their efforts to a new level. For Halloween, they went all out in the Activity Room on the main level. There was a photo booth, magician, and even a puppet show. "Ariel" was also there. During our reprieve at the beginning of the month, we had made plans for Natalie for her first Trick-or-Treating. She was going to be a bumble bee for Halloween. We had picked up the costume back in August at a garage sale and it was adorable. I had brought the Bee Costume hospital the weekend before and was able to have the day off to spend it with Kelly and Natalie. Her little costume was extremely cute, with a small hood with two small antennae and even a small stinger that came off her rump. The nursing staff loved her costume and, randomly, one of her doctors had also dressed as a bee, so when they came to round on us it was very fun surprise. We were given a "hall pass". With our permission to roam and Dressed as out Bee, we loaded Natalie into one of the in hospital strollers and traveled down to the main floor of the hospital. Inside the Activity Center on the main level, many of the other kids there had costumes on too! Natalie was mildly entertained by the puppet show and we even were able to decorate cupcakes.

While we had a very fun day, the doctors were having an important meeting back up in 11 West. They were unsure what to do about Natalie's symptoms. She was still having the occasional blood in little specs even with the elecare. We had follow up imaging which had been negative for the pneumatosis. When we returned to the floor, the nurse let us know that the plan had not changed and we were still in "watch and wait mode. This was pretty disheartening for Kelly and I. We wanted to go home and almost felt trapped. We wondered privately that, if it was just milk allergies, maybe we should go home and see what happened.

Our mood was improved when a special package arrived. There was a small box, flowers and a balloon. My Brother Tyler and his Wife Tracy are quite the fan Halloween and had sent a Halloween themed "Get Well" Package. Inside the small box was two things. One was a small little critter with fluffy orange hair. It had large eyes and would make a funny noise when you squeezed it. "Woo-be-da-do-wo-da-da-wo' it would let out in a high pitched voice. Natalie loved it, immediately trying to eat it. I would fluff it against her face so the long orange hair would tickle her. She would laugh so hard. The other item was just as good. It was a A pink panther wubbanub just like Puppy Pacie!

That night, the first snow of the season came, covering the college town in a blanket of white. This was Natalie's first snow. I was tempted to snatch her up and take her outside, but we were told it was not a good idea. I tended to be pretty excitable early on in my "fatherhood" and did not always think things through. As weak as she was, this was probably a good idea.

Luckily, we had nowhere else to be and it was warm and cozy in our hospital room. I was able to find the Red Wings game on the TV in our room. Natalie always enjoyed watching Hockey with me and we were able to cuddle up in one of those big blue chairs and enjoy the game. To keep her warm, we snuggled in close and I covered her in the Rainbow knit blanket my Aunt Diane had made her. We sat there for hours, watching our team fight to start the season off right. I looked down at her, eyes focused intently on the large LG TV on the far wall and reflected how proud my Grandfather would have been. He was a huge hockey fan back in the day and had gotten my brother and I into it.

Overnight, Natalie had a small set back. Her Oxygen saturation dropped down to an unacceptable level. This tended to happen from time to time with her, usually when she was upset, but it always gets the night time team in a bit of a tizzy. By the time the sun came up, things were back to normal, but the event seemed to concern our doctors. That next morning the Team of Doctors came around for rounds and gave us an update. They had a meeting that morning as a team with Dr. Gelehrter and decided to make a big change in our plan. They felt that Natalie was no longer "tolerating" her shunt and this was causing some of her issues. One of the young female doctors told us that, as a group, they felt that there was likely little benefit in prolonging the next surgery until December. They felt that we should just do surgery now. It was stunning how quickly Open Heart surgery seemed to come up and the decision made to move forward with it. Kelly and I looked at each other, a little concerned about how fast things were moving. Natalie was happy as a clam and suddenly we were talking open heart surgery. There was a lot of head nodding and then the team left, leaving Kelly, Natalie and I in the room alone in silence.

CHAPTER 31

FIX YOU... AGAIN

"But the Lord stood with me and gave me strength." *2 Timothy 4:17*

After a little over 3 weeks in the hospital, struggling with oxygen saturation and bloody stools, we finally had a plan. We had almost escaped 2 weeks into it, even having our discharge papers drawn up, when she started having more bloody stools. The doctors had told us that, hopefully with her surgery, she would have more permanent blood flow to her very small arteries in her lungs and this would stimulate them to grow. As the month switched to November, we geared up for the surgery. Natalie started to improve with the stools and the blood actually stopped while on the special formula. The doctors had their mind made up, and the plan pushed forward for surgery on November 4th 2014.

We were told to expect the surgeon to come by sometime on the 3rd. Dr. Ohye came into the room quickly, speeding through the door on a metal scooter. He had recently been in some sort of hiking accident and had broken his leg. He had just gotten back into things at the hospital and had taken our case. He introduced himself with a bright smile. He was a little older, thin Asian fellow with his long black hair pulled back in a ponytail. He wore thick rimmed black glasses and was wearing pale blue scrubs. After introductions, he explained how he would be the one taking care of our girl and described the procedure, moving to the dry erase board to draw out his plan. He was going to take a "conduit" and attach it to

Natalie's heart where her pulmonary artery was supposed to be. In this case, the conduit would be from a cadaver. After attaching the conduit to her heart, he would attach it to the small remaining arteries that go to her lungs, hopefully increasing blood flow. He would also take down the shunt. This was a palliative procedure, which means it was meant to improve her quality of life but not really correct her heart defect. He said that it should fix most of our problems and, depending how things go, it may allow us to discuss a more permanent "repair" down the road. Kelly asked him if he was sure he would be able to complete the surgery with a broken leg. He nodded, smiling and assured us it would be "no problem". We were a little unsure about the whole thing, but I had heard his name before among parents on the floor and had been told "he was the best". He explained the risks and the word "death" echoed through my head. He assured us we were in good hands and I signed the paperwork.

The night before Natalie's second open heart surgery, we had most of the family there to visit. Kelly's parents came in from Kansas. My Dad was there as was my grandparents. The mood was actually pretty bright for such a difficult occasion. There was plenty of laughing and snuggling all around. Natalee had never been more happy as she snuggled with her visitors and Puppy Pacie. It was hard to believe how "sick" she would be just 24 hours from than. She was so vibrant and happy.

Later that night, Kelly, Natalie and I cuddled as a family on the couch in our room watching a movie on the television. We sat, surrounded by a large thick blue and gold knit blanket. Kelly looked at me, worry in her eyes, asking what I thought. Looking at Natalie, who sat in my lap looking at the TV with a little black and white beanie on her head, I told Kelly that we had to just trust in our Doctors and trust in the Lord above. I looked her in the eyes and told her it would all work out.

They took her the next morning. It was difficult. The process was much like our catheterization from just 3 weeks before. Natalie never seemed to be nervous at this age, but I always had that sinking feeling as I handed her off to the nursing staff. Just as they were taking her from me, I squeezed her hand three times, hoping that by some miracle she would give me the two squeezes back. She didn't.

At Mott's there is a waiting room right off the PICU on the 12th floor. We would start on one of the lower floors in the pre-op area and then, once things were moving in the operating room, move up the PICU area. The lounge on 12 was large with multiple things for families to distract their minds with. They had a small playroom when you first come in with a small play house, board games and computers for parents to use. Through another door the lounge becomes much bigger seating on the left around a large television and a small kitchen on the right. There were some old arcade games that took quarters along the left glass wall. If someone continued to talk straight, past the kitchen, they would stumble on a small hallway at the far side of the room which leads to another, quieter room. We set up shop in that back room as a family, hoping for privacy. There was nothing really to "do" in this back area as it was basically just a bunch of chairs spread out in a circle, but I think we were ok with that. The laughter and jovial energy from the night before was gone, replaced by a high tension silence. Most of us sat alone, keeping ourselves busy on one task or another. I played my PlayStation Vita, messed around on the iPad or read a book. As I sat there, I remember wondering to myself how things would be after this. Would this "fix" Natalie for the time being? Would this help us finally escape the hospital? Would it allow our family to feel "normal"? There was really no way to tell.

A local restaurant catered lunch for us, providing gyros which were unexpected and fantastic. We all spent the next 6 hours together in the room, mostly in silence. A nurse or social worker would visit us every 30-60 minutes to give updates.

CHAPTER 32

RESEARCH MONTH

Have you ever had a song stuck in your head and no matter what you try, it doesn't go away? I think most people have this trouble. For me, on the day of Natalie's second surgery, the first verse of "Skyfall" by Adele kept circulating through my brain. The lines, if you think about them, are very "doom and gloom", speaking to the end and how you just need to breath and let it happen. Not exactly what you want to be thinking about as you wait for your daughter to come out of major heart surgery.

As I walked down the hall towards the most acute area of the PICU, the song once again was on my mind. I did not know what to expect as I walked to the large "bay" that was the PICU after Natalie's surgery was completed. The "bay" was circular in design with a large nurses station in the middle. If felt was very large and open. The outside walls were made up of large glass windows that gave an excellent view of the outside world for miles. The outside world was covered in a layer of white. The rooms in this PICU were spread out around the space, separated by curtains. The rooms were made up of the child's bed, which was placed in the middle of the "room", surrounded by numerous pumps and monitors. There was a small couch and refrigerator along the back wall behind the bed. For entertainment, a TV on a stand was off to the side, almost as an afterthought.

The area was very bright and when I walked into the space, my breath was taken away at how critical all the children looked. Most of them were post-surgical just like my daughter. Whenever a child came in from surgery, most parents were asked to leave so they could be "stabilized" the child in peace. When I came in, many of the other parents were just getting settled back in from when Natalie had come in. Natalie was in one of the middle bays in a large white bed. She was unconscious and surrounded with more monitors then I had ever seen. Her robot had grown quite a bit, even sprouting another pole. Her saturations were poor and her skin was an odd grey color. She looked puffy around her face and I could see the irritation around her eyes from where they had tapped them shut.

My heart stopped in my chest when I saw her. They had a towel wrapped around her chest, similar to how she looked after her first surgery. I could see two drainage tubes coming out from under the towel and down to the side of the bed, draining blood. It was as bad as I feared. Our nurse was very friendly, which was typical for most of our experience, and told us Natalie was "having a hard time" but was coming around. I was asked not to touch her, but they did allow me to lean over and give her a kiss. I then went to look for Puppy Pacie. She "needed" him and I did not see him right away. Natalie had been allowed to take him back with her for comfort during the surgery and I found him in a "biohazard' bag at the foot of the bed. I unpacked him and made sure he took his rightful place next to her arm.

The PICU was loud, full of alarms and noises similar to the other ICU's we had stayed in before. After a short while, I told Natalie I would be back and left the area. Only two visitors were allowed in the PICU and I wanted to give others a chance. As I walked down the hall back to the waiting area, I fought back tears. She had been doing so WELL, relatively speaking, and it was worse than I had feared. With her pale, grey color, she looked to me like she almost didn't make it back to us, and it is feeling that haunts me sometimes even to this day.

Things did not improve quickly. In fact, the next day, it seemed to me that she just seemed to worsen. She would be lucid and fight her sedation due to being in so much discomfort, needing quite a bit of support and sedation to keep her going. As I sat there, book in lap with my bright orange Browns Sweatshirt, I would watch her start to flail and hear the familiar sound of her fighting the ventilator. I would drop my stuff and go to her, placing my hand on her head and try to speak to her in a calm voice and I tried to sing her the "Hallelujah" song. It didn't seem to work. Even on a ventalator with 100% oxygen, her oxygen saturation down into the 40's. The nurse would come over calm but quickly and give her more medications and she would calm down. As terrifying as it was, the

Cardiology team told me they were happy with her progress. Plan was a simple but familiar one. They wanted to try to wean her down off some of the oxygen and seeing how she does. She was to stay off of food, demanding "bowel rest" to be extra careful. They didn't want a return of the dreaded "NEC".

The next day, November 6th 2014, Natalie was still having a hard time with sedation and being agitated. The Doctors were continuing to try to wean her oxygen support down and were making slow but steady progress. She had been extubated and was semi-awake. I had camped out in the back on the couch, large, heavy, blue and gold blanket keeping me warm in the PICU. I had moved her Yellow and Pink "Natalie" sign from her room on 11 West to the window along the back wall once things had calmed down and I looked at it as it sat still against the cold glass of the window to my left. Kelly and I took shifts sitting on a chair next to Natalie's bed, holding her hand and reading to her.

With everything going on with Natalie, my residency program offered me some different options. One of my attending doctors from my program, Dr. Oram, paid me a visit. I had enormous respect for Dr. Oram, not just because of how smart he was but because he was always just so calm. He gave me a long hung, holding onto me a moment after I released and told me that the program was here for me with whatever I needed. He brought up the different options. One was to go on leave from the program. I was so nervous, feeling adrenaline rush through my body as he spoke. I was terrified of "being let go' from the job I had worked so hard to get. Things were tough and I had responsibilities that were falling to the side. My residency mates had been picking up the slack, but what if they grew tired of the extra work.

Thankfully, there were other options. One of them was to allow me to change my rotation to something less "stressful". This was pretty atypical for an Intern as the rotations first year are very structured. I was overjoyed by this option. I was grateful the program was not making me step away from work. Instead of pediatrics, I would be doing a "research month" for the month of November. I would be dismissed from clinic duty and my fellow residents would cover my tasks. This allowed me to move in with Kelly into the Ronald McDonald house in Ann Arbor and be with Natalie in this difficult time. I was more than thankful, hugging Dr. Oram and thanking him over and over again.

Back in the PICU sometime later, while I sat on the couch, I skimmed the internet to pass the time. Sitting alone in my own thoughts, beeps and alarms in the background, I felt guilty for wasting time. Part of my time off from work for my "Research Month" required I actually did some research. I was unsure what I wanted to do at first, but as time when on, I realized my case was right in front of me.

Up until now, I had not looked at data and long term in regards to Pulmonary Atresia. Our situation always seemed so rough and uncertain and it didn't really seem all that important. I was focused on going day to day. Who really could worry about how long she "may" live when we are talking open heart surgeries. I decided, sitting right there on that couch in the PICU to open Pandora's Box and look into it. Luckily, there was plenty of data to sift through. The numbers flooded in as I read paper after paper. The biggest indicator of survival was the ability to get a complete repair. A full repair refers to basically surgically correcting whatever the defect was, returning blood flow to close to "normal". With a complete repair, there was no telling how long she could go. Data seemed to be limited by surgical advancement. Who knew if she could live to be 50 as kids born 50 years ago did not have the options we had now. The good news was that most recent data showed that almost 80% of Pulmonary Atresia kids were alive at their 5th birthday. This gave me quite a bit of hope.

During those long days In the PICU, I became consumed with my research, looking into all sorts of different procedures and outcomes. My paper would look into survival rates based upon timing of repair. I was comparing babies repaired before they turned 1 and those babies repaired after the age of 1.

Natalie was slowly improving and, later that night, we were able to hold her.

CHAPTER 33

EMILIO

Much like in Kansas City, I frequently found myself walking to the hospital early in the morning to check on Natalie. My overnight anxiety was back and it could be crippling at times. Earlier in the year, walking the streets in Kansas City was mildly soothing. Now, in mid-November, it was dark and cold as I walked across the gravel lot to visit Natalie in the PICU. I tried not to worry about what had been happened, pushing aside the thoughts of almost losing her to this disease. I focused on being able to hold her again and how nice it felt having her little body against mine. As I approached the hospital, I prayed that we would soon find ourselves back at home and things back to normal. It seemed unrealistic, but I prayed it nevertheless.

When a child gets admitted to Mott's, parents and visitors are given a flimsy paper ID badge with your name, picture and a number designating where you "belong". It is one way to bypass the security desk when you enter the hospital. If the hospital stay is prolonged, parents are given more permanent badges made of plastic. As you walk around campus, you would see other parents with their badges. Even from a distance, you could see the "11W" on the parents badge and knew they were walking a similar path as you. It was almost a strange badge of honor representing your membership in the "heart warrior" club. Many parents would also have special shirts with their sick child's name on it. Most of them use Heart Warrior as a theme, or things like "Caleb's Cheer Club", "Brittany's

Battlers" for example. Another popular theme was the "zipper" club. This referred to a nick name some parents give the scar their child has from surgery across their chest. While it seems kind of cute and silly, I always thought of it as grotesque and morbid.

When we had been moved to the PICU the desk attendant switched out my 11W badge for a "12". I flashed the badge to the check in guard at the front desk and made my way through the large lobby to the elevators off to the left. After saluting Superman, who keeps watch over the lobby just before the elevators, I pressed the button and waited. There are 6 elevators at Mott's, each with a smiling face of a child or mother happy to relay the greatest of the care provided to them here at Motts. The elevators run randomly so you never know what you would get.

As I went down the colorful hall off the elevator, my nerves started up again. The wall inside the walkway to the PICU is very colorful with small clear glass tiles, each with a child's hand print on it. There are also success stories printed out on the wall, most from Heart Warriors just like mine and how they were winning their fight. I remember praying that someday we may find ourselves on that wall. I entered the bay, walked around the nurses desk in the middle to find Natalie extubated. She was just sitting there, her bed raised to help her breathing.

She looked exhausted, large brown eyes staring off at nothing with a terribly tired, sad look on her face. They had placed a large oxygen cannula on face, taping it to her cheeks with ng tube under it. Her chest was uncovered with the little white EKG patches covered with the purple hearts on her chest. Natalie seemed to struggle with adhesives with these monitors. They tended to cause her skin to break out but that was nowhere near a concern at the moment to me. I was so excited. I walked over quickly, saying "Hey Nat!" in a slightly excited, nervous voice. She turned to look at me, eyes glazed over and it was like she was not yet awake yet. It did not look like she even recognized me.

Kelly arrived soon after me and was just as excited as I was to our little girl awake. The nursing staff told us she was making great progress but was still pretty weak. With her awake, I went to work put out all the things that make her happy along the foot of her bed. Her two sound machines, the fan and her "friends". She was a zombie right now, but I hoped that seeing them would help bring my happy Natalie back.

I don't know if it was the stuff we brought, being awake or what, but Natalie really came around as they day went along, even giving me a smile at one point. The nurse brought out a device to help "keep her lungs open". It looked like a tongue depressor with a suction cup on the end. To use it, you would repetitively hit her back and side with it, over and over again. I do not know what the official name of this device is, but I affectionately referred to it as the "baby beater". The Nurse encouraged us to use the baby beater often to help keep Natalie's lungs open. That night, I made it a priority to get the Hockey game on the roller television so Natalie and I could watch it together. While we were distracted, Kelly was approached by another family as she returned from the pumping room.

Jorge was a young Spanish man, about my height and build. He seemed almost shy, introduced himself and his family to us. His wife Patricia had just gave birth to their beautiful son Emilio at 3AM this morning at Mott's. They had traveled all the way to Ann Arbor from El Salvador for the birth. They left EVERYTHING they knew to come to this Hospital because little Emilio also has Pulmonary Atresia. His doctors had been able to diagnose his condition at 20 weeks gestation and they had told Jorge and Patricia that if they wanted their baby to survive they had to come to either United States or Europe. Patricia explained that they had been watching us, watching Natalie all propped up in her bed and smiling at passersby. In their time of need, seeing her improve and happy gave them hope. I remember how awestruck I was at this statement. Not only had this family given up just about everything to get here but that somehow we had given them hope. It was an amazing feeling.

Emilio's room was two or three beds down from us in the far corner. I approached them later, saying hello and meeting the little guy. He was smaller than Natalie but was unconscious and under quite a bit of support. Looking at the way the family looked at their little boy, my heart went out for them. I knew the look and the feelings they must be going through all to well. Jorge explained that the doctors were discussing surgery soon for him. His heart was in worse shape than Natalie's. His atresia seemed advanced, affecting the right ventricle as well as the pulmonary arteries. Since things were more complicated Emilio could not have a repair similar to was planned for Natalie. Her right ventricle was in good working order which allowed doctors the possibility of creating a "normal" system later on. Instead, with Emilio, they would have to create a "single ventricle" system and he would need a heart transplant sometime in the future. His surgery was set for some time soon, may be as early as the 14th. It was tough to hear. We wished them the best and exchanged information. Kelly planned on writing them once things stabled out. Hopefully, Natalie would be back at home soon and could bring more hope for what would hopefully be a similar future for their little Emilio.

Later, on reflecting on this encounter, Kelly expressed her thoughts about how hard it would be to go through that much. "God is surely working through Natalie." She said to me. 'I just can't imagine how hard it must have been to leaving my country and emptying all of my bank accounts and selling my belongings to help my baby survive." she had said as we were getting ready to tuck into our separate beds at the Ronald

McDonald House. I agreed. Somehow all we had been through seem so small compared to theirs. I also knew that his road was going to be very rough in the future. We said a prayer together for their family and for little Emilio.

CHAPTER 34

THE FIRST SNOW

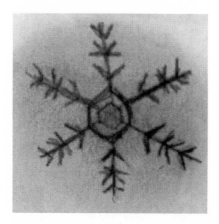

Natalie continued to improve as the days passed. She made it back to a room on 11 West on the 8th of November. It was nice to be back "home", taking up residence in room 64. The doctors started tube feeds and she was weaned off pain medication. By the 11th, one week after surgery, she was back to her normal happy self. She was doing so well that discharge became a real possibility. The Doctors that they felt they could pull her large IV that was kept in the right side of her neck. It had been in for some time, originally placed for her TPN when she was admitted in October and I had been worried about it for some time. I did not want it to get infected. I was happy to see it go. Natalie still has a scar to this day from that IV on the side of her neck.

That night, Natalie had another episode of bloody stools. It was in the middle of the night and most of the normal staff had left. I remember the stress in the room as the Nurse Practitioner for surgery came in to evaluate her. I was very frustrated as they had JUST removed her access line and here we were again. I remember commenting under my breath how the surgery was supposed to have fixed this. Step one was to get access. Natalie was quite small, so it was no easy task. One nurse came in and tried three times to place an IV and missed. I had to leave the room during the tries. Unlike when she was born, I had a hard time now dealing with seeing Natalie scream out in pain. When I came back, I was stunned to hear about the misses. I was even more stunned to see that they had tried to get a vein in her head. Now I was no expert, but I head learned that this was something you do not try on a child Natalie's age (6 months). The blood draw team had gone home so we were left with little options. They offered to have the PICU nurse to come try. I was fuming.

After they were able to place a line, start fluids and get blood, the Surgery Nurse Practitioner came back in and proposed a plan. They wanted to start back up "the 2 week treatment" again. It was like the straw that the broke the camel's back for me. We had just gone through this and I was not comfortable with going back. Natalie looked fine. I refused the plan, demanding evidence of NEC before we start down that path again. I had seen Natalie suffer too much already and was not happy with causing more pain. I wanted an xray showing pneumatosis before we would do this again. "She was just "repaired"! It SHOULDN'T be NEC." I had said sharply. I brought up that maybe it could be related to the feeding she was going through. Somehow, maybe Kelly's diet wasn't fully "dairy free" as she had "cheated" once or twice by mistake.

Initially, the Nurse Practitioner did not agree with me. She thought I was being emotional and not thinking clearly. She was 100% right of course, but I could not see it at that time. We had a little standoff, but she did respect my wishes. At the end, the Nurse Practitioner was gracious, agreeing to hold off until the AM to see how Natalie did. I was fine with this, praying to see the cardiology attending in the morning to discuss the case. I had been given my wish and our care was switched from the Surgery team to the Cardiology team that next day. To my delight, the agreed with my assessment and were fine to watch and wait. Natalie's stools cleared up over the next few days.

Looking back on that night, it is embarrassing. I was not a nice parent that day and I openly clashed with Natalie's provider. Heck, I even had informed them that I was a doctor and I knew what I was talking about. That said, I was not thinking like a doctor that night. I was thinking as a parent who had reached his limit of seeing his kid suffer. I was wrong and I realized it that next day and tried to use the whole experience as a learning experience.

I knew what the Nurse Practitioner was doing her best and it was wrong for me to act out. I apologized the next day, but it left a bad taste in my mouth. From that night forward, I promised myself I would no longer be Natalie's "doctor". I am her father and that job is hard enough.

We were given the go ahead to go home on November 13th after another month in the hospital. On the day we were leaving, it was snowing. Natalie was in pink and white striped pajamas with a cute little knit maroon hat for the trip. Kelly and I couldn't wait to escape, pacing Natalie's room.

Our discharge was delayed for an hour or so after a fire broke out on the 4th floor below us. No one was hurt and it was almost humorous. "God just doesn't want us to leave" I remember telling Kelly. After the discharge was made official, I brought Natalie down to the main lobby, wandering around the lobby as we waited. Kelly went and pulled the Brown Rav4 up to the front of the hospital and parked in the Valet Area.

I saw Kelly in the car and started to leave the hospital through the front door. I stopped in the Atrium and pointed out to Natalie the falling snow. A look of confusion and then curiosity came over her face. As we walked out, she looked up at the snow in amazement, large brown eyes trying to follow the flakes as they fell. I watched as she tracked a flake with her eyes. The flake fell on her nose, causing her eyes almost to cross. She squealed out and tried to wipe it off as it melted. It was a magical moment.

CHAPTER 35

THE BEST LAID PLANS...

Someone once told me that there is always a light at the end of the tunnel. At times you just need to look really hard to find it. Once we returned to the lonely home in Toledo, everything was suddenly back to "normal". We arrived home and it was like we hadn't left. Natalie was suddenly breastfeeding again while Kelly stuck to a strict "No Dairy" diet and there was no blood in her stool. It was nice being home with the family. I was able to focus on myself a little in the down time, which was something that had taken quite a hit with intern year. I worked to get back into the gym and spent several hours a day on my research paper. It was coming along nicely and I pushed forward with confidence, finding plenty of data to support my thesis.

Over the next few days, we started taking Natalie all over the place. This upset many of our relatives, namely my mother, but I felt it important for her to see and experience everything we could. My mom was likely correct about precautions, but she had not seen Natalie when she was "sick and grey" after surgery. Natalie had come so close to the possibility of losing her life and It had put a fear deep in my heart. I felt a need to give her experiences. One of those, was the pool at the YMCA down the street. It had been 2 weeks since surgery and her wounds were healed, so I felt it semi-safe. We dressed Natalie up in a yellow bathing suit with a big floppy hat. The pool water was cool and she was not a huge fan at first, but she spent some time splashing her mommy which makes every baby smile.

Things were going so well that we felt it safe to start making plans for the next few months. We were not due back in Ann Arbor for a few weeks and I was off work so this gave us plenty of time to have fun. We decided on visiting my Dad for Thanksgiving and I was going to learn all there was to learn about smoking a turkey. As the month moved forward, I had a familiar nervous feeling in my gut. I was gearing up to restart Inpatient medicine on December 1st. This was a hard rotation but one I enjoyed. My "pre-rotation jitters" was nothing now and seemed to be cropping up whenever I started a new rotation, but this was different. Natalie also had her follow up appointment with her cardiologist looming. I was not particularly worried. Natalie was doing so well, even working on crawling. What could go wrong?

On Tuesday November 25th, with Thanksgiving 2 days away, we made our way up the snowy route 23 to Mott's Children's hospital for our follow up with Dr. Gelehrter. It was routine for us to get imaging before we saw her, usually first an X-ray and then an Echo. Natalie had been growing used to Echocardiograms and no longer needed sedation as long as she had Sprout on the TV. She hated the X Rays. To get a clear view, the technicians had to put her in this little chair against the X ray Buckie, strapping her arms up and off to the side. Natalie would scream, crying hard with tears rolling down her face. Honestly, to me it looked like she was being crucified. We were allowed to stand behind the protection wall, watching through a glass window and offering words of encouragement. As soon as the image was taken, they allowed us to come comfort her. On this occasion, Kelly went to help Natalie. My attention was elsewhere.

Looking at the image on the computer screen, something didn't look right. I had seen Natalie's heart before on imaging. It was the typical "boot shaped" heart of a Tetralogy of Fallot baby, but this time the heart seemed much larger. It was almost as if it was moving into the left side of her chest and squishing her lung. After looking at Kelly, I could tell she saw something was off too. I did not know what to think, wondering to myself, "Is this just what her conduit looked like on x ray?" We were taken to a waiting room to await word from our Cardiologist.

Dr. Gelehrter and her fellow came in with stern and worried looks on their face. They explained that Natalie's "mediastinum was enlarged" which was pushing her heart to the side. They did not know what was causing it. Dr. Gelehrter asked about how Natalie was acting. We explained how she had never seemed better, happy, laughing and even working on crawling. They asked about specific symptoms of heart failure such as heavy breathing, swelling or sweating. Kelly explained how Natalie had been sweating quite a bit when she breast feeding but she had thought it was normal. I could tell the doctors were concerned. Dr. Gelehrter advised we come back into the hospital and get some work up done. They did not know what was going on, but it wasn't normal and surgery may be needed. She apologized and left to make arrangements. It seemed unreal. Everything had been going so well. Kelly and I looked to each other and then at Natalie. She sat on the table, innocently playing with the toys that was brought in for her, Puppy Pacie dangling from her mouth.

I fought off tears as I left the room. I had to tell Dad to see if he could come sit with us for procedure. He lived 2 hours away from Ann Arbor, and was always pretty busy. Even with his heavy work schedule, he seemed always willing to drop everything to be by our side during times like this. I also had to get a hold of my grandparents. My grandparents always bent over backwards for Natalie and us. It was hard telling them, and my grandfather took the news in silence. I felt so bad spreading the bad news. I knew what it did to people, but I needed help. Things had been going so well and we had not expected this. I had not even packed a bag.

Little sleep was gained that night as I sat in the blue chair in good ol' room 64. It was like we had never left. The happiness we had been building was suddenly replaced with a terrible emptiness of the unknown. I had an inner sense of dread that no amount of positive thinking could fix. A nurse took Natalie early in the morning for another test and It confirmed that there was a serious problem.

We were told that there was a "pseudo aneurysm" with her conduit that they had just surgically placed several weeks earlier. Simply put, some of the conduit was tearing loose from her heart due to the high pressures and blood was pooling around the heart. It had pushed the heart over, deflating her left lung. It amazing the doctors Natalie seemed to be doing as well as she had been based upon this. This situation was an emergency and they called for surgery that very day. We were taken down to the surgical floor, carrying Natalie in our arms in tears. It was like we had a backslide to a month ago, only this time the surgery was an emergency.

Kelly felt guilty terribly. She felt like there had been signs of something wrong and she had missed them. I tried to reassure her. Personally, after getting through the shock and fear, I felt lucky. Had we missed the appointment with Dr. Gelehrter Natalie would have likely died. At some point the thing around Natalie's heart would've ruptured and she would have bleed out quickly into her chest.

Our surgeon Dr. Ohye's schedule was full. We were assigned to one of the other surgeons named Dr. Si. While Dr. Ohye comes off as "cool and confident", Dr. Si comes off pretty serious. I have seen him smile before, but this was not one of those times. He was shorter and younger than Dr. Ohye. He explained when we met with him that he was going to go in and assess. They may need to replace the conduit. He was also going to try to "patch open" her arteries as well, which would decrease the pressure hopefully on the conduit. This meant cutting the arteries open and basically making them bigger with cadaver parts. He told us the risk. The word "Death" was thrown around. He mentioned that he may need to "keep her open" to help keep down pressure. This sounded terrifying but what choice did we have.

A short time, after we signed the paperwork, I watched as they wheeled Natalie down the hall away from me, Kelly in the bed with her to help with the transition. I buried my head into my Dad's chest and cried just as hard as that day at the airport right before Natalie's first surgery.

CHAPTER 36

BLACK FRIDAY

The "routine" for us was the same as the before Natalie's last surgery for the most part. After sending Natalie off with the nurses, we all sat in the PICU waiting area as a family, awaiting word on how things went. We would do what we could, finding ways to pass the time.

Unlike the surgery 3 weeks before, we no longer had a room at the Ronald McDonald House. As we were suddenly back in the hospital and things were pretty dire, a social worker offered us the option of staying in the "Mott House" inside the hospital itself. Located just off the elevators on the 12th Floor, the Mott House was a special designated area set aside for parents to rest when situations are dire, much like the "Ronald McDonald Room" at the hospital in Kansas City. Kelly and I agreed and went to go check it out, keeping a close eye on the beeper we had been given for updates on Natalie.

The Mott House, unlike the Ronald McDonald House in Ann Arbor, was very updated and nice. It had a large lounge area, a small kitchen with a microwave and fridge and then multiple single rooms along a back hallway. The rooms were small but had everything we would need. The floors were covered in a thin generic brown carpet and there was a small bed. Each room had a small private bathroom with a shower. The bathroom looked almost identical to the bathrooms in the patient rooms on 11 West. The floor had a mosaic tiles with black squares surrounded by white triangles.

The walls are pale brown with a very colorful "rainbow" pattern of titles making their way around the wall about halfway up.

In regards to the surgery itself, I do not remember much about what actually happened. similarly , round 3 in the PICU is also a blur. That sounds terrible, not remembering something as serious as this, but as I write this exactly 4 years later, all the details blend together. I know Natalie did well during the surgery. Dr. Si told us that it was difficult as the tissue was "seapy" due to the recent surgery but overall he was pleased with how things went. When we finally saw her 6 hours later she was back in the same area in the PICU that we had have just left 3 weeks ago. She had at least 7 pumps on 2 IV poles keeping her going. It was hard to be back right where we just had been. We had fought so hard to get back home, yet here we were. Our baby, once so smiley and happy, was unconscious with a tube in her throat and countless drugs keeping her alive.

Thanksgiving was canceled. There was no way we could make it with Natalie having surgery. Kelly, my grandparents and I were taking shifts watching over Natalie two days after her surgery when social work came in and told us a Thanksgiving meal was to be catered. I was not super excited, but Kelly perked right up. I have always been pretty picky when it comes to food, especially on Thanksgiving, and was not a fan of the "fixings". Kelly, on the other hand, loved ALL of it. We walked to the room outside the PICU and found a group of people dishing out the goods. Turkey, Potatoes, Stuffing, Pies. All you could want, they have. As I watched the server placing a large piece of white meat on my plate, I remember looking over at Kelly and she had a look of despair on her face. I was completely caught off guard and asked her what was up. She looked at me and, in her traditional Kelly "whiny", voice let me know that they used dairy in the potatoes. The used diary in everything except the stuffing and the turkey. She couldn't have all the fixings! I felt bad but I couldn't help but laugh.

The food was pretty good and really lifted the mood. We passed the time watching the Lions win and Cowboys lose, which never seems to happen on Thanksgiving. Before we knew it, we were sitting back with Natalie in the PICU, settling in for the night.

It was not all bad though! In life you always have to try some positive! One GOOD thing about being in the PICU with an unconscious child is the opportunity for Black Friday Shopping! Ann Arbor is a big town and normally it will take you 45 minutes to get just about everywhere. With Natalie under 24hr care, we decided to take the chance and try to see what we could get. We tucked Natalie in and left her in the hands of the caring nurses while we went out into the madness.

I was surprised to find much of the town deserted and almost no lines at the big box stores. In Missouri, people tend to form long lines days in advance. Hell, one year me and my three brothers sat outside a GameStop all night for a chance to get a Wii. It turned out that the college was out of session for the holiday thanks to a Thanksgiving break. The town was dead. We suddenly were the first in line for most of the sales and could basically find any of the deals we wanted to check out.

I wanted a new TV. Who doesn't want a new TV? My wife did not agree. "We don't need a TV! We have one!" She had said. She had to remind me multiple times that night of that fact as I walked passed all of the large boxes that lined the aisles at Target. Toys-R-Us was also very exciting. It was super busy with parents staking carts high up with discounted toys. I remember joining in on the fun. It was almost like a fever came over me. It was less about what she needed and more about "could she use this" or "would she like this". There was so much 'good stuff'. Overall, We did pick up a new sound bar, some things for ourselves as well as some good gifts for Natalie on her first Christmas. I came away feeling pretty good about myself.

Natalie recovered slowly but surely. They had her extubated before long, putting her on a Bipap to help with her breathing. She was quite upset that Puppy Pacie could not fit in her mouth with her Elephant like tube going to her nose. Remembering a lesson from the NICU, It was nothing a spare pacifier and a pair of scissors couldn't fix. Before long, we were back on the floor, sitting in the playroom on 11 West working on the same old things including eating and weight gain. As the month of November drew to a close we had hopes of escaping and enjoying our first Christmas together as a family

.

CHAPTER 37

REVENGE OF THE STUFFING

I started my second Inpatient Hospital rotation that December. I woke up the morning of December 1st, a Monday, a little nervous. I tried to focus on how much I had enjoyed the work on Inpatient the first time around, but it seemed to do little to calm the nerves. Natalie and Kelly were still in the hospital an hour to the north. After leaving our empty house, I made my way to the Toledo Hospital, parking in the Resident lot next to the hospital and made my way to the building for morning rounds. While this rotation was very difficult, I rather enjoyed it. There was something really rewarding about caring for someone when they are truly in need and getting them back home feeling much better. My shift that first day was to see my list of patients, present them at rounds and then go to my outpatient clinic in the Afternoon. I tended to always be nervous for new rotations, but I was extra nervous this month as I had been gone for the whole month of November doing "research".

I had nothing to worry about, while challenging, I found the work really enjoyable. One really good thing about being back at work is that it took my mind of my Daughter. I was able to focus on the task at hand instead of constantly watching monitors, jumping at every alarm. I rounded on my patients, wrote up my notes and presented my patients to my attending at 9 am. We would walk through our patients, telling our attending what had been going on and what we thought we should do.

They would ask us questions and together we would lay out a plan for the day. We also had a team of pharmacists present to help with medication questions. It was exactly like what the "Team of Doctors" did for Natalie on a daily basis. After we discussed all of the patients on the list, we would go see all of our patients together. Once they were all seen, we would monitor for results and handle any new admissions for the day. We also had clinic once a week, so one of the interns would disappear for a bit to handle that. During Residency, we also had lunch "didactics" or lectures every day. These were mandatory and discussed different topics to help our education. I attended my outpatient clinic and knocked it out pretty well. Initially, the program started us off with patient slots every 30 to 60 minutes, so clinic was pretty light.

After clinic, I called the inpatient team to check in and was told to take the rest of the day off. Things were quiet and they did not need me. I was excited to escape earlier and I was able to go back to Mott's to visit my family. Kelly had texted me and there were plans that maybe we could take her home that day.

Natalie had done quite well, moving from the ICU to a normal room on 11 West and spending her days breast feeding and playing in the playroom. I arrived just in time for the nurse to hand Kelly the discharge paperwork. We had effectively escaped! I gave Natalie a snuggle and started packing up all of her gear. I had grabbed up her swing, picked up her friends and placed it on a cart to load to the car. Before leaving, there was one last duty to take care of: Diaper duty. Kelly was changing it as I loaded the suitcase onto the cart. "Uhhhhh!" Kelly said in an odd voice, I turned and I knew it was bad by her face. The stool had little flecks of blood in it.

It was terrible frustrating and disheartening. We had already been told that we were going to get to go home. We already had gotten Natalie excited about seeing the "Fishies" at Cabela's on the way home. It is not like Natalie could really complain about missing out on these things, but it felt like we were suddenly back at the starting line again. We looked at each other, unsure how to proceed. Kelly became frustrated, "She has been doing so well!" She started in a high pitched voice, flailing her arms a little. "She has been well tolerating her feeds and everything seemed normal. Since I am on a dairy free diet she shouldn't be having bloody stools." I think we both had the same thought at that point: Do we say something?

I was trying to calm Kelly down struggling to mask the unsteadiness in my voice as the nurse came in. She saw the diaper and gave us a sad sideways glance. I think the tension in the room was thick and the nurse picked up on that. She paged the doctor to come check things out. The doctor came in and started asking about how Natalie's activity was and Kelly's diet. Kelly explained to the doctor that Natalie was feeding well with breast milk and acting like her normal self. In regards to the diet, Kelly had been very careful, taking in nothing that even remotely could be considered dairy. Then her eyes grew and you could tell she had just thought of something. After a moment of reflection, Kelly told the doctor and nurse that the only thing she had eaten recently that she wasn't 100% about was turkey at the Thanksgiving dinner in the PICU.

Kelly took a moment and called the restaurant that catered the meal. As I watched he speak to the manager, I knew the answer based upon the look on her face. She hung up the phone and told the room in a defeated voice that the stuffing she ate did in fact contain butter. The doctor seemed reassured. Kelly was very upset. This diet had been very hard on her, making it hard to eat just about anywhere. She felt she had been sabotaged and Natalie's bloody stools were now somehow her fault.

Initially, the Resident felt the episode was likely just due to the stuffing and offered a "watchful waiting approach" as opposed to anything more invasive. I was thankful that this was the plan. The hospital still had some of Kelly's breast milk from before thanksgiving frozen in storage and decided to start thawing it out to give to Natalie. The Nurse practitioner felt that the milk from before should be fine to give her until Kelly's system rids the butter laden stuffing.

Unfortunately, sometimes the best laid plans don't always work out. Natalie had another bloody stool an hour later, leading to the doctors to throw out the "watch and wait plan". They made her NPO (nothing by mouth) and ordering imaging. Natalie had to have another IV placed and she was getting hungry. An Echocardiogram was completed that came back stable and her X Ray of her abdomen looked ok. The resident came back and gave us the update. For now, we went back to 'watchful waiting. They recommended the Elecare be started back up and we would hopefully just stay in observation.

Elecare is terrible. It smelled so bad and Natalie hated it. No matter how hungry she seemed to be, she would spit out anything you tried to giver her and even start dry heave. They tell you that babies cannot express complex emotions, but it felt to me like she was doing it on purpose. It actually reminded me of myself when I was a kid and my dad tried to force me to eat Sloppy Joes. I could vomit on demand.

The nurse was not playing around though. She placed an NG tube into Natalie's left nostril and started Elecare on a pump. Natalie seemed to do well with this. That night, we saw a Gastroenterologist for a second opinion on the bloody stools. After reviewing the studies, He explained to Kelly and I that he felt that two things were likely going on. The very bloody stools Natalie was having in the past were likely NEC and had been treated appropriately. That said, the stools more recently with the small flecks of blood were more likely some sort of irritation colitis, either from a small amount of diary or some other protein. Either way, he felt it was not a big deal. As long as she was not acting sick and it was "frank" (which means a lot) he was ok with observation.

We were still encouraged to stay in the hospital for observation. The hospital itself started to prepare itself for the season, putting up a large Christmas Tree in the lobby. We took Natalie to the "lighting ceremony" that night. They had one of the kids from the floor push a large switch to light it all up. We took Natalie to the tree, her first Christmas Tree, and she stared at it, eyes wide open and mouth agape. She smiled as I pointed to the bulbs that were larger than her head. She even giggled. I could tell it was fun for her which warmed my heart. I can still see our reflection in my mind to this day and hopefully will never forget that golden reflection of her looking back at me in one of those bulbs.

With the NG tube, Natalie was able to take the Elecare without issue. The focus from the doctors shifted the next morning from her stools to weight gain, something we constantly seemed to be dealing with. She had lost some weight with everything going on the past month and the doctors wanted to see some gains. We were going to have to stay in the hospital until she showed she could gain weight.

After what felt like months in the hospital, what harm could come from a few more days? We settled back in, fully unpacking our stuff and prepared for another week or so of "hanging out". Another exciting thing offered by child life at Mott's is a visit from some of the student athletes from Michigan. From gymnasts to wrestlers, we would get visits from athletes from time to time as they donating their time and gear hoping to make a sick child's day just a little better. Most of the time, I had not ever heard of these athletes, but I really appreciated the time they took to stop by. On the December 4th, Devin Gardner, starting Quarterback of the football team, came to visit. As huge Michigan fans, I may have been more excited than anyone. Natalie seemed mesmerized by him. I think it was because he was so tall. I always heard that football and hockey players were big in real life, but this guy was HUGE. Like, I came up to his belly button huge. He introduced himself to us and asked how Natalie was doing. He was so nice, with a calm voice. After sharing some stories, I asked if he would be ok with us taking a picture. He smiled, agreeing to the photo opportunity. It was a real highlight.

Natalie gained some weight steadily with the Elecare and was even taking some of Kelly's frozen milk by bottle. We were discharged from the hospital on December 5th with plans for follow up mid-December. While we left, I felt cautiously optimistic that we could hopefully stay away for a month. I was also hopefully to stay out of the hospital for Christmas. We had spent Halloween and Thanksgiving at Mott's and I was really looking forward to being able to celebrate with just our family. We took Natalie to

Cabela's on the way back, just as we promised. She has always loved looking at the fish, especially the catfish. Once she was a few years older, if you asked her what sound a catfish makes, she would tell you in a very excited fashion "Rmiaow!".

CHAPTER 38

BREAK OUT THE UGLY SWEATERS

Things went back to normal quicker than you would think. While Kelly and Natalie were back in routine back at home, I was busy with my heavy work hours at Toledo Hospital. Kelly continued the absolutely insane dairy free diet and Natalie was able to breastfeed without any more blood in her stool. We were weighing with her daily and she was making progress. Mott's had arrange for home nurses to come out with scales as well and visits from a support group called "Help Me Grow" to see us. I think this gave our doctors more confidence with how we were doing at home. They were very nice people and seemed to really look out for Natalie's interests and make sure nothing was falling behind.

Natalie did so well with breastfeeding that her NG tube was out before we knew it. Natalie also said her first words: Mama. I was not thrilled. I had been coaching her on "dada" aggressively and It didn't seem to have paid off. I was very excited as we were able to visit Santa Claus at the Franklin Park Mall. If you think about it, visiting Santa is a little bit of an odd thing to do. When else in your child's life would you be ok with setting your kid on some old strangers lap and telling him what you want. Well, traditions are traditions so we rushed to do it the first chance we had. Natalie looked at Santa as she sat in his lap with a very concerned look and he just looked back. She was uncertain who this guy was and was unsure what to think of his beard. It may have concerned Natalie, but it made for an excellent photo.

Otherwise, life was back to normal. Our television died on us sometime soon after we had gotten home, almost rubbing salt in my "black Friday" wound. Talk about first world problems, right? Kelly and I still giggle about this today. We had a follow up appointment with Dr. Gelehrter on December 21st which included an x ray and echocardiogram. I was so nervous as they took the x ray but everything came back great. Natalie was gaining weight. They gave us permission to "stay home".

For Christmas, we really went overboard for Natalie. It is hard to buy toys for a 6 month old, mostly because you are not sure what exactly is "appropriate". We had gone to Toys-R-Us on Black Friday and picked out all these little toys, new clothes and dolls. One idea I had was to get her a replacement for Puppy Pacie. Kelly and I had talked about weaning Natalie from the pacifier and I voiced my concern about how difficult this could be. How could we ever wean her pacifier from her if it was attached to her best friend. I came up with an excellent solution. We needed to find a stuffed animal that LOOKED like Puppy Pacie but did not have the pacifier. I learned that makers of wubbanub actually has larger stuffed animal versions of their animals so a child's best friend could grow with them. I leaned over my laptop, excited to find the bigger Puppy Pacie. When I found it, i was frustrated to realized that the larger "bear" stuffed animal did not look like the wubbanub version.

Her Puppy Pacie was relatively flat with a little head and arms poking out. The larger bear version sat up like a normal teddy bear. Sure, the color was the same grey with the bright spots, but it didn't "look" like her friend and I was worried Natalie wouldn't get the connections. The Puppy on the other hand, had the same design as the smaller bear. It was almost identical except for the colorful ears. I decided that Natalie was likely young enough to fall for my charade and this would be her new best friend.

On Christmas, I held Natalie on my lap as we (I) opened her gifts. Natalie loved the paper flying everywhere and was having a good time playing with the boys. As more and more gifts were opened, she started to lose interest, being distracted by the toys piling up around us. After casting aside the last box of "uhhh cloths", I snagged the box wrapped in red and green paper with small Santas on it. Of course, I knew what was in there and could not wait to see how Natalie would react. As I started ripping off the paper, Natalie was pretty distracted. I squeezed the brown box open so Natalie could see inside. I was a little disappointed that she didn't even seem to want to look inside. I reached in and pulled out the gift and placed it right in front of her. When I brought out the puppy, she initially didn't know what to think. I held my breath as she inspected the stuffed animal.

Suddenly, Natalie recognized her friend and a huge smile came over her face. She wrapped her arms around it, rocking back and forth, squealing with glee. I encouraged her, telling her it's BIG PUPPY PACIE! She started playing with it, placing the dogs orange ear in her mouth. Pure joy overcame me as I felt like I had "won" Christmas and was winning as a parent.

Later that night, the pacifier fairy came 'officially" and turned Puppy Pacie into a Puppy Pal. Wanting to begin the wean, we took Puppy Pacy and just left the big one behind. Natalie transitioned without any issues, sleeping with her new best friend snuggled tightly in her arms.

As the new year came around, things started to speed up, but in a good way. Natalie had a follow up in the first week of January with her Cardiologist who felt she was doing great. The plan was to repeat testing in April. This was surprising. We had not been out of the hospital for more than a month her entire life so three months seemed like an eternity to us. Days turned to weeks without incident. While I worked long hours at the hospital learning my profession, Kelly and Natalie worked together to help her grow stronger. In the first few weeks of the year Natalie went from barely sitting to rolling all over, almost escaping her Bumpo seat on her own. In March, while I was slaving away on Round Two of Inpatient Pediatrics, Natalie was preparing to make a trip to visit Bubbe in Kansas City. She had to first see Cardiology and they were amazed with her progress. She was "Exceeding goals" they had said. She was even now on the growth chart! Kelly was very proud with the whole situation. When she told me about the visit, she proudly proclaimed, "My mommy milk must be good stuff because it is workin'!!". I could almost see the smile on her face through the phone based on how her voice sounded. Kelly and Natalie took the train to Missouri and was gone for 3 weeks.

As spring turned to summer, we spent quite a bit of time outdoors. Natalie's first birthday was quite a big deal indeed. It was "Chicka-Chicka Boom-Boom" themed and everybody came to the extravaganza. We even hired a professional photographer to document the date. One image that is burned in my mind is her sitting there, large hat with palm trees on it, smashing cake in her face.

Natalie soon learned to walk and talk. Every day when I come home you squeal and run to me yelling "dada" looking for a hug. It was like having a normal little girl. I recall how this was one of the greatest things I had ever known up to this point. "Pup Pup" went everywhere with Natalie. He had to come with us to the store, the mall, and ALWAYS to doctor's appointments. Natalie had a follow-up heart catheterization in July, forcing me to spend yet another one of my "vacations" in the hospital. That said, it was worth it. We did well and only had to stay for the weekend. It was frustrating on some level never getting to go anywhere during my time off, but I never minded missing "vacations". Any time away from the grueling hours of residency was a plus. Having the time to just sit and cuddling my girl was a blessing.

We found out we were pregnant in the summer of 2015. Natalie was going to be a Big Sister. I was watching Television and Kelly had set the pregnancy test near me and just waited. I remember reacting "well", as it was pretty exciting, but inside I was terrified. I feared deep down in my soul that I would bring another child into this world just to watch them suffer. The geneticist put that chance at 5%. I worried what challenges a new baby would bring to our family, especially if it was born sick.

Kelly and I had a good honest conversation about it. It did little to ease my nerves but I was glad to let my feelings be known. After a month or so, we rented a Lake house in the Irish Hills of Michigan and invited quite a bit of family members up for the announcement. Kelly had bought a shirt with a big heart on it that read "Big Sister" for Natalie. We had her wear it the day everyone arrived and waited to see who would notice. It was quite a bit of fun. Honestly, It was like my life was so perfect all of a sudden. With Natalie doing well and a new one on the way, we felt like a normal family.

PART IV

Falling for the Illusion of Normalcy

CHAPTER 39

SOMETIMES YOU FORGET

Some of the most difficult times in all of this have come when we almost forget how sick my daughter is and then have a "day of reckoning". Somehow, though the grind of normal life, the thoughts of her illness falls out the back of your mind. You almost no longer notice the thick scar on her chest or the way she huffs and puffs when she runs. You forget that, at any time, things could drastically change. Forgetting is a blessing that many parents of sick children never get to experience, and I am thankful we are able to forget, but sooner or later the truth will flair up and you get shocked back to reality. It is a life altering experience that I would not ever wish on anyone.

By the time Fall had rolled around in 2015, we had fallen into a very "normal" routine. Kelly was 19 weeks pregnant with our son Lucas and we were making plans to visit Missouri for Christmas. We were going to take the train, just like in March. Natalie had stayed out of the hospital for most of the year, only making a small stint for bronchiolitis in march. She could walk and talk now. We used FaceTime more than ever while I was at work. Nothing wiped away a tough patient encounter from my mind then an "Lub You" from my little Nat. She enjoyed playing at the park, begging us to push her "as high as the clouds" on the swing.

Residency had been going very well, and I was cruising in my second year of residency. At my program, you are designated a "senior" resident during your second year and the work load significantly lightens. Rotations also focus more "outpatient" with things like Cardiology, Orthopedics and Outpatient pediatrics. This brought a much needed break from the heavy workload as well as more personal freedom.

On another snowy day in November 23rd 2015, we made our way back to the hospital in Ann Arbor for a routine echocardiogram and checkup. Everything felt routine, including our plans to head to the small cafeteria to pick out smoothies afterwards. I was secretly planning a trip to the M DEN as well, but had not yet told my wife. I wanted to get my Dad something special as we would be spending Christmas in Missouri.

Her routine Echo quickly became anything but routine, revealing what appears to be a recurrence of the pseudoanurysm. That something was wrong on the monitor as she was getting the testing and my heart sank. It is hard to explain, but looked like a pocket next to a pocket. I immediately having flashbacks of the year before, my mind flooded with the crushing, overwhelming feelings of anxiety. People have talked to me about Post Traumatic Stress Disorder, having recurrent thoughts about a traumatic experiences and panic. This had to be close to that.

As we sat in the waiting room for Dr. Gelehrter, doubt creeping into the back of my head. I was holding Natalie close, rocking her and singing to her as she held Pup Pup. I wondered if this was the end. We met up with her cardiologist, who was just as shocked as we were. "She always looks so good." Dr. Gelehrter had said, "If she ever looks BAD then we know we are really in trouble." The attempt at humor was appreciated, but unfortunately we were emotionally no longer present. We were almost shell shocked. I handled it in stride, pushing my emotions down into my core and focusing on trying to be positive. Once again, Natalie had a medical emergency and we had randomly caught it. I looked out the window as the storm picked up. "At Least we don't have to drive home in this…" I had said. They took Natalie for a CT of her chest and it confirmed the diagnosis. We were immediately admitted with plans to undergo a second repair the next day. I was given the privilege of spreading the news to our family members.

We spent the night the best way we could, trying to keep the spirits high. Natalie was dressed in her traditional Hospital garb, a small light blue gown that buttoned in the front. Pup Pup was given a gown as well. She was given an IV and was finally formally introduced to her new Robot. She did not remember it from the year before. We tried to keep things up beat, showing her the picture of her amongst the others listed as "11 West All Stars" hanging on one of the main walls just off the nurses station. We played in the play room for hours, carefully guarding the "Goalie" pad on the right hand and IV secured there. I sat there, rubbing the small tufts of her dirty blond hair that was finally coming in after 18 months and smiled. I will never forget how "normal it felt" watching her run around in her gown and exploring the 11th floor. IV and all, she was happy. She never let anything bother her for long at this age.

Dr. Si came in to see us the next morning. It was nice to see his face, so calm with a slight smile. He made an offhand comment on how we were making a routine of this. The surgery plan was to completely replace her conduit either with cadaver material, gortex, or an adult artificial graft. He said they may not be able to replace it, but he would have to wait until he "got in there". Surgery would likely take 4-6 hours. He mentioned scar tissue and how sometimes it makes the surgery take longer. After answering our questions, he gave us that yellow piece of paper to sign our daughters life away. I signed it, once again pushing bad thoughts out of my mind. Once he was gone, things started to speed up. Nurses came in and hooked Natalie up to her robot and started her on IV fluids. They also gave her a special bath meant to decrease risk of infection.

"Should we give her something?" The anesthetist asked, sensing our anxiety as we sat in Preop. We agreed and they gave Natalie something by mouth through a little syringe. We were unsure what it was, but it took effect quickly. While I was holding her, I watched as her eyes seemed to come out of focus. Natalie then wobbled a little, leaning her head back and let out a funniest laugh/chuckle. With tensions running so high, seeing our daughter "drunk" helped the mood. In fact, it was hilarious.

We sat in the waiting area, much like we had one year ago with our family and anxiously awaited hearing from the team. To be completely honest, time spent waiting in the PICU area has become such a blur between the three times we spent half a day there. Usually, we all sit in the large back room, each working on their own project. I remember "drawing with friends" back and forth with my Dad. Clash of Clans was blocked by the Wi-Fi at Mott's, so I would go back to playing Farmtown to pass the time. My grandfather would work on the cross word in the paper. Kelly and I would take trips to the big cafeteria, the chapel or gift shop. There is also a large indoor garden waterfall deep in the hospital we would visit. The team would tell us when the procedure started and then when Natalie was started on heart bypass. They would come out at later intervals later, telling us how she was doing, and then when we were closing. Nerves would start up for me near the end as I awaited to speak to the surgeon. After a short while, the Nurse returned to let us know that Natalie was being weaned off of the bypass machine and the surgeon will likely be coming to speak with us in the next hour or so. That was always the part where I was afraid what they may say. What sort of news was he going to share. The nurse told us that the plan was, Once Dr. Si updated us himself, Natalie would be taken to PICU and it'll be another 45-60 min before we could see her. The nurse said they will most likely extubate her in the PICU and it sounded like her chest would be closed too.

The surgeon Dr. Si, came into the room with a very serious look on his face. Kelly and I were sitting in chairs near each other, but he basically stood in the center of the large room explaining what he found and what he did for Natalie. He explained that once they "got in there" the aneurysm was quite enlarged and had some clots in it. He also said the conduit itself was almost unrecognizable. He fully replaced it with a cadaver homograft and was able to patch out part of her left Pulmonary Artery but the right one was just too small. The tissue he attached the new conduit to was kind of frail so he had to put a bunch of packing in to control the bleeding and had to leave her chest open. They hope to close in two days. He answered our questions and then let us know they would let us know when we could see her.

CHAPTER 40

LIKE LAST TIME, BUT WORSE

When we finally were able to go to see Natalie after her fourth open heart surgery, I was terrified with what I would see. I vividly remembered how hard it was the year before after her last surgery. She had been so pale, grey almost, and had such a hard time recovering. I did not know what to expect with her "open chest". I visualized some huge, grotesque hole with ribs sticking out or something in my mind as I walked down the hall to the PICU bay. Natalie was located in the "room" in the corner where Emilio had been a year ago. I was instantly relieved that it was not grotesque at all. She was intubated and her robot had returned and grown bigger than ever. Her face was partially covered with a thick tape holding the tube in place and she had a tube through her nose that was decompressing her stomach. Her chest was covered with a towel to hide the fact that her chest was left "open". She had a chest tube in place just below her incision mark, poking out from under the white towel. Somehow, in all of that Natalie looked so peaceful, resting calmly with a small raccoon blanket propped up as a small pillow/support on the left side of her face. She looked like an angel. The story of the raccoon blanket, later named "Ringo" is a story for another book.

To me, it was like all of my nightmares come true. I had woken up at times over the past year drenched in sweat after a nightmare about those long days in the PICU. In the dream, a doctor would tell me some terrible news. I would wake up in a panic only to find myself in my bed. I would sneak out and across the hall to check on Natalie, just to be sure it was really just a dream.

There was no waking up from this. It was like a sick case of Deja Vu, only it wasn't just that odd feeling in my gut that I had lived this before. Here we were, in the same place at the same time in roughly the same situation as we had 1 year ago. It makes the mind question what is real sometimes. You cannot make this stuff up. After the family was able to see Natalie, kiss her, and say prayers over her, the company cleared out, leaving Kelly and I alone with her. Well, as alone as you can be in a PICU. It hurt my heart to be back here so suddenly. It is like your entire world view comes crashing down. Things had seemed to be going so well in our lives, like we were past all of this. I have read before the idea that you should never go to bed mad at the ones you love as you do not know if they will be there when you will wake up the next day. I felt that statement was wise, but never thought it may hit home so hard.

The first night for Natalie was difficult. When I came into the PICU, Natalie seemed to be doing well. That said, I felt very uncomfortable when I came in and her chest was uncovered. I averted my eyes as quickly as I noticed it, but I got an eye full. The hole was smaller than I thought it would be, and ribs were not poking out. It was like just a weird blood red colored hole in her chest. I asked the nurse to cover it and she quickly moved a blanket over it. She apologized but I brushed it off. I told her it's just my issue and she didn't know I was sensitive to that sort of thing. She was young, with her long dirty blonde hair pulled back into a ponytail. She seemed to know her stuff though as she relayed the what had happened overnight to me. Natalie had a bit of a rough night while we slept in at our little room in the "Mott House". The doctors had discontinued the paralytic and Natalie started having a hard trying to keep her sedated and comfortable. She kept moving a lot so they are having to add more drugs to keep her calm.

Looking at my little girl, who was resting peacefully, I felt really bad that she had suffered while I slept in. I expressed my feelings to her nurse and she gave me some positive feedback. Most kids did not do well right out the gate and we had made it through the worst of it now. Hopefully, we would be able to wean support sometime soon and start feeds .

This made me feel somewhat better. I pulled up a chair next to her bed and took my seat at her side. It was then that I noticed someone had painted Natalie's toenails. My mother had come in town for the surgery and to help. There is nothing like holding your mother when you are anxious or scared. During some of the slow times the night before, probably when Kelly and I were getting something to eat, my Mom must have taken advantage of the paralytics and her time alone with Natalie to paint her toenails.

This made me smile. I took the opportunity, while Natalie was unconscious, to do my part and do something I always wanted to do: Paint her fingernails! She was a little girl, but with her lack of earrings and hair, sometimes she didn't always look it. I had been begging Kelly to paint her fingernails for months, but she always shot me down. "She'll put it in her mouth!" she would yell back at my complaining. Now was my chance. Kelly was not in the room and I had her all to myself. I pulled out the bottle of Coral red/orange paint my mom left on the bedside table and went to work on the hands. I was very proud of the job I did, but I will admit, painting nails is tough work! When Kelly came in, I had a huge grin on my face, trying to hide my anticipation. She did not notice right away, but when she did, she tilted her head to the side and make a smirk with her mouth. It was one of those faces that said "Really?" without having to say anything. Kelly shook her head no slowly, then we both broke out in laughter. It was something be both really needed and really set a good tone for the day.

That night, I retrieved the TV cart and brought it over to Natalie's Bed. I was able to find a hockey game and turned it on. "Just like old times" I said as I sat next to her. I had the whole thing set up, feet propped up, when I realized that Natalie was facing the wrong way. Her head was facing me and not the TV I had moved in close to her bed. I looked over at my wife who was playing a game on the iPad. "Now how do I explain to the nurse that Natalie is facing the wrong way and needs to be moved....." I asked Kelly. She gave me one of those looks again. I decided it did not really matter. Natalie was knocked out anyway. I sat back and enjoyed the game for the rest of the night.

We had been given a room at the Ronald McDonald house across the street to stay in overnight and had tucked in pretty late. This room was on the second floor which was quite a bit less "depressing" compared to the basement. When I came in the next morning bright and early, Natalie was no longer in her place out in the PICU bay. Panicked, wondering where Natalie was. Kelly and I walked over to the nurses station and asked where our daughter was. The nurse pulled up the charts and found Natalie was in a separate private room. This did not make me feel any better and unfortunately this nurse was not "our" nurse so she had little information to add.

Our new room was right outside the PICU bay. These rooms were private, but walled off with glass walls and a sliding glass door separating it from the main hallway. As the nurse showed me to the room, I noticed the "Contact

Precaution" gear on a cart outside. I knew something was up. I feared for the worst.

CHAPTER 41

QUARANTINE AND ISOLATION

The nurse inside Natalie's new room was draped a paper thin yellow gown, gloves and a mask as she worked to clear out Natalie's secretions from her airways. Natalie looked about the same, unconscious and unclothed. Her sensitive areas were covered with a small white towel. Wires and tubes seem to be everywhere. Her bed was propped up at about 40 degrees and it almost looked as if she was on display. Pup Pup sat with his head on her left thigh. The nurse was young, maybe late 20s, and was pretty short, with her dark hair pulled back in a ponytail.

Isolation was nothing new to me. On my pediatric rotations back in Toledo I had plenty of experiences with isolation gowns. Any child thought to have a respiratory infection that was contagious was typically placed in precautions. This meant that any visitors had to place a gown and mask on before they entered the room to try to limit the spread of infection. During the winter months, it seemed like most admissions were for influenza or bronchiolitis, so you ended up gowning up to go into every room. I was a professional at this point. Knowing how this worked, I placed on the gown and entered Natalie's room.

While working on my daughter as she coughed, our new nurse explained what had happened. Natalie had spiked a fever overnight and the doctors ran quite a few tests to find a cause. After surgery, it is not uncommon that a person can spike a fever. It was important to try to nail down a cause as the fever could be a sign of a serious problem or infection. In medical school, professors love their mnemonics to help memorize different things. For postoperative fevers there was the "5 W's": Wind, Water, Wound, Walking and Wonder drug. It was one of the countless acronyms pounded into my brain. Wind was associated with pneumonia, water was urinary tract infections due to catheters, wound referred to wound infection, walking was to remind you about blood clots in the leg and wonder drug made you think about medication side effects. These are not the only cause of fevers after an infection, heck some people spike fevers just due to the stress of the procedure. These were just things you did not want to forget.

One of the tests that they had completed on Natalie was a respiratory pathogen panel. This tests for 10-12 common viruses that cause infection such as Rhinovirus, Adenovirus, Influenza, RSV, Human Metapneumovirus and several others. It is a common test ordered in urgent cares and emergency rooms to try to pick up a cause of an infant's infection. While the test is great at helping determine if a person may need antibiotics or antivirals, the swab is was nonspecific to how long the person has had the infection. Natalie's swab came back positive for several of the cold viruses, Rhinovirus and Enterovirus . She had a case of the sniffles about a week before her checkup and was just getting over it when we were admitted.

The swab told us she had the virus in her system at some point recently, but It could not tell if she was actively sick and contagious now or just getting over it. Due to the positive test, she was placed in precautions. It really bothered Kelly and I that they moved her to a new room without notifying us. Nothing puts the scare of a lifetime into you like walking into a postoperative ICU and seeing your child's bed empty. I was bothered they did not think to notify us about the fever. Natalie was sick enough with this fever to do testing and then mover her but not sick enough that they thought to let us know about it.

I was also mildly irritated about the "big' deal they seemed to be making about this virus. Natalie had been improving before our appointment which meant she likely was not contagious. Now, with this positive culture, Kelly and I were no longer allowed in the normal PICU waiting area for fear of contamination and anyone visiting Natalie had to wear gowns, masks and gloves. I tried to go with it. I tried to tell myself that it didn't really matter that much and we would be out of the ICU and isolation before long, or so I hoped.

I was in the room with when the Doctor team came around. I expressed my concern for the precautions and they told me that it was not going to be that big of deal. They heard my concerns about how she was likely not contagious but could not have other patients who were ill at risk of being exposed. This made pretty good sense to me. Overall, the doctor felt that Natalie was doing much better and the fever had resolved. The plan for the day was to close Natalie's chest wound and pull back on sedation. After that, they planned to put in an NG tube and start feeds. They asked if I would to leave the room so they could get started on it. I did not mind at all. I had no interest in seeing that, so I thanked them for their time and left, kissing Natalie's head before I left.

CHAPTER 42

HOLIDAY TRADITIONS

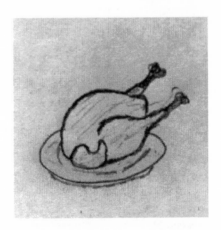

It was once again we were given the privilege to celebrate Thanksgiving in the PICU. It was suddenly becoming an unwelcome family tradition. We decided that, at least with Natalie as a daughter, it was becoming obvious that it was probably not a good idea to plan to do anything around Thanksgiving in the future. Much like the year before, a local charity brought in a catered Thanksgiving dinner with all of the fixings for families to share. Due to the quarantine, Kelly and I were not allowed to go to the dinner, instead staff had to go get plates for us. While I really appreciated the effort the staff was putting in to try and help us, it was very frustrating being basically trapped in Natalie's room for something that was not "a big deal". My Grandparents visited and we were able to enjoy the turkey dinner while watching the Lions game with Natalie, who was sound asleep for most of the day. As the day turned to night, Natalie started to struggled. She would "wake up" for a minute and open her eyes. I would notice her eyes and come over, trying to speak softly. I could tell that she was not really there, her eyes would be glazed over, and she would start holding her breath and thrashing out. Her saturations would drop and alarms would sound. The nurse would give her some medications and she would drift off to sleep.

Kelly and I sat in the room with Natalie in almost silence. I suddenly realized that our trip to Missouri was likely compromised. I looked at Kelly, who was wrapped up in that large blue and gold blanket watching the TV. "I ..." I hesitated. "I don't know if it is the best idea to go to Missouri for Christmas." She looked at me, in thought, then nodded her head. "What about the train tickets?" she had asked. We had already paid for the three tickets in a sleeper car. I told her I would handle it. I walked into the hallway and called the customer service line for Amtrak and was greeted by a robot voice. After a few phone tree prompts, I was given a live person. I explained I needed to cancel a reservation. At first, I was given some pushback as we were so close to our departure date. After explaining the situation though, they were happy to refund the cost of tickets.

Unlike the past, Natalie seemed to be handling the weans well. She was coming off support and even was stirring a little without freaking out. The next morning, Natalie had not had any additional fevers. Now, Natalie's skin is very sensitive, and she has had issues with adhesives in the past. We noticed she had a few areas that were really irritated from the adhesive and that morning we also noticed an abrasion at her internal jugular site from the prep soap on the side of her neck. It was like her skin was peeling off, leaving what looked almost like a popped blister rash the pads. She also had this odd square shaped rash on her side which I could not figure out. After thinking about it, we realized it was from the conduction pads used during surgery. We brought it to her nurse's attention, who commented, "but those are the sensitive pads..." Of course it didn't matter WHAT kind of pads they are. The kids skin is peeling off. We switched her back to the normal pads with the little trains and cars and things actually improved.

Once again, we found ourselves in the PICU on Black Friday. We learned last year how dead the area gets during the Thanksgiving break and decided to make another run at it. This time, we coordinated it with our family back in Missouri. We really wanted to try to get my Grandfather a television for his living room. He has always done so much for the family and it seemed right. He needed a new television and would never go buy it for himself. Even if he tried, it would take him 6 months of research before he decided what he wanted. He would then try to price shop and it would take another month before he made a purchase.
It would be much easier if we just picked one out for him and surprise him for Christmas.

After planning some coordinated moves, Kelly and I were going to check out Target and Best Buy. The weather did not help the trip as a large snow and ice storm had been pummeling Ann Arbor. The storm made the trek harder than last time, our poor RAV4 slipping down the hills even in "Sports Mode". To our surprise, the city was a little bit busier than it had been the year before, but the hunt was on which made it exciting for us. I remember finding a big Westinghouse in Target and reached out to my Mom and Foster Sister Monica to see if it was the winner. They were in line at Best Buy back in Missouri and let me know that they were eyeing something better, so I let the deal it go. We picked up some stuff for Natalie at Target and then made our way to Kohl's and Best Buy which was right located across the street. I really wanted a new Sound Bar for myself for the TV we had bought to replace our old one last year. Kelly was interest in clothes from Kohl's. After a pretty "meh" walkthrough Kohl's, which was insanely busy, we went into Best Buy. The TVs they had on crazy discount were long gone, but they still had some good stuff in the back. I found a good LG Television that looked perfect. It was 55 inches and pricier than the ones Monica was looking at, but if I picked it up, it would have "free shipping". We were already in Michigan. The family agreed on this one. We purchased it along with a nice sound bar, but then I had a dilemma. Where were we going to keep it? I had not thought that part through, It fit in the RAV4, but I couldn't leave it out in the car while we stayed at Mott's with Natalie. That was asking to get stolen.

Really, there was only one option. I could not risk my grandfather seeing it and ruining the surprise. I took the big TV back to the Ronald McDonald house, pushing it across the floor to our room. I remember feeling a little guilty pushing that thing around in a place of such sorrow. Seemed so materialistic of me. We placed the TV box in between the two twin beds and used it as a night stand. In the end, it was worth it. Later, once we were out of the hospital several weeks later, I called my grandfather on the phone in a panic and told him our basement toilet was leaking and sewage was flooding my basement. He ran over to our house, wearing his dirty overalls, with two buckets of tools only to find the giant present on my dining room table. He cried.

On November 28th, I came in to find Natalie asleep with her pink giraffe blanket and Pup Pup covering her up and keeping her warm. We were told that she did very well overnight, tolerating her "sprints" well and the plan was to extubate that morning. Things progressed nicely and she was to be extubated just in time to be able to scream for the Michigan - Ohio State game that we planned to watch that day.

Extubation went well. We were asked to leave while they took out her tube and, when they let us come back, Natalie was wide awake laying on her back with a large nasal cannula on her face. It was blowing air pretty hard in her nose, making a sound like a weird vacuum or loud fan. She looked very miserable when we came back in, her eyes sunken and sad. Over the past year, we had put in a lot of effort weaning her off of her pacifier, but the first words out of her mouth after she was saw us was as a very harsh, crackly "PACCEEEEEEE". Luckily, the pacifier on a zebra string had been packed. We handed it over to her and it seemed to help her calm down. We had fought so hard to wean her off of it for the past six months, but neither Kelly nor I minded her sucking on it now.

There is something freeing sometimes about shutting off a football game in anger. Along with shouting your frustration at your team due to failure, it is something most fans do when things are not going right. The Michigan-OSU game that day had been one of those games. Usually, in a game like the one that day, I would have pulled off the jersey, thrown the hat and called it quits at the beginning of the fourth quarter. When you are stuck in a room with nothing else to do, what choice do you have except to watch the punishment. After watching Michigan get absolutely obliterated by OSU, I spent much of the day singing and talking to my little girl as she was slowly was waking up and coming back to me. By the time the sun went down, Natalie was wide wake and HUNGRY. She had not eaten in a week. Sadly, the doctors would now allow her anything by mouth yet. They did allow her a wet surgical sponge. I will never forget, watching her sitting up on the propped up hospital bed, nurse blowing by oxygen in her face, trying her best to eat the sponge on a stick. She chomped and chomped for what seemed like hours on that thing. I know it probably did not solve her hunger but she sure worked on it like it was going to. Baby beater made another appearance, so we took turns hitting her with it to keep her lungs open and improve oxygenation.

CHAPTER 43

HOLD YOU ME

The next day, Natalie was continuing to get better. She had another good night and they were able to wean her off of the high flow. She no longer sounded like she was sitting next to an airplane and the plan that day was to work on getting chest tube out and maybe try feeding her by mouth. The doctors advised us that they did not want Natalie to eat until she had her chest tubes out. She still couldn't form words well, instead speaking in grunts and high pitched scratchy whispers. They doctors did allow her to have a sucker, so Natalie ate about an entire pack of Dum-Dums that day.

Pulling out a chest tube is never fun. Luckily, we were not in the room when this came out. I discussed earlier the process and I was glad to not be involved this time. The nurse invited us back after the tube was out to help calm Natalie down. She was screaming, face purple and cheeks covered with tears. It was Pacie Time and Pup Pup time for sure. We had basically abandoned putting on the yellow garments by now. I had convinced myself that the positive test Natalie had was from something she had encountered before admission and likely nothing to worry about now. Natalie had not had another fever after that first night and seemed to be doing well. The staff still wore the garments but they didn't seem to care if we did.

As the day went on, Natalie slowly started to regain her sweet little voice. She was more aware as well, reaching towards me and asking me to

"Hold You Me" in scratchy words. Back when Natalie was learning to talk, when she wanted us to hold her she would ask us to "Hold You", mimicking how we spoke when we would reach towards her. It was very cute and we never thought to correct her. In time, it slowly became "Hold You Me". Standing next to her bed, looking into those tired eyes, it broke my heart to tell her that I could not "Hold You Me". The doctors wanted to observer her for a short while and make sure her lungs were ready to go on their own, but Natalie couldn't understand that. She just wanted to be in the comfort of my arms. I tried to comfort her, laying my head next to her in bed and singing to her. I made sure she had her puppy. I had hope that, with the chest tube out, it was only a matter of time before she would be allowed to get out of bed.

With Natalie starting to do well in the PICU, we were given the option to go to the Red Wings game. While watching the game the day before, our nurse had asked us if we liked Hockey. I had given her almost a "duh" look, teasing with her. She explained that had tickets to the game on Sunday and could not go. We jumped all over that offer.

After Natalie was settled in after a morning from hell, Kelly went back to our room get ready to the game. When she came back, she had concern on her face. Kelly pulled me aside, letting me know that she had wet herself earlier. I gave her a funny look. That is not something you expect to hear in a situation like this. She said it was weird as she had just gone to the bathroom and did not feel like she had an "accident". Kelly told me she tried to hold her legs together and it just kept coming. In my experience, this sounded like one thing. "Do you think my water broke?" I had asked her. She denied any cramping and said it had stopped after a moment.

Personally, I had no idea what to make of it. I knew that it was a risky situation. Had a patient described this to me as a doctor, I would have had them get checked out. It sounded like someone's water breaking. That said, it had stopped, there was no bleeding and Kelly was only 20 weeks along. This would not be typical. Then, there was also the issue of her doctors being an hour away in Toledo. Kelly asked if she should go to the ER and I could tell she was worried. We talked about it, talked about the risk and decided to just wait to see what happened. Besides, we had a hockey game to go to.

We left Natalie with my Grandparents and made the hour long track to Joe Louis Arena in Detroit. The Red Wings were playing the Florida Panthers and I was sure Kelly would finally get to see a win. Our teams never seem to win whenever we go to the arena, but they were playing Florida who, historically, was not a very good team. Heck, in the two Red Wing games we had attended together in the past with my Dad and the Wings did not even score a goal. There was hope today as the Red Wings had good motivation. They were fighting to keep their historic "active playoff streak" alive. Since we were from Missouri, we had not had a chance to make it to many games in the past and we were both pretty excited. As we entered the area, the atmosphere was excited and I was SURE it would work out for the "Good Guys". The seats were perfect, located right at the red line, about half way up.

After the second intermission, while stuffing my face with boneless Buffalo Wild Wings, Kelly had another incident of wetting herself. This seemed really odd, and deep in my mind, I honestly asked myself, "Do we have to go to the hospital?" She was not cramping and it seemed to go away as fast as it came. We thought maybe Lucas was sitting on her bladder. Kelly has an appointment with her Obstetrician in several days. We decided to just watch it and go to the ER at Mott's if it came back. It didn't happen again during the game. Sadly, the Red Wings lost though, prolonging the losing streak that continues to this day. The ride home has been uneventful. Kelly reported no more leaking and Natalie had done well without us.

That next few days were pretty uneventful. Natalie slowly returned to the girl I knew, insisting on hanging out in my lap as she recovered. I was overjoyed to be able to hold her again. She tried to eat, taking down 5 fruit loops, 1 bite of strawberry yogurt, Pediasure, Apple juice, and 1/4 peach slice. I caught a ride with my grandparents that night back to Toledo who dropped me off at my empty house. It was never easy coming home alone and with a difficult rotation this month, it made sleep very important. I had clinic all day the next day with ER shifts sprinkled in throughout the month. My rotation for December was Pediatric ER which let you set your own schedule, which was a really cool thing for residents at this point. I had originally planned on making the first part of the month work heavy so I could take most of the second part December off for our trip to Missouri.

While I lay in bed counting my blessings, Kelly called me. She told me that as she stepped out of the shower just now and the leaking had happened again. She told me that it leaked out and she was sure she was not wetting herself. "Well, does it smell like urine?" I had asked. I figured that if it didn't, that would be more worrisome. She was unsure. I asked her what it smelled like and she couldn't tell me. She was really worried. I told her to go to the ER. No more playing around. I would pack up and head that way for the night and call into work. She didn't want to do that. Kelly was tired and wanted to sleep. She didn't want to be up all night in the ER. I was not happy with this, but I could understand what she was trying to say. We agreed she would lay down and if it got worse she would go down to the ER at the hospital there. As I laid my head down after all of that, oddly enough, I fell to sleep pretty quickly.

The next day things were much better. I called Kelly as soon as I woke up and she was still asleep. To me, this was probably a good sign. I called out to the PICU and they told me that Natalie had a good night. They had plans to start feeding her real food that day. This all sounded great to me.

In reality, Natalie did have some side effects to her surgery. At rounds, the doctors were happy with her overall progress, but something came up on imaging. She had a chest x-ray that showed her diaphragm higher on one side, which was not normal. Dr. Si explained that it could have been caused from her open heart surgery if the surgeon accidentally damaged the nerve that causes the diaphragm to go up and down. So there is a chance her diaphragm could be permanently paralyzed. Looking at Natalie, he had explained that her oxygen stats were still seems to be doing great and she didn't seem to have any issues breathing. They planned to get an echocardiogram to check on it the next day, but otherwise it was watchful waiting.

While I started my shift in Toledo, Kelly and Natalie were hosting some visitors at Mott's. Kelly's Dad and Stepmom had just arrived for a visit from Kansas and were excited to hang out with our little warrior. Otherwise, it was another day of cuddling and weaning. Kelly had an appointment with her Obstetrician scheduled for the afternoon and I planned to meet up with her after my clinic shift. My grandparents came up to stay with Natalie while she was gone.

CHAPTER 44

ATONEMENT

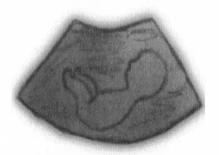

My day had gone pretty well. Kelly had told me about the diaphragm thing on the phone at lunch, which I had not really heard of before. I knew about the phrenic nerve, its course and what it did, but I was not yet familiar with how easily it can be damaged in heart surgery. Kelly told me that the doctors "didn't seem too worried about it", so neither was I. I had finished clinic early, so I got out early and wanted to surprise Kelly at her appointment

I drove down Sylvania Avenue towards the Sunflower clinic, windows down and feeling pretty darn good on my way to surprise Kelly. I distinctly remember how GOOD it felt, being back at work and things seeming to have been going smoothly. I had no need for all the anxiety that had been building up inside me the past few weeks. Maybe it might just work out in the end. I called Kelly to let her know I had gotten off early and was going to meet up with her at her Obstetrician's office. Kelly was hesitant, and the excitement I was hoping to hear in her voice was simply not there. I knew something was up long before she told me something was wrong with the baby in a panic voiced. I did not know what to say in the moment. My initial thought was that something had happened with Natalie and the idea something could be wrong with Lucas was foreign. It was like I could not think past Natalie. "With the baby? What's wrong?!? Is he ok?!" I blurted out. She had a hard time explaining what had happened and, since I was just down the street, we decided to wait until I could talk to her doctor.

Dr. Litt was Kelly's obstetrician. She was fresh out of residency, but I had worked with her on my OB rotations back when I was an intern. She was just a few years older than me with long brown curly hair and a big smile. Kelly had come to the appointment feeling things were ok. The leaking had stopped and she actually had almost canceled the appointment. While the nurse was taking her vitals, after exchanging pleasantries, Kelly explained that she had a weird gush of fluid a few days before. It had stopped and we had decided it may have just been an accident. The nurse stopped, looking at her with a "deer in headlights" look. "Oh.. a gush of fluid huh, tell me more." she had said, calmly.

Dr. Litt came into the room to see Kelly looking a little anxious. She asked some specific questions about the leaking episodes and performed an exam. She told Kelly that she did not see any fluid on exam and the "Nitrazine" test was negative. Nitrazine test refers to placing a little piece of litmus paper near the cervix. Amniotic fluid is more neutral than the normal secretions down there, so if the testing comes back showing acidic secretions, it is considered normal. "Well, testing so far is normal," Dr. Litt had said, calmer than when she came in, "Let's get you into the ultrasound just to make sure things are ok."

During the ultrasound, Kelly knew something was up. Normally the technician will say something like "well, good to go" or something similar when they are done with the exam. After her examination, the Ultrasound Technician sort of stopped and said "Stay right here, I am going to go talk to Dr. Litt real quick and will be back" and left the room. Kelly thought this was odd and suddenly worried what it could be.

Instead of the technician, Dr. Litt came in. She had pictures in her hands. "This was your fluid levels the last time we checked. This is where they are today " She explained calmly but obviously concerned, showing pictures to Kelly as she did. "As you can see, it significantly dropped. In fact, it is low enough that I can say that your water did break." Dr. Litt told her this last part with a very serious look on her face and instructed her that she had to get to the hospital right away. "Wait.. what?!" Kelly had said, mildly surprised. She had feared something was wrong after all of the fluid loss, but running emergently to the hospital was not something she had expected. She started to panic a little, starting to cry. Kelly was worried, not just about the baby, but what the news would do to me. So much had happened with Natalie recently and now this. Kelly felt that she had been holding herself together pretty well throughout this whole thing and dealing with the stress well. Obviously, she had not been doing as well as she thought mentally and it had taken a toll on her body. She expressed her fear to Dr. Litt, explaining how she was afraid it may push me over the edge.

I arrived quickly, feeling that surge of adrenaline as I walked across the parking lot. I was also getting very nauseous as went through the front door of the clinic. I tried not to think about the whole thing. I told myself there was no use getting anxious when I had no idea what was going on. I said a prayed to myself as I walked past the people waiting in the waiting room, begging for this to be some sort of false alarm. I approached the front desk and was directed back to one of the rooms just through the waiting room. It was a small ultrasound room and was pretty cramped. Kelly was sitting on the exam table when I walked in. She had a terrified look on her face when she saw me and I could tell she had been crying recently. I tried to stay calm, giving her a hug and fearing the worst. My immediate fear was that the baby had died.

Kelly blurted out that her fluid was low, like really low. She told me that the baby looked ok but she was going to have to go get checked out at the hospital. I tried to process this, feeling my heart beat pick up and my face turn red. I remember wondering how the hell that could have happened and wondering what it meant. Before we could discuss it further, Dr. Litt came in. She showed me the images they had taken that showed the lack of fluid. She explained that a normal "Amniotic index" at this point in Kelly's pregnancy is around 14 and hers today was a 2. Dr. Litt could tell that both Kelly and I were both beyond distraught. She gave me a hug. She looked me in the eye, placing her hand on my shoulder. "I know this is scary and I know you guys have so much going on with your Daughter." She said, looking directly in my eyes. "It will be ok. Get Kelly to the hospital and we will get her taken care of." My mind was racing and I nodded.

I don't think I understood the gravity of the situation. That or I was in shock. Even as we went to the hospital, Kelly having to stay there and leaving Natalie alone was the last thing in my mind. Before everything had fallen apart, Kelly and I had made plans to meet up at the house after her appointment to check out the Christmas Tree I had picked out to surprise Natalie. This plan was thrown out the window and, instead, we went directly to the hospital. We arrived at the Toledo Hospital and were admitted right away. Kelly was given a room in the antepartum area on the 3rd floor. Her room seemed really small, with a typical hospital bed and an old rocking chair and absolutely no view.

We met several doctors pretty quickly. Dr. Litt had called ahead and given them some of the story. We were first evaluated by an OB resident as well as the attending. They placed Kelly on the heart monitor for the baby and the plan was to meet with the neonatologist and develop a plan from there. Personally, I knew the baby would die if he was born right then as he was simply too young. The Neonatologist at Toledo confirmed my thoughts, explaining to us, "When your water breaks at this age, babies just don't do well." they had said. In addition, even if Lucas stayed inside for a while, most babies born to mothers whose water break this early do not survive. Those that do survive tended to have lung problems the rest of their lives. One option was "expectant management" where the doctors would admit Kelly and watch her and deliver the baby if it came. They could not give steroids or anything to try to help his lungs as he was simply too young. They also offered us the option of an elective abortion "as the child was not viable". Either way, if we decided to forego the abortion, they recommended Kelly to stay in the hospital until she gave birth.

It was an extremely hard to hear and left Kelly and I with a hard decision. Natalie needed us, but here was our other child and he needed Kelly to stay in the hospital on bedrest if we wanted to give him any chance at life. I remember being angry, but having a hard time explaining why. I didn't know what was bothering me more. Was it the fact that Kelly would not be able to be there for Natalie, the fact that Lucas was in danger, or the simple fact that the holiday season we had been planning for was not going to occur. On top of this, I had some other disappointment that I held to myself. I think, deep down, I always feared what Natalie's future would look like. I never knew if she would grow up, go to school or have a family of her own. Up until that moment I had almost assumed that Lucas was the answer. Lucas would have at least a chance to be "normal" and would grow up, have a family and carry on the family name and traditions. Suddenly, this was all in doubt. I know this all sounds silly, but your mind goes to weird places in times of distress.

Abortion was out of the question for us. So, the plan offered to us was simple. Kelly would have to stay at Toledo Hospital, indefinitely, until she delivered.

CHAPTER 45

ONE DAY AT A TIME

There is something about taking this life "one day at a time". I mean really taking it one day at a time. It is cliché and really kind of a silly term, but what does it really mean? In this life don't we as humans usually take things one day at a time? Don't we usually focus on what is in front of us and what we have to complete in our cycle of sleep, wake, work, play and repeat? I feel like I wrote about this already when explaining how Kelly and I "lived" during those first few weeks of Natalie's life. What I am trying to describe here is more of how things needed to go with we were going to make it through the challenges of December 2015 as a family.

I somehow knew that things could not continue as they had. It would not work. I knew I had to change something so, instead of waking up and allowing myself to stress out about "What am I going to do once we get out of the hospital" or "How are we going to have Christmas in two different hospitals", I tried to focus instead on "I wonder what Natalie would like for breakfast" and shaking off all of those other anxiety driven thoughts. I really tried to just allow things to come to me and react accordingly and it seemed to serve me well. I was too overwhelmed to really sit down and think on things and that was probably a good thing. I also knew that I would need quite a bit of help if we were going to make it and my family really stepped up.

While our life in Toledo seemed to be actively burning down, back in Ann Arbor, things seemed to be going really well. Natalie was getting back to her normal self, smiling, playing with her Pup Pup and enjoying her visitors. I arrived there a little bit later that day, hugging my grandfather as I broke out into tears. He rubbed my neck, trying to comfort me and letting me know it would work out. I remember him saying how unfair it all was under his breath. He was right. This was not "fair", but what in life usually is? I was fighting my own demons, trying to push those old feelings of guilt out of my mind. Natalie was happy to see me. She had no comprehension that her mother was out of the picture and I had no intention of trying to explain it to her.

As Holiday decorations started to show up around the hospital, Natalie continued to make steps to get out of the ICU. She was weaned to normal oxygen and then room air. On December 2nd, Natalie had an echocardiogram and her doctors felt that her heart looks pretty good. It did confirm that left diaphragm appeared to be paralyzed. It had occurred during her last surgery, the nerve to that side of her diaphragm was likely irritated or cut and unfortunately there was not much can do about that but watch it. Dr. Si expressed hope that it might improve in six months or so. It did not seem to be causing Natalie too much trouble. If it did start to affect her breathing, they could try some procedures. Otherwise, they felt that Natalie could possibly be discharged soon, aiming at allowing us to escaping that upcoming weekend.

Back in Toledo, the long term picture slowly was becoming more clear. While the doctors initially felt Kelly would deliver Lucas at any time, soon it seemed that this may not be the case. After a few days, it was apparent that we may be in this for the long haul. This was a good thing. The longer he was in there the better he may do. The Doctors gave her steroid shots as she moved closer to 23 weeks, which is the point of "Viability". The Neonatologist even gave us a chart of numbers. If he was born now, his chance of survival was 23% and each week that passed that he "stayed inside" the numbers improved.

While every day she stayed there meant a greater chance for Lucas to live, I don't think this provided me any sort of emotional "hope". The scariest part of the whole situation with Kelly was that, at any moment, she could go into labor and that would be it. She would get to come home, but she would come home empty handed. I think I was just overwhelmed and none of it felt "real". Not yet. Kelly had not been home in weeks and, soon it became evident that she would not see the lights or decorations I had put up. This really bothered me. It seems silly, but sometimes when things are tough you hold onto whatever you can to feel "normal" and putting up lights and a tree are as normal as it can get. A fellow resident, Nate, heard be talking in the resident room about it to my friends. He brought me in an artificial Christmas tree. Overjoyed I promptly took back to the hospital and set it up in Kelly's room. I had some sideways glances from the nursing staff as I walked in with the large box, but no one stopped me. I did not ask permission. It is always better to ask forgiveness, or so I am told. Once it was up, it really helped me inside feel just a small amount better.

In Ann Arbor, Natalie was transitioned to a normal room. For her, the hardest part was the quarantine. The "contact precautions" followed us back to 11 West. What was supposed to be "not a big deal" was still making our day more difficult. Because of that silly positive test a week prior, Natalie was not allowed out of her room or into the play room. I was very upset by this, and while I understood not wanting to get anyone else sick, Natalie was not sick and had been well past the point of being "contagious" at this point. That said, I had learned the tough lesson in the past on speaking out. I vowed to not being the "difficult" parent again. I worked with childlife and they would bring toys and projects to our room to play with. In time, they brought us a little green car and allowed us to explore the hallways in it as long as we wore a mask.

I was struggling at being the only parent for Natalie. I tended to be the "goofy" parent but having to entertain her all day was becoming difficult. 1 week prior, I had been down in the gift shop wasting time and found a giant Yeti that I adored. He was rounded, fluffy with a big smile. It seemed so darn happy. I wanted to get it and give it to Natalie when she woke up from her anesthesia, but the big one was like $60. Kelly told me no. She actually had to tell me more that more than once.

With Kelly gone, and our general mood and outlook shot, I went down and bought two of them: One medium white Yeti and one large pink Yeti. I took one to Kelly in Toledo and the other, I put in Natalie's crib. When she woke up, she was stunned. I watched with glee as she inspected it. It seemed bigger than her. After a moment's hesitation, she gave it a large hug and insisted it follow her around and ride in the car with her and puppy the entire day of December 5th. She suddenly had a new best friend and I felt like I was finally winning at something.

As I mentioned earlier, I had adjusted my work schedule to free up much of the second half of the month of December. That meant I still needed to put in some time during the first few weeks and I had ER shifts most days. Most of them were at night, 11am to 2am. This meant I could not be with Natalie. My program offered to allow me to take the month of, but that would mean delaying graduation and I was not a fan of that. As I could not be with Natalie 24 hours a day every day, we set up shifts to cover the times I was away either with work or spending time with Kelly. My grandparents, Dad or my Aunt Diane would sit with her while I worked and Kelly sat in the hospital 1 hour to the south. It was very difficult and I put quite a bit of miles jumping back and forth to Ann Arbor multiple times a day. We depended on family and I don't know how we would have gotten through it without that help.

One morning, while packing up to visit Natalie, I found a drawing Natalie had made with a black and pink marker sometime before she had gotten sick. The image itself, at first glance, did not make any rhyme or reason. It was a typical random drawing obviously created by a child, yet somehow, to me, I saw my daughter in it. As I held it in my hand, standing in the hallway of my empty house, my other hand went to my mouth to cover a gasp. I could see, as clear as day, a little girl in a small dress looking down at what appeared to be flower petals around her feet. I knew it was my imagination, but once I saw it I could not see anything but this image. I was amazed by it. I knew could never create something like this and there was no way my toddler could put something on paper that clear, but here it was. Inspecting it, I felt a feeling of sadness. I found myself asking in my mind if those were really flower petals around her feet or was it a representation blood. It was a dark thought, yet somehow mystifying and predictive of what happened after she created the image. I did not know what to do with the picture, but I knew that it was beautiful and important. I took it to Michael's and had it framed, excited to show it to my wife if and when she ever came home. Who knew, my Daughter was an artist.

Kelly and I did what we could to stay in contact throughout the week and it was now Kelly's turn to FaceTime us. We would have family FaceTime sessions that would last almost an hour. Later that night, during a family FaceTime, Kelly had white yeti slowly come into the picture. Natalie was surprised and I watched as she looked from the phone, to her pink yeti and back to the phone, trying to figure out how it could be in two places. I don't know what was going through her head, but after several moments she started laughing with a huge grin on her face. I captured that image with the phone, Natalie sitting there, light blue gown hanging off her thin frame with healing incision poking through the top, a huge smile on her face. It is an image I treasure and keep it on my desk to this day.

Natalie was so weak at first, unable to even walk after her major operation. We worked with physical therapy and she slowly able to regain her ability to move her little body around. Her next hurdle was eating. Natalie had never been a "good eater" and we had struggled with weight gain her entire life. When she was born, after she was finally extubated, she had struggled with breastfeeding. Over the last year, Kelly had worked very hard on this and Natalie had finally started gaining weight at the start of summer. Kelly had been advised that she needed to wean Natalie by her OB, and she tried. Kelly had been working on real food at home, but it was not going exceptionally well. To keep up her weight, Kelly had been forced to continue to breastfeed Natalie.

Now, that was gone and I was forced to try to meet her caloric needs by mouth. Every morning I would have to order her food. I had no idea what Natalie liked, but I tried to pick things out that sounded easy. I knew she loved grapes, but the hospital was not keen on giving grapes to kids under 4. It was a choking hazard so I had to verbally confirm whenever I would order grapes that I understood the dangers of eating grapes at her young age. We tried cereal, pancakes, apples and juice, all with little success. The dieticians would come in, asking me how much she took in and I would have no clue. I was extremely frustrated. I had always thought I was a relatively 'ok' father but I was failing. In a last ditch effort, I started FaceTiming Kelly during meals to try to talk Natalie into food. It was only mildly successful and Kelly was able to get Natalie to eat a single a piece of frosted mini wheat.

Even without food, Natalie continued to power forward. She worked though PT and made enough progress that the doctors felt she would be safe to go home. Even without food, Natalie seemed to have plenty of energy, playing all over our room and acted like she needed zero sleep. The night of the 5th, my grandparents come to watch Spartans play in the Big Ten Championship. In her crib, Natalie refused to go to sleep, sitting up and watching the game with us. Just past midnight, MSU claimed victory and a berth in the playoff on a last second field goal. I was proud my kid could hang with us for such a fun event. Kelly would have been disappointed most likely. We were ruining her "routine" after all.

Natalie was discharged home on 12/6. The doctors wanted to get us out so Natalie could spend some time with Kelly. We were to keep a close eye on her diet and follow up on the 17th. Suddenly, we were home, sitting on the beanbag in front of the television before lunch time. We made it a priority to get to the Toledo Hospital to see Kelly. Natalie was so excited to see her Mom, squealing and hugging her. They sat together on her bed, first introducing the Yeti's to each other in person and then watching a show called Dinosaur Train.

CHAPTER 46

FAILING AT THE ROUTINE

Natalie was so happy to be home. I did my best to fill the time. Initially, it was like an extended weekend. We would screw around, cuddle and play with her toys in the attic. She would look through the windows of the doll house for me, smiling ear to ear with a blue sucker hanging from her mouth. During the day we would sit on the floor in the living room with Yeti and watch her favorite show on Sprout: Ruff Ruff Tweet and Dave. At night, we would watch movies before drifting off to bed. One night, we even had a driving in movie night. I brought in her "Cozy Coupe" inside and she sat in it and watched a movie, her fluffy kitty friend by her side.

Let's be honest at this point. For the most part, up to this point in her life, I felt deep down that Natalie never liked me. Not really. This was very true when she was young and persisted up until she was a toddler. . She was always excited when I would come home from work, running to the door, arms open and screaming "Dadddddddddyyyyyy". Sure, she would tolerate me, smiling at me with those big dark brown doe eyes, but the second Mommy would walk into the room, it would be all over. She was definitely not a daddy's girl. I adored her, living to come home and see that smiling face. Even with that, I was an auxiliary piece in her life. I spent much of my time during the first year of her life at the hospital, even sleeping there at times, due to residency requirements. I was a play thing that would come home on weekends to "spice things up. I was there for ruff housing and pushing the stroller. I think it is fair to say I was a solid "Number 2" parent.

When Kelly was admitted to the hospital, suddenly there was a large void in both of our lives. Natalie was too young to really express her thoughts, but for the first few days to weeks, she was exceptionally upset. She cried for her mother frequently. I was so out of my element trying to care for a 18 month old child. I knew Natalie loved me, all joking aside, but I was struggling deeply and was overwhelmed. It seemed I would frequently forget the small things such as bathing or brushing teeth. Luckily, Kelly would prod me with reminders enough to help me learn. Seriously, you would be surprised how many times you have to be asked "DID YOU BRUSH HER TEETH?!" before it gets added into the chaotic bedtime routine. It was very hard trying to balance out my emotions and frustration.

My Mom flew in to help me with Natalie around this time. She told me that she just knew, somehow, that I needed help. Moms have a way of knowing things like that I guess. It was nice to have someone to help around the house, especially since I was used to being a loner due to my heavy work schedule. She would watch Nat while I went to clinic or did my ER shifts.

On the 15th, we decided to head to the Franklin Park Mall to visit Santa. I felt bad that Kelly could not be with us, but that was something we could not change. Natalie seemed super happy when we arrived, taking her time exploring the Christmas village in her little red fluffy dress and black top with a small pink bow in her hair. I was excited to see what she would think when she saw Santa. The year before she had been amazed by him. Not this time. This year, she was terrified of Santa. As soon as she saw him she made it known she wanted nothing to do with him. We finally got her on his lap and she started crying, holding puppy close. It was difficult to see but made for an excellent picture. She refused to talk to Santa, just crying and asking me to "Hold You". It was a bit of an odd exchange between St. Nick and myself. I didn't know if he remembered us from last year, but somehow we got on the topic of Kelly not being there. We explained how Kelly was trapped in the hospital due to her water breaking with our son. His response was, "I know." He made some small talk with my Mom, who explained how she was visiting to help out with Kelly at the hospital. He responded, "Oh, I know." It was like his answer for everything. Truthfully, it made you almost wonder HOW he knew. Was it really Santa?! Santa gave Natalie a plate with her name on it and also gave us one for Lucas.

CHAPTER 47

ALWAYS PACK A BAG

On our way to Natalie's follow up appointment with her cardiologist, trying to ease the tension in my gut, I said it. "I mean it can't get any worse, right?" I knew it was a bad idea as soon as the words left my lips, but I had said it. Natalie has been out of the hospital for a week and seemed to be her normal self. Things had been a little hectic at home, but luckily, my Mom had been there to help. Natalie was continuing to be stubborn and not eating by mouth just yet.

My Mom accompanied Natalie and I to our 1 week checkup at Mott's on December 17th 2015. We had an echocardiogram ordered before we met with the Cardiologist. This was standard procedure really. We sat, comfortably on the hospital bed in the dark as the Echo technician scanned Natalie's chest. My Mom sat on the chair across the room from us, looking at her phone. Natalie was enjoying a sucker and watching "Nina" on the TV set just over the Technician's shoulder. I was making small talk with the technician, purposefully not looking at the images. If something was wrong, I did not want to see it. The Tech was very friendly, which was typical, and happy to talk to me as she worked. I asked if the Natalie's diaphragm was still down. She looked at me funny and I realized it was a misunderstanding with the words. I clarified that by "down", I had meant not working. We both had a laugh and she checked. The diaphragm was still elevated on the left. "Rats" I said out loud.

"Remind me, what is wrong with her Superior Vena Cava again?" the tech asked me. I was slightly confused by this. "Nothing is wrong with her Vena Cava. It is her pulmonary arteries that have the issues." I had said in a calm tone, figuring she was just mistaken. She made a funny face, taking a few more pictures with the Ultrasound machine. "Are you sure?" She asked in a curious voice. I took a moment, but I knew Natalie's anatomy and what we had struggled with in the past. If she had something wrong with her vena cava, it would be news to me. I told her that I was 100% sure. "No one has ever mentioned it to me." Normally, this wouldn't mean anything. Doctors don't always mention every abnormality they see, especially when there is a lot wrong, but something about this situation felt off.

I tried to not be anxious about it, but sometimes you cannot help yourself. We returned out to the waiting room and Natalie went to play with some of the toys. Normally, we would be called back to a waiting room to see Dr. Gelehrter, but instead she came out to meet us in the waiting room with her fellow at her side. My Mom and I met with her in the middle of the empty waiting room and I was anxious with what news she would bring me this time.

Dr. Gelehrter explained that me that the Echo showed what they thought was a pocket of fluid building up around her vena cava. They did not know what it was but Natalie would need to be readmitted and they would need to repeat testing and have Dr. Si come see here.

Though most of this experience, overall I feel I had remained pretty stoic. Except for the few cases well documented in this book, I managed to take most bad news without much emotional response. At least on the outside. I also managed to temper my expectations with focusing on the positive. I can only remember one time when I completely shut down and basically lost it and this was it. I slammed my fists on the couch arm, interrupting the doctor as she spoke. "Wait.. Wait…" I said, voice cracking and thoughts racing. I could no longer take it "I… I.. need a moment.." I said very quickly, stood up and left before she had a chance to respond.

I was in tears before I reached the hallway. I moved quickly to the elevators and the random hallway next to them and called the residency coordinator, Chris Miller. I was supposed to work a shift and had clinic and for some reason that seemed like the first thing to address.

Chris, as usually, was very understanding. They canceled clinic for the next day and my fellow residents agreed to cover my responsibilities until I was able to return. I called my Dad, in tears and frantic. He asked me to calm down so he could understand me. It took me a while, but talking through it for a second time was easier. I explained that I had no idea what was going on but Natalie was being admitted and maybe would be getting surgery. He told me he would be there for whatever I needed.

After I calmed down a bit, I was able to regain what little composure I had left. I returned to the clinic to face whatever was next. I could tell that my Mom was handling the situation as I approached, hearing the three of them laugh about one thing or another. After getting settled Dr. Gelehrter asked me if Natalie had been sweating or breathing harder than usual?" . My answered always tended to be the same, "Not that I know of." I realized quickly that I just did not know much about my daughters day to day routine and what was "normal" for her. "Has she been swelling." There it was. My eyes grew as I realized that Natalie had been swelling in the morning. Every morning when I would walk her down stairs to get ready for work I had noticed her face was puffy. Before Kelly was admitted, I was always out of the house before Natalie would wake up. I did not know what she looked like in the morning and I figured that maybe the puffiness was just because she was tired. I thought it was normal. I expressed what I had experienced and the Fellow gave me an "ahhhhh" look. I felt like an inadequate parent and a failure. Here I sat again, feeling like a jackass. How had I not noticed that Natalie was failing. I did not know what to say, except, "I thought she looked ok…" it came out as sheepish, but I think the doctors understood. "She always looks so good" Dr. Gelehrter said with an understanding smile, "But she is… Natalie".

The first major concern was infection. If this was some sort of large pocket of infection, it could turn deadly quick. We met with Dr. Si and he expressed his concern about "going back in so soon". The fluid pocket had too many viral structures nearby to try to use a needle to take some out or drain it. He was honest and said that he was unsure what to do. I was included in the discussions when trying to determine a plan, which was nice. Between doctor visits, I tried not to think about spending Christmas in the hospital, trying to focus on the concerns at hand, but it was difficult.

After things were stable, I felt a strong need to be with Kelly and to cry with her. I needed her embrace. My Mom stayed with Nat, playing in the playroom on 11 West and I took the 1 hour trip south to Toledo Hospital. I was having a hard time keeping myself together. I tried to push terrible thoughts from my mind, but it took almost all my will to keep a level head. As I entered town, "My Immortal" came over the radio. It is a sad solemn song and one I knew well. Songs just speak to me sometimes and in that instant, that song seemed to hit that certain spot in my heart that makes me lose control of my emotions. There was something about the first verse and the idea that not all wounds can be healed by time.

All the stress and fear overcame me and I started to cry. As I continued to sing along, my voice became higher pitched and then started to break up as

I cried harder and harder. At one point, I realized I could no longer see the road through my tears. I had to pull over in a parking lot out of fear of getting in an accident. I prayed very hard sitting there in the car, pleading and begging God to help me. Help me through this time and give me the strength to face the trials ahead. It took me a little while, but soon enough I was back on the road with my emotions coming around. By the time I arrived to the hospital in Toledo, I was doing ok. I never mentioned this to anyone.

CHAPTER 48

THE BEST DAY EVER

Sometimes in life you find inspiration in odd places. Natalie had grown to really enjoy the Sprout Channel. It was not something I was happy with, but when we were in the hospital so much, sometimes we had to find ways to pass the time. She started at age 6 months watching the "Good Night Show" with Nina and Star as she rocked to sleep in her rocker. She loved "Ruff Ruff" but she would tolerate just about anything on that channel. During our admission near Christmas of 2016, Sprout started showing a new cartoon called "Nina's World" and in the theme song there is a line "Gonna be the best day ever!". Natalie seemed to love the show and hearing that theme over and over caused the tune to stick in my head. It is odd sometimes the things that stick with you, but soon I started every day with the idea that every day should be the "Best Day Ever". When people called in to check on her, I would tell them how we were having the Best Day Ever. It somehow became an odd mantra for me. If I said it enough, I would will it to be true. It didn't matter what was going on, as long as we stayed positive and made sure it was "The Best Day Ever", it would be. With that, nothing was going to be able to get us down.

The plan for our Admission ended up being pretty simple: watch and wait. We would watch for signs of infection and were going to have repeat echocardiograms daily to look for changes in the pressures around the heart. In the meantime, the Cardiology fellow and the resident who were part of our team were going to look into research and try to figure out if intervention was needed and what the benefits may be. I was ok with this. Not having emergency surgery while Kelly was locked up in Toledo seemed like a great idea. Kelly was torn about the whole thing. She wanted to be with Natalie so bad at this point and simply couldn't. We discussed it with her neonatology specialists back in Toledo and they felt the risk was simply too great for to leave the hospital to be with Natalie and I in Ann Arbor. They felt that, at any moment, she could go into labor or her placenta could fall out and it would be a medical emergency. We discussed leaving against medical advice, but this just sounded too risky. Instead, we decided just to keep in close contact and take it one day at a time. Luckily, after my clinic was covered on our first day in the hospital, I did not have any additional shifts for several days and we had family around to help. I was able to spend most days with Natalie or running back and forth to spend time with Kelly. I was really appreciative of everyone volunteering their time to take a "shift" at Natalie's side. My grandparents even came up one night so my Mom and I could escape to see the premier of "Star Wars: Force Awakens".

Over the next few days, nothing seemed to change. I was terrified at any moment I would hear that "Lucas" was on the way, but that never seemed to happen. Kelly and I joked back and forth about having a baby on Christmas and how "cool" that could be, aside from the prematurity. Heck, we could even name him "Jesus".

On our third night in the Hospital I had a visit from my Residency mates. Jeff and JD had been in the area and thought to come by and bring me a Sandwich from Zingerman's Delicatessen. For those who do not know the area, Zingerman's Delicatessen is the home of the single best Reuben in this fine country. As I stuffed my face in the cafeteria, my Dad watched Natalie and my friends and I played Pass the Pig. It was an amazing thing for them to do and it meant the world to me. For just a moment, it felt like I was just hanging out with the guys on some weekend game night. After they left, I thanked my Dad for holding down the fort and took over. He had kept Natalie busy in the big playroom just off the 11 West nurses station. We slept well that night, minus a few alarms from the IV pump that was attached to her hand.

Besides the everyday fear that the doctors would walk in and say the word "surgery", concern about Natalie's weight suddenly became a major issue. She had been losing weight since her last discharge. Personally, I knew things were not going well and mealtimes were becoming a high stress situations. It did not help that the nursing staff seemed to not understand how difficult it was becoming. They would constantly ask me about calories and "how many mL of juice did she drink". I had no idea. Natalie just seemed to pick at everything and I was unsure on how to count the amount of fluid coming from a juice box.

Before they would even consider letting us go home, the doctors needed to Natalie her eat. She was "failing to thrive" at this point and, while they did not say it out loud, I knew it was more or less my fault. We met with a dietician. They asked me what she liked to eat. Sadly, I had no idea. I knew she loved sweets.

After trying some different techniques the first few days, the nurse placed an NG tube with plans to start feeding Natalie overnight while she slept. I had to leave when they first placed the tube. I never did well with her screaming. I don't know if it was from the screams itself, the alarms from the monitors due to her saturations dropping or a mixture of both. After she calmed down, things seemed to go back to "normal" with her, playing throughout the day and sleeping well enough at night, even with the NG tube taped to her face.

The tube feed at night did not seem to be to bad. They would plug her into a pump once she was asleep and were able to get a can or two of pediasure into her stomach. She even started to gain weight. The dietician was encouraged. We discussed diet and discharge planning. One of the "goals" for discharge was that I would be able to place and manage the NG tube.

While I was visiting Kelly on the Day of Discharge, my Dad took Natalie to a small "shop" that the Mott's team had set up for the kids. They were given tickets and could pick out gifts for family members. Natalie picked out a gift for Kelly, Myself and Lucas. When I returned, she was so excited to show them to me. She had four gift bags of differing sizes. We held off on opening them until Christmas, but I can tell you now that mine was a screwdriver set and Natalie had picked out a Kitty blanket for herself.

With the NG tube in place and close follow up plans, we escaped the hospital on 12/21. The dietician recommend trying to push food by mouth, no matter the substance. At this point, things were so poor with Natalie's intake that her doctors even approved of candy and fruit snacks. I knew Kelly would have concerns about this, including the risk of childhood obesity and cavities, so I brought it up to the discharging doctor. They almost laughed when I asked this, gesturing towards a very thin Natalie. I recall them saying that we had little to worry about in regards to obesity at this point. In regards to cavities, they felt that a dentist could likely deal with anything that comes up cavity wise down the road. For now, Natalie needed calories. Any Calories.

CHAPTER 49

NG TUBES SUCK

Inserting a feeding tube can be difficult. When someone teaches it to you on a dummy, it is portrayed as "idiot proof". After placing the tube on the patient's nostril, you stretch it to the ear and then down to the very end of the breast bone and place a mark at that length. You then simply lubricate up the tube, pick a nostril and push. Keep feeding it until you reach the little mark that you made when you measured. Then tape it down.

In real life, it was anything but easy. I tried to take all the emotion out of it and to do that, I made a routine. I would set Nat off to the side and then lay out a grey towel that I stored next to the bill pay station where the NG supplies were kept. Sometimes, the procedure would lead to vomiting so I had the towel to try to keep things tidy. I would next gather all the supplies: Tape, tube, pad, lubrication, syringe. Natalie has a hard time with tape causing rashes so we had been given a barrier pad that had to go on her face first. I would cut the support pad into a shape matching her cheek, then also prep some bandages. Two were usually enough for the job. After moving Natalie over to the towel, I would place the pad sticker on whichever unlucky cheek I had decided not to see for the next week. I would then measure the tube, placing it on her nose, down to her ear and then to the lower part of the middle of her chest. She usually would get pretty upset at this point as she knew what was coming. I marked the measurement with a piece of tape and applied the jelly to the yellow NG tube.

Then came the hard part. Sometimes I had help, but most of the time I had to almost sit on Natalie's arms to keep them down. The technique is as described. Pick a Nostril and start pushing. Her face would squish up and she would start screaming and choking at the same time as I frantically tried to push the tube in place. Vomiting occurred at least half of the time. Sometimes other weird stuff happens, like the end of the tube would come out of her mouth or end up in her lungs and I would have to frantically take it out and start the process over. The whole thing was absolutely heartbreaking and I hated every moment of it. After the tube was pushed in to the mark, I would try my best to hold it there while checking placement with the syringe. You would attach it to the end and draw off the tube, looking for gastric juices. If the juices showed up when I pulled on the strange, we were good and I would tape half of her face up with bandages and then flush with water. I would quickly try to apply tape before it was knocked loose. More than once, before I could take it down Natalie would slip her finger in between her nose and mouth and hook the tube, pulling it out.

Afterwards, I would take Natalie in my arms and try to calm her down. This was not easy as she was furious but in time things slowed down. Suckers helped. Natalie caught on pretty quick, crying and screaming any time I would lay her on the floor in the dining room while I prepped my supplies. There was no way around it. This was keeping her alive and became part of our weekly routine. Some parents change out the tube daily. The benefit is that your child is allowed to be "normal" during the day and you avoid the funny looks everywhere you go by passersby. My constitution simply could not take that. It was simply too hard to do that to my daughter period, let alone every night.

We also had a pretty tight bedtime routine. Every night, I would hook a bag up to Natalie's feeding tube and fill it with two cans of formula. It never mattered what flavor, Natalie would not be tasting it. Sometimes I would even mix flavors. I would then prime it through the pump, and hang it on the IV pole next to her bed. Then it was time to get Natalie ready. After brushing her teeth, I would lay her on the floor, change her diaper, being sure to tickle both feet. She always would laugh and squirm, bringing a smile to my face. After I put on whatever PJs I had picked out (Cupcake Girl was my favorite), I would pick her up, turn of the light and rock her in the rocker we had in her room. I would go back and forth, watching our shadow move across the wall as we did. I would say the same prayer, begging god to keep us safe, help Natalie eat and to keep Lucas "inside". I was also sure to always thanking God at the end for the Best Day Ever. With that done, I would sing her the same thing, in order, every night. First the Our Father Prayer, then "You are my Sunshine" and finally "Hallelujah". I frequently started crying at the "Please don't take my sunshine away" verse. Natalie would drift off and I would take her and set her on her small mattress that was on the floor. She had a normal twin bed, but she had not like her bed frame, so we had just set the twin mattress on the floor.

Then it was time to set up the pump. It had to be set to deliver a certain amount of fluid and at a certain rate. If the fluid went in too fast and it would make Natalie sick. If it went in too slow, she would not get the full amount and therefore not get the calories she needed. After I had the pump set, I would attach the pump to Natalie's NG tube and kiss her on the forehead and leave her room.

I would then spend the next few hours alone, reflecting on the day. I would spend most nights on the phone with Kelly or spend some time playing video games. Fallout 4 had just come out and it was amazing. Frequently though, I would spend time on the phone with my Step Brother Ben. He had just lost his wife to Cancer recently and had a son of his own. While our situation was not the same, and Kelly was going to come back sooner or later, it felt very similar and I think it was beneficial to both of us to talk it out for an hour or so most nights. It helped me not feel so lonely.

I would not turn on the pump until right as I went to bed and prayed it would not clog overnight. When it clogged, it would let out a shriek of an alarm that still haunts my dreams. It probably went off once or twice per night. The most common reason for the alarm would be if the line was kinked from Natalie moving. Every once in a while though, it would be something much much worse.

The worst I can remember was during the night after my Mom had gone back to Missouri. Natalie retching is what woke me from my sleep. I have no idea how this woke my up, we were not even in the same room, but it did and I flew into her room just in time to catch her chocolate vomit in my hand. After cursing, which is something you could not really control in a situation like this, I lifted Natalie from the bed with plans to take her to the trash can. As I pulled her onto my lap, the vomiting became more aggressive. All I could do was continue to catch it in my other hand. Soon, NG tube came out of her mouth and started adding to the craziness, shooting out stream of pediasure every 3 seconds. I wanted to grab the trash can but couldn't move, I wanted to scream for help, but I knew no one was there. I remember screaming out loud in frustrations. Natalie was crying and suddenly, I realized so was I. I took a deep breathing, trying to get my panicking mind to slow down. In the heat of battle, I somehow was able to remind myself that it was my duty to handle it. Now determined, I took my hand, now full of regurgitated pediasure, and rubbed it all over my shirt. It had nowhere else to go. It was slimy and terrible. With my hand clear and my mind straight, I moved quickly, pulling the tape from Natalie's face and quickly pulling her NG tube. I dropped the end in the trash nearby. Natalie was surprised, pausing her vomiting for a second and then started screaming. I took that momentary pause to pick her up and run her to the toilet.

Afterwards, after changing Natalie and placing her down to sleep in my bed, I tried to assess the damage. Natalie's room looked like someone had just been killed, except instead of blood they had pediasure flowing through their veins. The NG tube pump had done a good job spraying it all over. There was chocolate on the floor, the bed, the wall, the end table. I looked like the murder victim, my yellow shirt dripping with chocolate oozy goodness. The good news was that, while chocolate sucks to clean up, at least it did not smell like vomit.

I waited until the next afternoon to replace the NG tube. I thought both of us could use a break that night. I resisted the urge to bring her into my bed, as this was something Kelly and I had felt strongly about. Overall, I was rather proud of myself how I had handled the situation. While it was a terrible event, it was just what I needed. I found myself suddenly gaining confidence in my ability to actually do the job. When the pediasure hits the fan, I really did have what it takes to be the parent Natalie needed. Taking emotion out of it seemed to be the answer. Trying not to focus on the fact that it was "my daughter", I was dealing with helped. Instead, just focus on what I had to do on that exact moment, much like emergencies at the hospital, was the key. I had to treat Natalie like a patient. It became automatic, almost robotic and it was how I survived emotionally. I looked forward to my nightly talks with Ben. Something about sharing our daily struggles over a cold beer helped me vent. He was basically my therapist and it something I will be forever grateful for.

CHAPTER 50

CHRISTMAS IN THE HOSPITAL

Besides the obvious difficulty with raising a child on your own during residency, things slowly improved over the next week or so. Personally, I was just excited to not have a family member in two different hospitals for a holiday. Christmas can improve most people's moods, even when things are not the easiest.

It was my goal to continue to make every day 'The Best Day Ever". We visited Kelly frequently, coming to visit in the afternoon after Natalie's nap time. Kelly insisted on me keeping Natalie's "schedule" the best I could and quickly learned how useful it was. I had to apologize for teasing her for the past year when it came to this crazy "schedule". When Natalie had a strict schedule, she seemed to know what to expect and it helped her mood. Turns out, Mom knows best.

Christmas Eve approached quickly. My Dad throws a party every year for the family and Natalie and I were planning on attending. After loading Natalie in the car for the drive to Findlay, I left her in the car for a moment so I could play "Santa". There was a hidden area in the bench in the entryway of my house that designed for shoe storages but ended up being a great place for presents to hide. I retrieved all the gifts from the hiding spot in the entryway and quickly placed the presents around the tree and filled the stockings, whistling a Christmas tune as I worked. It was not short work, We had gone a little overboard on Black Friday again during Natalie's

PICU stay. Going overboard was becoming a bit of a routine. Have I admitted yet in this book that Natalie is a little bit spoiled? Well, it was a magnificent spread of presents and I stood for a moment and enjoyed my display. It really was excellent.

It was not perfect though, and I had a pain in my heart when I looked at the scene. Any child would be overjoyed to wake up to this scene on Christmas morning. I had picked out the real tree from Home Depot while Natalie was in the hospital and decorated it. It even had tinsel!
As the smile on my face started to fade, I was reminded that my wife had not ever even seen the tree except in pictures. She would be here to see the smile on Natalie's face when she saw it. Her presents would not be opened with the rest, instead sitting off to the side waiting for her to get home. With mixed emotions, I closed the door and joined Natalie for the drive down.

When we arrived in Findlay, I was surprised to find out that this was to be the first year in recent memory for me that the "Christmas-Eve Party' was not at my Dads House. It was going to be held at one of my Step-Mother's brother's house. This was not discouraging in the slightest. These parties had been one of the highlight of my childhood and I was very excited as I drove up to his house.. Typically there was quite a bit of commotion and tons of food. There would be people you knew well and those you didn't know so well. It was basically the family reunion from my Dad side the family. The best part though, was the White Elephant gift exchange. It was always entertaining with a few recurring Gag gifts to keep in interesting.

After the White Elephant gift exchange, people would hand out gifts for one another. This was Natalie's first real time going to this party and she had received quite a few gifts. I spent most of the night showing her off. She looked so cute with her little dress and pacifier in her mouth. Her face was heavily taped, trying to keep the NG tube in as long as possible. It covered almost half her face. Looking back now, the tape may have been a little excessive and did make Natalie appear sick. At the time, I think I was just used to it and didn't notice how it made her look. All I knew is that I hated changing that damn thing and wanted it to last as long as possible.

That night, after hooking up Natalie to her robot and feeding pump in the spare bedroom upstairs at my Dad's, we exchanged gifts. This was another tradition that had been going on for about 5 years. Someone finally had asked, "Why wait until morning? It is not like Santa is coming!". The logic was undeniable. Instead, the next morning became filled with a new tradition. My Dad would get the leftover shrimp from the night before and make omelets out of it. I know that sounds weird but it is simply the best. The old saying is true: Don't knock it until you have tried it. I sent Kelly pictures of mine before I stuffed my face. She sent me back an image of her hospital eggs which looked like they came out of a box. Looking back, it was probably not a nice thing to do but I was simply that excited. Traditionally, after breakfast we would go to my Great Grandma Connie's house in North Baltimore. That year though, I had somewhere else to be.

Kelly's bleeding had gotten worse and, for Christmas, she had been moved into a labor and delivery room. She had gone through this routine many times, transferring room to room. It was quite a big ordeal, not only for her own comfort, but also because we had to move all of her "gear" and her Christmas tree. Luckily, the L&D rooms were large and allowed us to bring in quite a few presents. When Natalie and I arrived back in town, we first made a pit stop at the house to see if Santa had came. Upon entering the house, Natalie immediately saw all the presents I had left around the tree and she was so excited. She moved present to present, unable to really open them but pushed the boxes around. She tried to ride the power wheels ATV we had picked out for her but was unable to work the controls. After the initial excitement died down, we packed everything up, including Kelly's gifts from my Dad and Natalie, and took them all to the hospital. With all the boxes and gift bags, I had to make quite a few trips to get everything unloaded. I also received many odd looks from other patients and staff, but it was worth it. For just a moment, nothing else seemed to matter. In our large room on L&D, we were a happy "normal" family.

PART V

Afterward

CHAPTER 51

DADDY'S GIRL

After Christmas, I doubled down on the routine. Kelly had been right and keeping a routine was vital. Even with good structure, Natalie continued to struggle eating much of anything by mouth. If it was not sweet (fruit snacks, suckers, fruit) she would not eat it. I tried not to worry about it, realizing that I was supplementing at night, but it made every meal a battle. She would eat a little better when we would visit Kelly, taking in a cracker or part of a banana, but at home, I had yet to figure it out.

Part of our "discharge" plan for Christmas had mandated that we come back relatively soon. The follow up visit was on December 28. With the Pink Yeti, large wooden rosary around his neck, buckled into the passenger seat next me, Natalie and I made our way through the snow in the early morning hours back to Mott's. We definitely packed a bag this time. My nerves started to spike during out Echocardiogram. Natalie sat perfectly still, hypnotized by "Ruff Ruff" on the TV on the wall. I refused to look at the Echo as I was sure I would find something else that would only add to my panic. While I feared for the worst, I was relieved to hear that the fluid collection had gone down ever so slightly on imaging. It also seemed that the steady diet of fruit snacks and nightly tube feeds was working. Natalie's weight was stable. We were told to come back in 1 week on the 4th of January and recheck things.

After the New Year, Natalie and I fell into a routine all of our own. Residency rotations change at the first of every month and my new rotation, Geriatrics, was starting up. Remember, the month before I had cleared out much of the end of December of shifts by working frequently in the beginning of the month. Now, I was going to go back to a relatively steady workload. The rotation was not "difficult" and designed to help me learn about nursing home care. It was not terribly time consuming, but did take me away from my girls.

As I was starting to work again, things in our old routine, such as feeding times, nap time and visits to Mommy were now going to be in my control. Every morning became the same. I would wake up and get dressed. Then, I would wake up Natalie and get her ready. I would take her downstairs and turn on her favorite thing in the world: Sprout. I would proper her up with pillows and a blanket and there she would sit with Pup Pup and watch either 'Tree-Fu Tom" or "Lazytown" while I warmed up the car and finished getting ready. Then we would leave together off to the babysitter Nancy's house

Nancy was one of my mom's friend from high school. She came in to save the day when everything fell apart. She was middle aged with short blond hair and a big smile. She was just finishing raising her kids and somehow volunteered to help us with Natalie, her "little friend". My Mom had gotten me in touch with her and she took excellent care of Natalie and it did not take Natalie long to grow attached. Sometimes, I would wonder if she thought Nancy and my Mom were the same person. They looked very similar and I guess that didn't hurt.

After one more week of the routine, we packed back up with our bags and headed back to Mott's for our next Echo. The message was the same. "Things are stable, come back in a week" they would say. I would meet with the dietician who tried to come up with strategies to increase Natalie's calories. She talked about putting butter or mayonnaise on chicken nuggets or adding yogurt to different mixtures. They seemed to miss the simple fact that Natalie would not take things by mouth. After I pushed hard, the dietician also increased the tube feeding amounts. I prayed it would not mean more vomiting at night.

Back home, things started to feel actually "normal". As the days passed, I became more confident in my skills and our new "routine". Natalie needed me and I was finding that I had the ability and desire to help her. I also noticed that her feelings towards me seemed to change. While she was excited to see Mommy, calling out her name every time we drove up to "Daddy's Work", she became more and more attached to me. Sometimes, she would refuse to even sit with Kelly in her hospital bed, instead electing to stay in my embrace. I know that this hurt Kelly's feelings, but it was what needed to happen for us to make it. My Mom suggested to me later that maybe Natalie was reacting to "losing her caregiver" and this is why she clung to me so much. Either way, she was now Daddy's Girl and it is something that has stayed the same ever since.

We had yet another follow up in Ann Arbor one week later on the 11th. We did pack a bag and the visit ended the same way as it had a week before. I found myself suddenly having hope again. I prayed that maybe this was not a big deal and we wouldn't need surgery. I also started to wonder if maybe packing a bag was the key to leaving.

Even with Natalie doing well and work coming along, there was enough stress with Kelly and Lucas to keep me off balance. Kelly not being around did complicate things, but what made things much more difficult were the frequent "alarms" at the hospital. More than once I had to call my grandparents to watch Natalie in the middle of the night due to issues with Kelly and bleeding. Most of the time it was a false alarm, and Kelly would be shuffled around the unit until she stabilized again, but it was hard on both of us.

We took the track back up north for the next follow up with Cardiology on the 25th. Nancy decided to come with us for this trip. She did not "need" to come, but I think deep down I just craved support. It was a lonely life at times. At the visit, Natalie's Echocardiogram showed improvement in the blood flow which suggests that the fluid collection was decreasing. I was shocked when Dr. Gelehrter offered up a follow up appointment in six weeks. It felt freeing and "forever" away. What would we do with our time, not having to drive to Ann Arbor on a weekly basis? The answer was actually quite simple and came to us unexpectedly: deal with baby brother.

CHAPTER 52

ON A TUESDAY

I have not mentioned it yet, but that winter, EVERYTHING seemed to happen on a Tuesday. Natalie's 4th Surgery was on a Tuesday. Kelly's Appointment with her **Obstetrician** where we found out her water broken was on a Tuesday, and Lucas would frequently have issues leading to Kelly being transferred to the "high risk" area on Labor and Delivery on Tuesdays. Kelly and I had noticed the trend sometime in January and made light about it. It was almost as if we feared Tuesdays due to what may or may not happen. On one of those Tuesdays, Kelly's doctors decided that Kelly had to be bed bound and we could no longer go on walks around the Hospital. It stunk as that was Kelly's only outlet to freedom. When we would visit, frequently we would go explore the hospital, taking in the Christmas decorations around Toledo Hospital or having lunch in the Cafe. Now we were limited to a wheelchair. Sure, we were still able to wheel around the hospital when we would visit, Natalie in Kelly's lap, but it just was not the same.

On February 2nd, a Tuesday, things once again became complicated. For several weeks Kelly had bleeding pretty constantly but she never really had any pain. Suddenly, there was pain. Lucky for us, her OB-Gyn Dr. Litt was on call and came to evaluate her that night. She knew us very well and realized that Kelly was in labor. She made the call and Kelly was rushed back for a Cesarean Section. Lucas came into the world screaming at 31 weeks exactly. He was small, weighing only 3 pounds, and his head was shaped oddly due to the lack of fluid. They allowed Kelly to hold his hand for a moment in the incubator in the recovery room before shifting him off to the NICU. It felt eerie and unreal. Not only was he born the same way as Natalie, semi-emergent C-Section, but the entire post-delivery situation felt very felt familiar. I once again was stuck battening going with the baby or sticking with Kelly.

Toledo was much more "family friendly" than Kansas City, and they allowed my Grandparents to stay with Kelly. I went off to find Lucas in the NICU, which was on the same floor as Labor and Delivery but over in the newer side of the hospital. When I arrived, my son was already intubated as the doctors and staff were working on him. We had been prepared for this. While being born at 31 weeks causes babies plenty of issues, we knew that whenever he would be born he would have trouble with his lungs. The doctors could not tell me very much as they did not know much. It was too soon. They knew that Lucas's lung function could be very very bad due to his prematurity and lack of amniotic fluid. We would have to wait and see how he did. One doctor mentioned that he had hope that maybe Lucas had kept his mouth in the small amounts of fluid present and things could have partially developed. All we could do was pray.

Kelly's post-partum course was anything but easy. Due to her heart condition, her doctors wanted her to be on a heart monitor after surgery. The monitor picked up some funny heart beats, leading to her being transferred to the cardiology floor in another section of the hospital. She hated this as she had grown quite use to the antepartum staff. The other nurses were simply not as attentive or used to dealing with post-C-section patients. The Cardiologist who was consulted was concerned about a pulmonary embolism due to some blood work Kelly had done and felt she required a CT Scan. All of this freaked me out. I knew how hard it had been alone with Natalie and, after spending nights on the phone with Ben, deep down I was worried that maybe Kelly wouldn't make it home. The CT scan came back negative thankfully, but Kelly was started on heart medications which was new for her.

After several days of observation on the floor, Kelly was discharged home from the hospital. She had been at Toledo Hospital for 70 days. Lucas had to stay in the NICU and looked like he would be there for some time. Kelly was back to pumping and that drove her life once again.

With Kelly finally home, I initially felt a huge sense of relief. I had done it. For better or worse, I had done it. I had kept the little human alive in their mother's absence. However, it soon became apparent that things were not simply going back to the way they were. Our situation was not "fixed" with Kelly's return. Instead, Kelly being home seemed to just make things more complicated for Natalie and I. Kelly immediately struggled not getting around after her surgery, but also adapting to routine Natalie and I had grown accustomed to. We had developed our own way of doing things and she was the outsider. Kelly did not know what show to turn on the TV, which sippy cup we were trying out now, what time we had snack, and other simple things that made up our daily lives. Natalie and I had developed our own code and "Daddy" had become the one she looked for when she needed help. When Kelly would try to help her with something, Natalie would say something along the lines of "No! Daddy Do it!". When Natalie would call out at night or fall and hurt herself, it was my name she called. This was emotionally hard on Kelly. It was almost as if she was replaced.

I tried to teach Kelly the routine, but that was difficult and she became frustrated. It was like she could not see "why" we did things a certain way and not her way. I tried to have patience but it was not easy. I now understood how she felt every time I questioned her routine back before her admission. I showed Kelly how I had been taught to place Natalie's NG tube, hoping she could help with this terrible procedure that killed me every time. Kelly watched intently, but seconded guessed my lesson when it came time to do it. Children's Mercy taught her one way to measure and insert the NG tube and that was the way she had done it when Natalie was brand new. She had to place it many times those first 6 months and she was pretty comfortable with that method. Now, I was sitting over her shoulder trying to show her a different way to do it. Our frustration with each other boiled over that night, leading to first a shouting match and later a crying fit. The night ended though with us expressing each of our personal frustration. She shared her feelings of inadequacy and how she felt replaced with me. I pledged to have more patience and not to nick pick so much. She pledged to try not to question my every suggestion. We both went to bed happy.

Over time, Kelly was able to focus on overcoming these frustrations and establish a new hybrid routine with Natalie. I was glad things were improving for them but I struggled with letting go of the controls. My Mom gave me some advice, explain how Natalie was torn and was having a hard time "trusting" that Kelly would be there. She told me that "Natalie needs her Mother" and to allow Kelly to do her job. She felt Natalie's fear of Kelly disappearing suddenly had been driving some of her budding behavioral issues. I forced myself to take a step back, focusing on work. Kelly and I tried to get the parenting rolls closer to the way she was used to, closer to the way they were before our hospitalization.

It was a good time to do so as things were getting much more difficult at work. February was Cardiology month and, while it was intense, the hours were not bad. I was allowed to help with heart caths, taught to read echocardiograms and attend cardiology clinic. To keep the routine somewhat in place, Natalie was to visit Nancy several times a week which would allow Kelly time to visit Lucas.

As February moved to March, Kelly took back over the role of primary caregiver. Both her and Natalie seemed to be growing accustomed to this but from this point on, she was "Daddy's Girl". Kelly was able to go with us to our follow up in Ann Arbor near the end of March. The echocardiogram showed that the fluid pocket around Natalie's heart continued to just "be there" and, miraculously, Natalie was 5% on the growth curve! The NG tube feeds were working. Dr. Gelehrter gave us a pass for 3 months, with plan to have a G tube placed sometime in May.

CHAPTER 53

CAREGIVERS ARE USUALLY RIGHT

When you have once child who is in the NICU, it can be easy to stay by their side. For those parents who have other children at home or have demanding jobs, it is simply not possible being with your baby every moment of every day. I remember how I was obsessed with making sure Natalie had company any time she was in the hospital. I remember how unkind i had been in my own mind in regards to parents in Children's Mercy who always seemed to be absent. This is something, as I sat with Lucas in the NICU, that I felt guilt about. I had known nothing about those other parents in Kansas City and it had been very wrong of me to question their motives when they were not around. Sure, there are bad parents out there, but I am positive, living through it both ways, that no parent would leave their kid alone in the NICU if they can help it.

In March of 2016, I was assigned Inpatient work as a Senior. The hours were still pretty intense, but you would alternate a week of being on day shift with a week of being on night shift. Our night shifts were pretty relaxed and for the most part, much easier on me. Being at the hospital frequently made it easy for me to visit Lucas every day. I would finish my rounds and pop my head in to check up my little guy. Once rounds were completed, I would spend my downtime sitting in Lucas's room waiting for the pager to go off. Initially, Lucas was on a ventilator, much like Natalie was back in Missouri. My grandparents were there most days as well for the first month or so.

The trouble was, besides work, I also had to spend time at home with the rest of my family. Natalie was not allowed into the NICU as she was not yet 2 years old. She couldn't see her new brother, not that she really knew what this meant. To complicate the matter, she also came down with a respiratory infection and that meant going to the Emergency to get checked out. Any sickness can quickly become deadly in heart babies.

Going to the Emergency Room is always stressful for us. I have always had the worry that someone would just look at Natalie's chart and just decide she needed admitted even before laying eyes on her. At the Toledo ER, Natalie was more than just a little sick. Her oxygen saturations were in the high 60's. Dr. Gladieux had admitting privileges and agreed with the ER physician that she needed to to be admitted. The doctors started her on high flow oxygen, nasal suction and albuterol treatments for bronchiolitis. Bronchiolitis is a common lung infection in young children and infants. It causes inflammation and congestion in the small airways from a viral infection. Bronchitis tends to last 5 days but worsens around day 2-3. It can be very dangerous in sick children and has even been known to kill heart babies. Natalie had been given a "vaccine" to prevent this but unfortunately she had come into contact with one of the bugs that was not part of the vaccine.

With two kids in the hospital being at the hospital 12-16 hours a day most days suddenly had its benefit. Now, not only could I visit Lucas daily, but I also was able to visit and spend time with Natalie too. Things were a bit rough at first for Natalie as she was choking on the excess "secretions, vomiting and coughing frequently. The doctors started putting "super" pediasure with 1.5x the calories through her NG tube to keep her both hydrated and meet her caloric needs as she was not eating. Toledo Hospital does not carry the "Sprout" channel, so we lived on the pull out couch in our room watching reruns of Ruff Ruff, Tweet and Dave on the iPad. Thank God for the 'Sprout Online" streaming app.

Once Natalie started to improve, it became difficult relaying the information and recommendations we normally followed from Mott's to the care team to our doctors in Toledo. While in Ann Arbor on the cardiac floor, we were usually cared for by Fellows or Nurse practitioners. They knew our kid inside and out and frequently consulted with Dr. Gelehrter about Natalie's care. On the Children's Floor at Toledo Hospital ,things were a little different. There is not a designated "Cardiac" area and it is the Pediatric Residents who have a strong presence there and takes care of most of the patients. Personally, I love education, so I never thought of this as a bad thing. Heck, I was trained on these same floors. There are attending doctors nearby who are very seasoned can really handle any issue.

That said, if the attending is not one of the in house Hospitalists, the process can be more complicated. While Dr. Gladieux was the attending overseeing care for Natalie, he also sees patients all day in his clinic. He is not there seeing his hospitalized patients with the residents and reviewing their work and that can create some anxiety amongst the residents as well as parents. In our case, the Pediatric Residents just did not seem to feel comfortable with how Natalie looked, worrying about her retraction and oxygen levels. Her oxygen levels were in the 70s', which was not that abnormal for her but they insisted that we keep her on oxygen.
They seemed to constantly want to transfer her to the ICU. I tried to explain that she has the retractions at baseline and her oxygen is usually poor, but it did little to make them feel more comfortable. In this moment, I wanted to scream, and this reminded me of another lesson I had learned before with Natalie. Always trust the parent of sick children. As the child's primary caregiver, they are the ones that live with this child and know what is normal and what is not for them. I have seen kids that looked fine, but the parents were concerned. I would admit them for the child to suddenly crash. I have also seen kids that look terrible, but parents tell me that things are ok. We would discharge them and the child would come to their ER follow up in clinic and be doing great. Trusting the parent is key.

The Pediatric Residents seemed to not understand this lesson. After they pushed again to send Natalie to the ICU, I asked them to let Dr. Gladieux evaluate her first. Unfortunately, he was unavailable, but they told me that they had spoken to him and he recommended the transfer.
Remembering my experiences with the staff at Mott's, and the lesson I had learned in the past, I swallowed my pride and asked them to do whatever they felt was right. I was not her doctor, they were and I would trust their judgement. I was not happy about it, but I would trust them. Before I knew it, Natalie was rushed to the PICU, which is in a separate area in the hospital and very different from the normal rooms at Toledo. The walls were all glass with a centralized nurses station. It is loud, cramped and uncomfortable. In the PICU, the Residents are no longer in charge of the child, instead there is a Pediatric Intensivist who takes over. The PICU Attending was a middle aged Asian woman. She looked like someone who had seen quite a lot and knew what she was doing. She came in calmly and spoke with us. We discussed what had been going on, how things were going at home and gave Natalie a thorough look over. For the most part, she actually thought Natalie did not look too bad. Plan was just to keep doing what we were doing with the high flow oxygen and nebulizer `treatments and go from there. Dr. Gladieux came by later after clinic and I was thrilled to see him. He laughed as he came in, explaining how the texts he had received it sounded as if Natalie was crashing. To him, he said, she looked absolutely normal for the most part. "She probably didn't need to

have been transferred." He said in a jovial manner, "That's what I said!!" We had a laugh together. Somehow seeing his smiling face made everything seem better.

We spent a few more days in the hospital in Toledo and was sent home near the end of the month. I went on to inpatient pediatrics for the month of April, which historically had always been one of our most difficult rotations at our Program. It was supposed to be easier as a second year, mostly because you had an intern under you, but I had drawn the short straw and we were down a resident. Even though I was a Second Year Resident, on this rotation I was suddenly treated like an intern again and thrusted back into skut duty. It did not go well.

CHAPTER 54

TROUBLE IN PARADISE

April 2016 was a very tough month for me personally. You would think that, with everything we had gone through over the past year, nothing could phase me, but you would be wrong. Pediatric hours were grueling and I would only have 2 hours of free time at home per night. Lucas was at the hospital in the NICU but pressure mounted at home. Kelly's mother, who lived in Missouri, had passed at the beginning of the month unexpectedly and, with Natalie being ill, Kelly was not able to go to the funeral. Kelly was able to FaceTime with family members who attended the funeral in her stead, but it was not the same. I remember sitting on the pediatric ward, working on orders, and receiving a text from Kelly. It was a screenshot of the funeral. I never saw eye to eye with Kelly's Mom, but this still kicked me in the gut. Natalie would never remember her. She had not seen her that often, but she still cared for my little girl. Now she was gone and, while no one deserves to die, her mother was only in her 50s. It was just really unfortunate and made for a rough time on the wards.

One bright spot of the month was being able to rotate with Dr. Gladieux. I quickly observed the difficult nature of his job. He was not part of an organized health system. This gave him freedom in regard to his practice, but he had to take on the burden of the cost of running said clinic. He was responsible for staff and was basically on call all the time. He would go to the hospital before and after clinic. It sounded extremely difficult, but he seemed to love it. I learned that almost every one of his families were "one of his favorite families". It made me feel slightly less special, but it also illustrated how much he cared for each kid. He was not being disingenuous. He meant it. He had many patients whose parents he took care of when they were young. Most kids would squeal when he asked to take them home. It was how he said it, making a funny face and pointing to himself with his thumbs. They would go "Nooooo!" and he'd respond with a "Awww! Come on!" in a loud dramatic fashion. You could tell that he loved his work and it was inspiring. He'd ask about Natalie frequently and even would load me up with Pediasure samples every week.

Meanwhile, at home, Natalie was recovering well. The NG tube was working and she was climbing on the growth chart. It still was very difficult to maintain. We struggled with "what to do" with the NG tube. Usually, it is not recommended to have an NG tube long term and her heart doctor had recommended getting a G-Tube. While I was enjoying Natalie finally gaining weight, she continued to not take food by mouth. I wondered if the tube could be irritating and making things worse. I was afraid of the G-Tube. I knew that they were not as simple as the doctors seem to suggest they were. I also struggled with the idea of yet another surgery for Natalie. I feared the additional scars and pain that would be put onto my little girl.

Natalie had a vomiting episode and spewed out her tube in the week leading up to her surgery, and I just did not have the heart to put it back. The more she would fight it, the harder it was to place and our success rate was dropping. Without the tube, while we waited for Monday for the procedure, Natalie seemed much happier and was even eating a little. We spoke with Dr. Gladieux about it and he seemed to be against it the surgery. He asked if we would be willing to try something else. I trusted him completely and enjoyed an "alternative" to surgery. After talking it over, we decided to take his advice and canceled the procedure with plans to see how Natalie would do with oral feeds and feeding therapy "tubeless". We planned for close follow up with our PCP.

When Lucas first came home in April, I was shell shocked. It was very hard to balance the needs of the new baby as well as trying to keep Kelly as Natalie's "primary" caregiver. I found that I seemed to struggle with him much more than Natalie. I did not know if it was just a memory bias, but it did not seem to be THIS hard with Natalie. Lucas was fussy with me and there was nothing I seemed to be able to do to help. He was great with Kelly. Adding on the rough hours did not help. I learned that, when I am stressed, I tended to snap a little more at home. I made a conscious effort to leave "work at work" and it seemed to help.

As Spring turned to Summer, things slowly started to get into a new routine. I was afraid of our appointment on June 6th at Mott's. Dr. Gelehrter asked us to get the G-Tube and we did not. Would they be mad at us? After packing our bags, we made the trip. If the doctors were upset, they did not seem to show it. Her Echocardiogram came back "stable". The fluid was there but was about the same. They felt like things were going in the right direction, and recommended working on "calorie dense food" and repeating her heart catheterization in august. With a shake of the hand, we were free for the rest of the summer.

We spent the next two months in blissful ignorance of the rest of the world. You really did not have time to go anywhere with a toddler and a new baby. I became a Third Year resident which came with benefit of being the "big guy on campus". You were responsible for training the newest class of interns. I began to really have a passion for sharing what I learned. Others had sacrificed to get me where I was in my career and it was only right that I should turn back around and help the next guy. Things at home slowly became "normal".

Work grew easier as well. As a third year, except for the two Inpatient Months which were scheduled for me in October and March, most rotations were only 40-60 hours per week. I would come home to find Natalie outside kicking a kickball, goofy look on her face or maybe she would be way back in the big backyard pushing her little lawn mower with a large white hat on her head shading her from the sun. Without the NG tube, she no longer looked ill and she seemed so happy. She was just a normal little girl and it was such a blessing to have that feeling. Natalie was learning many words. When she first told me "I la you" it was through FaceTime. She also started to laugh all the time. She would close one eye, stick out her tongue and then let out a quick laugh consisting of a high squeal, finishing with a "heh heh Heeeeh!" She still makes this face to this day when she is truly happy or finds something really funny.

Near the end of the summer, we had another Heart Catheterization planned for the end of August. By now, close follow up was routine but the constant fear of readmission had subsided. Lucas was doing well and was slowly becoming a "normal" baby himself. Having a second child changes the way things work, ruining the "routine" she had worked so hard to build. Kelly could no longer get the Naps she used to treasure with Natalie every day, but, for the most part, things were going well.

We went up to the hospital early in the morning and Natalie was prepped and taken from us. She went away in one of the Nurse's arms, rocking out to "Troll Songs" on the iPod. We waited in the same old waiting room, counting down the minutes until we heard word from the team. The nurse came out and let us know that the doctor was done, rather quicker than expected, and that he would meet with us soon. I was worried as usually, in my line of work, finishing earlier is rarely a "good thing".

About 15 minutes later, Dr. Bocks called us into the little conference room off to the side of the waiting room to review the case. The right side of

Natalie's arteries were very stenosed and he felt it was better to work on the left. We had discussed Stents and cutting balloons in the past. "Stents do not grow with the child and can cause a problem later on." he had told us. He explained that the procedure went well and made some progress with the cutting balloons. His hope was that it would scar down helping us long-term with growth and we could avoid stents. Dr. Bocks showed us a picture of Natalie's chest that showed blood flow before the cutting balloons and then another picture after. The blood full look significantly better in the after picture. He was happy that we were making progress. Shortly after this meeting ended, we were allowed to go see Natalie who was awake in the recovery area down the hall. She laid there, arms to her side watching her favorite television show with her Puppy cuddled up next to her. I laughed when I noticed that Puppy had been given a name bracelet of his own. There was a cup of apple juice nearby, which was her favorite. When she saw us, she asked calmly if she could watch "Butterflies" on Kelly's phone. It was very different compared to our experiences in the past.

We had planned to stay the night as this was what was typical for us in the past, but Natalie bounced back very well and they let us go home. This was the first time they let us go home so easily after a heart test. It was like we suddenly turned some imaginary corner.

CHAPTER 55

IS EVERYTHING OK?

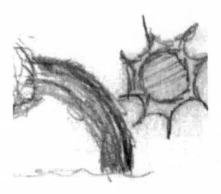

One thing that is both a curse and a blessing with all of this is social media. It allowed us to share information about Natalie quickly and help others stay in contact. It also has support groups that many people find helpful during difficult times. I had joined a "Pulmonary Atresia" as well as a "Tetralogy of Fallot" group mid-June that year and had been keeping up to date on many of the other kids in our area. It was awesome to be able to post your stories and be there for people experiencing similar things as your child and relay your experience. It could also be terrible. You hear about other kids and some of the things they went through. You follow closely, offering prayers and words of support as other children suffer.

For instance, there was one child who had a similar case to Natalie. She had a pseudoaneurysm of her conduit, just like Natalie. It all sounded so familiar as I read her mother's post. Then, when she went in for the emergent repair, just as we had done twice by now, she had a blood clot for that went to her brain during surgery and this caused a stroke. While the doctors were able to fix the heart, the damage was done to the little girls brain. She now was having seizures most of the day, every day and the seizures were resistant to medication. The mom, posting from recovery, explained how her happy little girl was gone, replaced by something she didn't recognize. She was at a loss and hurting. I had no idea what to say. This could have easily been us. This is not the only example of heartache I ran into. There are other cases too. Some you follow closely and watch as their child spirals downhill and pass. It is gut wrenching and terrible. What do you say to a mother who is grieving at the loss of their baby? You find yourself lying in bed at night crying thinking about possible futures. A fellow parent of a heart warrior shared her story with me. Her daughter was 10 and had been on hospice for 4 years. They had decided against more procedures, focusing instead on just having a life. The little girl had to wear oxygen, but was able to go to school and was otherwise happy. When I asked her how she handles it, She seemed to relate to our story well and shared something with me that was very heartwarming. "You will not always be able to tell her it is going to be ok. What you can always do is give her a hug, tell her that you love her and let her know that you are in it together".

On September 26, 2016, we met with Dr. Gelehrter to go over the results of the catheterization from August and make a plan for the future. We tested fate by not packing a bag was things were going so well, so we did not feel it necessary. Sounds familiar right? We also showed up late, which was becoming a trend for us. I was surprised how much more difficult it was with adding in another human in the mix when it comes to appointments. They saw us anyway. After exchanging pleasantries, Dr. Gelehrter sat on the rolly chair and sort of had a funny look on her face. She asked how things were going and we explained how it was going well. Lucas was home, off Oxygen and "a normal baby".

The Doctor expressed her concerns. Based upon all she could see, we simply were not making good progress with the heart catheterizations. Natalie's arteries did not seem to be responding as we had hoped. Natalie's growth also had seemed to level off. She was not exactly sure how to proceed. "If this was Boston," She had said, "they would probably perform interventional catheterizations every 2-3 months, but I am not certain it was worth the risk." Boston is a leading children's center for congenital heart disease. Many of the most complex cases go there.

I agreed with her. I knew heart catheterizations were a big deal. I have seen adult patients have to have "cut downs" to the artery due to bleeding or even worse things happen during a cath. Natalie had been very blessed and had little side effects of all of her procedures, but that did not make my anxiety any less about having them done.

After a pause, Dr. Gelehrter followed up with, "As long as she continues to tolerate things, maybe we should do them every 6-12 months instead." This seemed logical to me. She gestured to Natalie, who was stuffing her face with fruit snacks. "She seems to be tolerating things ok." She said, then adding almost as if she was thinking out loud to herself, "I do not know if she is small because she doesn't eat or if it is just what her heart can tolerate."

She asked if we had any questions. Kelly had come in wanting to know prognosis. I didn't. I didn't want to have some number stuck in my head. What if it was bad news. Kelly spoke up. "What are we thinking prognosis wise. What is her long term outlook?"

I let out an anxious sigh. My wife had a history of asking questions I found off the wall or uncomfortable. I was terrified of what Dr. Gelehrter was going to say. What if the answer was 4 or 5. I looked at Natalie sitting next to me. She was wearing her black and red polka dot Minnie dress and that ridiculously large and bright rainbow sequin bingo hat Aunt Diane had given her, totally oblivious to the conversation topic.

Dr. Gelehrter took the question in stride, not showing any sign of anxiety or even hesitation. "That would depend. It would depend on how she does with the procedures and if anything else happens along the way. Plus, there are always medical advancements to consider. I know they are working on some pretty cool stuff in Europe." She paused, then continued. "If they came up with something that grows arteries, who knows how long she will live. Transplanting hearts for these patients has been falling out of favor as of late as it has not really been shown to extended patients quality of life." She paused again, "If everything stays the same, I'd say 10 years…"

EPILOGUE
WHERE ARE WE NOW

This story was never meant to have a beginning, middle or an end. This Journey will never end for us. All we knew for years was this fight. Lately, we have been very blessed, having more "good days" than "bad days". That's all you can ask for when you have a child with an uncorrected heart defect.

Throughout this book, and even after it, we have been through so much as a family. We never did get around to "Fixing" Natalie. At some point along the way our goal seemed to shift away from finding a permanent solution to her heart defect. Instead, we focused on just trying keep things going. In my soul, I selfishly just wanted to find a way to get just a little more time with her. I wanted one more Christmas Morning, one more birthday or one more day at the beach. For the most part, these prayers were answered. We have had many opportunities to fall back into a normal life. When you look around our house, it does not look like a sick child lives here. We have the chance to forget how things are, and I thank God that we have had those opportunities.

Sadly, nothing has really changed with Natalie's prognosis since that office visit with our cardiologist. We have had more procedures, more surgeries, but sadly Natalie is not making much progress. We are still are in watch, wait and pray mode. Natalie has thrived the best she can and, at completing this book, she is a happy 5 year old girl just getting into kindergarten. This is a miracle as far as I am concerned.

When I initially heard the prognosis from our Cardiologist, I had a very mixed reaction. My first thought was joy. In my soul, when Kelly asked the question, I feared the doctor would give us a much smaller number. I had been reflecting on the NICU in Kansas City when prognosis was days to weeks. Ten years seemed almost like a miracle. Plenty of things happen to kids unexpectantly and out of the blue in this world all the time. They are taken from their parents way before their time. I would at least be prepared. If ten years is all we had, then I would spend it making sure Natalie had a life filled with happiness and one worth living.

Kelly and I spent many hours a night for several weeks after that visit crying together as we tried to work out what it meant for us. Kelly had a much harder time dealing with it, focusing on the fact that our girl may never get the chance to grow up. I just tried to keep things in perspective. Like most things in life, those worries slowly faded off into the background and we were able to get back to our normal life. When surgeries or procedures would creep up on us on the horizon, many of these feelings resurface, bringing with them haunting thoughts. I struggle at times to remind myself where we have come from. I reflect on the blessings we have been given and memories made and this sometimes helps. "We never expected our child to make it this far" seems like a typical sentiment from other "heart warriors" I follow on facebook, but it is a true statement.

I still hold out hope that one day we may get there and we will "Fix" Natale, but I have accepted that we may simply never get there. There is no failure in that. Afterall, my job is to lover her, not fix her. This life is all about the journey and the memories and not about how or when it ends. Things may not turn out as you hoped they would, but it is up to you to find ways to accept this.

I believe that all parents with sick children come away with scars. I know that personally, while holding in my emotions served me well initially, it left me deeply scared. I now find myself with a deep seeded anxiety that can be difficult to control at times. I probably need therapy, medication or both, but am too stubborn to ask for help. No matter how calm things are, I still find myself crying at random times and worrying about losing my little girl. It seems to crop up at random times, like when I am singing Natalie to sleep at night. I try to shake off these dreadful thoughts, but it can be difficult. I rarely speak to anyone about these things and it is hard for me even to put those words on paper for fear of embarrassment or fear of being perceived as weak. After all this though, an entire book about my feelings, I guess it is time to just get over that fear and share openly how I really doing when people ask.

Over the years, I have been asked frequently "How did you do it" and have to admit that I have asked myself it many times. The truth is that I really have no idea how I "did" it. During the slow times, the normal times, when things were good, I had a hard time remembering how it was having to live day to day, moment to moment as I had done in the past. Then tragedy tended to rear its ugly head again and we wouldn't have the chance to reflect on what we were doing. We just did what we had to and this frequently meant taking emotion out of the equation. I think the answer, although cliché, is literally taking things one day at a time. Remind yourself daily, just as I did, that "Today, Is the BEST DAY EVER!" and you will find things slowly coming around. Besides, what else can you do during times like that. The last thing you want to do is to ask "why" or feel sorry for yourself.

While it has been a difficult journey, I have said for some time that I would never have it any other way. I have been given a gift, and not one I feel like I deserve. I have memories now that mean more than gold to me. I get to have the honor and privilege of being Nat's Daddy. I reflect on a day this past summer. following little Natalie down the street as she pedals her big wheel tricycle ahead of me, singing a song she is making up on the spot. It was a magical sight. The memory of her on that bike is so vivid and special to me. It is something I thought years ago I would never get to experience. I am not sure what I have done to deserve that, but I know that it would have never happened without your help. What Natalie means to us as a family is priceless. She has touched so many lives. No matter how this journey ends, I will treasure my time spent with Natalie for my entire life. Remember that everything will work out in the end. You don't need to know how, just trust that it will.

To you, Reader, I hope that you have enjoyed this journey as much I have enjoyed putting it down on paper. I do not know who you are and how you found us, but I thank you for taking the time to hear our story and helping spread awareness for Congenital Heart Disease. Thank you so much for walking along with us on this journey. God

PHOTOGRAPHS

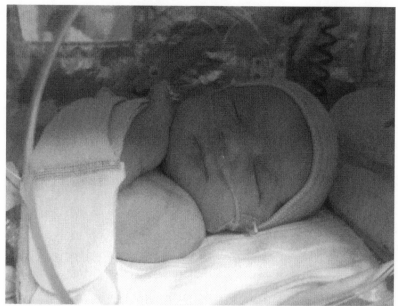

Natalie prepareing for transfer to Children's Mercy

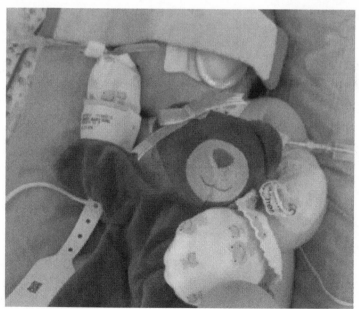

Growing Natalie in NICU with Colin's Bear

Trying on costumes in Mott's Gift Shop

Holloween in the Hospital

Natalies First Christmas in Mott's Lobby

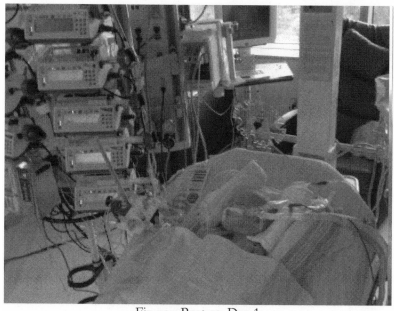

Fix you Post op Day 1

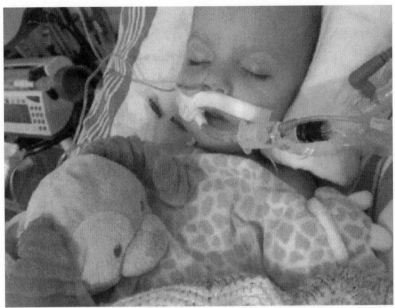

Just another day in the NICU. Fix You Part II

Natalie with Feeding tube

Natalie and Daddy Enjoying Florida

Natalie, Joey and Mommy

Natalie on her 5th Birthday

ACKNOWLEDGMENTS

I wanted to acknowledge all those who helped Natalie get to where she is today, but I quickly realized that if I tried to list all of you by name, that list would be longer than this book. From the amazing doctors and nurses, Ronald McDonald Charities, our family, friends and God, without all of your help, we would have never been able to experience all of the laughing, singing and pure happiness that has come our way. Without all of you, I do not know if we would of made it this far. In regards to this book, thank you for my Dad for reading through it to make sure it didn't completely stink and I thank my Mother for editing it line by line from a 300 page binder. I thank my wife for allowing me to cry on her shoulder as I worked my way through these difficult memories and I also have to thank Facebook for keeping a record of what happened along the way in a searchable manor.

ABOUT THE AUTHOR

Dr. Jordan Siewert is a Doctor of Osteopathy practicing Family Medicine in Toledo, Ohio, providing care to an underserved population. Dr. Siewert attended Kirksville College of Osteopathic Medicine in Kirksville, Missouri from 2010 to 2014 and trained at the Toledo Hospital Family Medicine Residency. He graduated in 2017. After graduation, Dr. Siewert moved his wife, Kelly and three children back to his hometown of Temperance, Michigan. Dr. Siewert has put in countless hours researching Congenital Heart Disease and hopes one day to be able to offer primary care services to children with these conditions at his practice. He enjoys the personal relationship he is able to have with his patients and treasures spending his down time with his children; Natalie, Lucas and Joey.

Made in the USA
Monee, IL
13 November 2019